PRAISE FOR DIANE FANNING

"Very few writers have the insight and gift to take a true story and make it one hell of a page-turner. In my opinion, Diane Fanning does just that in *A Poisoned Passion*."

—Susan Murphy Milano,
domestic violence victims' advocate

"Author Diane Fanning tirelessly recounts the young woman's lying ways, theorizes how Anthony might have disposed of her daughter, and concludes that Anthony is 'an individual whose self-absorption and insensitivity to others is a destructive force.'"

—*Orlando Sentinel* on *Mommy's Little Girl*

"Unbelievable stuff!"

—Mike DeForest, WKMG-TV, on *Mommy's Little Girl*

"I couldn't put it down until I had finished it . . . [A] story that's enjoyable to read and accurate to detail."

—Herb Betz on *Through the Window*

"I was astonished by how good this book was—insightful, well written, and fascinating."

—Hugh Aynesworth, four-time Pulitzer Prize nominee,
on *Out There*

Berkley titles by Diane Fanning

UNDER COVER OF THE NIGHT

BITTER REMAINS

BITTER REMAINS

A Custody Battle, a Gruesome Crime,
and the Mother Who Paid the Ultimate Price

DIANE FANNING

BERKLEY BOOKS, NEW YORK

BERKLEY

An imprint of Penguin Random House LLC
375 Hudson Street, New York, New York 10014

BITTER REMAINS

A Berkley Book / published by arrangement with the author

ISBN: 978-0-425-27848-2

PUBLISHING HISTORY
Berkley premium edition / January 2016

PRINTED IN THE UNITED STATES OF AMERICA

10 9 8 7 6 5 4

Cover art: *Dawn at Brazos Bend* @ Paul S. Wolf/Shutterstock.
Cover design by Jane Hammer.
Interior text design by Laura K. Corless.

Penguin
Random
House

Dedicated to
the memory of Laura Jean Ackerson
with the hope that Sha, little Grant, Gentle and Lily
find the healing and strength
to build happy and fulfilling lives

ACKNOWLEDGMENTS

I extend a very special thank-you to Sha Elmer for sharing so much with me, and to Tremayne Ward at the Wake County Courthouse. And thanks to Joseph Hardin and Mark Gierth, and to many others who chose to remain anonymous.

I also want to express deep appreciation to Detective Jerry Faulk and Assistant District Attorneys Boz Zellinger and Becky Holt for jobs well done.

To Jane Dystel, the intrepid warrior, who has been by my side throughout my writer's journey through fourteen true crime books and nine novels: I can never repay my debt to you or to all the staff in your office.

To my editor, Shannon Jamieson Vazquez, who helped me beat my last two true crime manuscripts into submission: thanks for shaping these books into the best they could be.

And, finally, I wish every woman could have a partner who is as compassionate, entertaining and supportive as my guy. Thank you, Wayne Fanning, for all you are and all you do every day.

NOTABLE PEOPLE

THE VICTIM

LAURA JEAN ACKERSON—Twenty-seven-year old entrepreneur, graphic artist and mother of two, aka Laura Hayes

THE ACCUSED

GRANT HAYES III—Musician, artist and father of Grant, Gentle and Lily Hayes. Husband of Amanda Hayes, aka Grant Haze

AMANDA HAYES—Actress, artist, mother of Sha Elmer and Lily Hayes and wife of Grant Hayes, aka Amanda Tucker, Amanda Smith, Amanda Haze

FRIENDS AND FAMILY

RETHA FAYE RYAN ABERNATHY—Mother of Amanda Hayes

JASON ACKERSON—Older half brother of Laura Jean Ackerson

PATRICIA BARAKAT—Inmate in the Wake County facility who befriended Amanda Hayes when she was incarcerated awaiting trial

DALTON BERRY—Son of Karen Berry and nephew of Amanda Hayes

KAREN BERRY—Older half sister of Amanda Hayes, lives in Texas

SHELTON BERRY—Son of Karen Berry and nephew of Amanda Hayes

SHA ELMER—Daughter of Amanda Hayes and Scott Elmer, aka Sha Guddat

GENTLE HAYES—Youngest son of Grant Hayes III and Laura Ackerson

GRANT HAYES II—Father of Grant and Grantina Hayes, husband of Patsy Hayes

GRANT HAYES IV—Oldest son of Grant Hayes III and Laura Ackerson, aka little Grant

GRANTINA HAYES—Sister of Grant Hayes III, aka Tina

LILLIAN ANN LOVE HAYES—Daughter of Grant Hayes III and Amanda Hayes, aka Lily

PATSY HAYES—Mother of Grant Hayes III, wife of Grant Hayes II

LAUREN HARRIS—Friend of Grant Hayes III and manager of the Monkey Joe's in Raleigh, North Carolina

JOSEPH "JOSE" HARDIN—Music promoter on St. John and friend of Grant Hayes III

MATT GUDDAT—Boyfriend and later husband of Sha Elmer

MARK GIERTH—A friend of Grant Hayes on St. John

CHEVON MATHES—Laura Ackerson's friend and business partner

BARBARA PATTY—Church friend and mentor of Laura Ackerson

KANDICE ROWLAND—Daughter of Karen Berry and niece of Amanda Hayes

OKSANA SAMARSKY—Artist and friend of Laura Ackerson

HEIDI SCHUMACHER—Laura Ackerson's closest friend

NICKY SMITH—Third husband of Amanda Hayes

PABLO TRINIDAD—Confidant of Grant Hayes III in Wake County jail

OFFICIALS

DR. GINGER CALLOWAY—Court-appointed psychologist who provided the psychological evaluation report about Laura Ackerson and Grant Hayes III in their custody fight

OFFICER KEVIN CROCKER—Policeman with the Raleigh Police Department in Raleigh, North Carolina

WILL DURHAM—One of two attorneys representing Grant Hayes III at trial

DETECTIVE JERRY FAULK—Raleigh Police Department's lead investigator in the Laura Ackerson case

AGENT MICHAEL GALLOWAY—Forensic investigator with the Raleigh/Wake City-County Bureau of Identification

JOHNNY GASKINS—Amanda Hayes's lead attorney

DETECTIVE DEXTER GILL—Investigator with the Raleigh Police Department

DETECTIVE JAMES GWARTNEY—Kinston, North Carolina, police department investigator who was the first to respond to Chevon Mathes's report of Laura Ackerson's disappearance

SERGEANT BRIAN HALL—Investigator with the Raleigh Police Department

BECKY HOLT—Assistant district attorney in Wake County, North Carolina

COURTNEY LAST—Computer forensics analyst with the Raleigh Police Department

DETECTIVE SERGEANT ROBERT LATOUR—Raleigh, North Carolina, homicide detective

DR. NOBBY MAMBO—Deputy chief medical examiner with the Galveston County Medical Examiner's Office in Galveston, Texas

DETECTIVE DAVID MOORE—Investigator with the Raleigh Police Department

DETECTIVE ZEKE MORSE—Investigator with the Fort Bend County Sheriff's Office in Fort Bend, Texas

KIM ORESKOVICH—Crime scene investigator with the Fort Bend County Sheriff's Office in Fort Bend, Texas

DETECTIVE THOMAS OUELLETTE—Investigator with the Raleigh Police Department

MEL PALMER—Investigator working for attorney Johnny Gaskins

DETECTIVE STEVE PREVITALI—Raleigh, North Carolina, homicide detective

DETECTIVE MARK QUAGLIARELLO—Investigator with the Raleigh Police Department

AGENT SHANNON QUICK—Senior agent with the Raleigh/Wake City-County Bureau of Identification

DR. DEBORAH RADISCH—Chief medical examiner for the North Carolina Office of the Chief Medical Examiner

JENNIFER REMY—Hair and fiber analyst for the North Carolina State Crime Lab

DETECTIVE AMANDA SALMON—Investigator with the Raleigh Police Department

JOHN SARGEANT—Laura Ackerson's custody attorney

JUDGE DONALD STEPHENS—Presided over both Grant Hayes's and Amanda Hayes's trials in the superior court of Wake County, North Carolina

DR. PAUL STIMSON—Forensic odontologist in Houston, Texas

SERGEANT DANA SUGGS—Assisted with logistics of the investigation for Raleigh Police Department

AGENT TIMOTHY SUGGS—Forensic chemist with the North Carolina State Bureau of Investigation

DETECTIVE BRAD WICHARD—Investigator with the Fort Bend County Sheriff's Office

BOZ ZELLINGER—Assistant district attorney in Wake County, North Carolina

CHAPTER ONE

OYSTER Creek leaped to the earth's surface in Fort Bend County, Texas, just north of the historic town of Richmond, about a half hour southwest of downtown Houston. Paralleling the Brazos River, it meandered through lush, semitropical countryside on its way to the Gulf of Mexico. Along the 4300 block of Skinner Lane, unruly brush and tall grasses crowded around as if trying to hide the creek from strangers' eyes. At one spot, a football field–size patch of lily pads consumed its whole width. Oyster shells littered its banks, hobby fishermen harvested its bounty and alligators patrolled its length for prey.

In July 2011, in the Pecan Grove community, another deadly creature desecrated its waters.

On Sunday afternoon, July 24, 2011, detectives searching for a missing North Carolina woman made a gruesome discovery tangled up in the weeds growing by the edge of the creek: a piece of armless female torso, severed at the neck and just above the hip area. By four o'clock, they'd found the rest of the torso. They strongly suspected that they'd found the body of the woman whom they were seeking, but without a head or hands, identification would depend on the slow, methodical process of DNA testing.

The next morning, just after nine, dive experts from the Richmond Fire Department and the Houston Police Department arrived at the scene. The near-100-degree sun beat down on their heads and stabbed into their backs with the single-minded intensity of a carrion crow. Humidity soared over 90 percent, adding to the oppressive atmosphere. Even the temperature of the water was 89 degrees. The smell of decomposition filled their lungs as they stood on the bank assessing the situation to help them define their target area.

Two divers, Brian Davis and Mark Thorsen of the Houston Police Department, plunged into the hot, dark, murky creek. They started their search at the boat secured to the bank. The tender stood still, holding a line connected to a diver, who traveled out in 180-degree arcs. Each time the man in the water completed a run, the man on the bank fed out more line, which slightly extended the distance from the bank and allowed the diver to traverse a wider semicircle. When searching for something large—like a car—the line feeds out fast; but today, as they were hunting for body parts, the process was far more deliberate, methodical and slow. Visibility was nonexistent, forcing the divers to feel blindly with their hands in the black water and to depend as much on luck as on skill in their search for more body parts.

Since the detectives were aware that the missing woman had a tattoo on her foot, they focused first on finding that, since it could be an easy and quick identifier. Since the foot has less muscular tissue than other body parts, it would not float to the surface readily, so they performed an underwater scuba search for one hundred feet in every direction. Sinking to the bottom, the divers made snow angels in the mud, seeking foreign objects on the riverbed—all to no avail.

The lily pads were a major nuisance, covering 50 to 60 percent of the surface of the designated search area. It was impossible to take a boat through them, and every time the divers pushed them out of the way, the current pushed them back. It was a constant struggle.

Noticing a spot of sheen on the surface of the water, an indicator of decomposition, divers Davis and Thorsen scooped up a sample and returned to shore. Cadaver-dog handlers presented it to their canines, who hit on the scent, indicating the presence of human remains and sending the divers back to that spot to continue their task. Near the area of the sheen, the smell of decomposition was strong. Searching on the surface, Davis spotted a suspicious object tangled among the roots of the lily pads. Pulling it upward, he saw a smooth, hairless bone in the middle of a dark mass. At first he thought he'd found a femur bone, and he called Thorsen over to help with the recovery. However, when they rolled it over, a face was revealed, and Davis realized what he had seen was actually the back of a skull. The water had held the skin and muscle in place, but when they pulled the head to the surface, it started sliding off the bone.

The two men placed a ribbon on the surface where they found the skull and made measurements of its location from two stationary objects. After shooting photos of the area of their find, they wrapped the head in a sheet and carried it to the bank.

The smell of decomposition was still strong at the spot of sheen, prompting the two divers to return to the water and continue searching. Fifteen to twenty feet deeper into the mass of lilies, they found a portion of a leg. Both of the parts they located that day were on the outer edges of the hot zone. Altogether, over two days, 60 percent of a body had been recovered and delivered to the Galveston County Medical Examiner's Office.

On Tuesday, the dive team returned, expanding the target area farther but finding nothing more. Nonetheless, they had all that was needed to make identification. The detectives had found the missing woman from Kinston, North Carolina, nearly thirteen hundred miles away, in Oyster Creek in Texas: twenty-seven-year-old business-woman and mother of two Laura Jean Ackerson.

CHAPTER TWO

LAURA Jean Ackerson was born on April 30, 1984, to Rodger and Brenda Ackerson in Hastings, Michigan, the only city in rural Barry County in the southwest corner of the state. There were six other children in the family, including her father's son, Jason, who was three years older than Laura.

When Laura was a toddler, Rodger and Brenda separated. The battle of unsubstantiated allegations and contentious finger-pointing that lead to the divorce inflicted emotional scars on everyone, fracturing family relationships and leaving the children with conflicting loyalties. In Laura, the long-term emotional damage was apparent even after she reached adulthood.

In 1996, Laura and her mother moved to Iowa. Laura attended Lynnville-Sully High School in the tiny town of

Sully and graduated in 2003 (a year later than she should have, due to the many disruptions in her home life).

Her half brother, Jason, left Michigan for North Carolina when he turned twenty-two, though he and Laura continued to keep in touch by phone a couple of times a month. Not long after Jason got a place in Youngsville, a half-hour drive northeast of Raleigh, Laura headed south to join him. Dead-end jobs, worse relationship choices, and frustrations with her home life had left Laura yearning for a new start. Although Youngsville was located in the prosperous and thriving Research Triangle area of North Carolina, it was still a small, rural town with a population under twelve hundred. It certainly wasn't a hotbed of employment opportunities, nor was it full of the entertainments and activities a twenty-year-old woman would crave. Laura lived there with her brother for six months before setting out for the brighter life of the far more cosmopolitan city of Raleigh to find a job and a place of her own.

In 2004, Laura started working for an Applebee's restaurant in Raleigh. She had the right stuff to be a good waitress: a cheerful, perky personality and girl-next-door good looks with an engaging smile and shoulder-length brown hair. There she met coworker Heidi Schumacher, a bright young woman with an equally sweet smile and longer hair that she sometimes wore up. The two women hit it off right away. After a short while, they both moved on to new jobs, initially together at the Front Row Sports Bar, though Heidi soon moved on to pursue an insurance career.

Laura had started taking online classes at Kirkwood Community College while living with her brother, and after earning her associate of arts degree from Kirkwood in 2005, she thought about a career in real estate, and took a seventy-five-hour prelicensing course at JY Monk Real Estate School that same year. Her natural talents and interests were stimulated, however, by two classes she took at the community college, one in graphic design and the other in marketing. She decided to focus on developing her graphic-arts skills and obtaining the necessary marketing acumen needed to start her own business. In her spare time, by using the Internet, the library and networking, Laura built on her academic introduction, absorbing all the knowledge she could to pave the path for her future. And to pay the bills in the meantime, she also worked for Bassett Furniture Direct in Raleigh doing retail sales and helping customers with decorating solutions.

Even though they were on different trajectories, the two friends continued to stay in contact through regular e-mail, live chat and phone calls along with occasional face-to-face meetings. From time to time, Heidi had Laura over to her parents' house in Wake Forest, situated between Raleigh and Youngsville. Before long, Laura was like a part of their family. It filled a void in her life since, except for her brother Jason, the rest of her relatives were in the Midwest.

In mid-April 2007, Laura called Jason bubbling over with excitement because of the new romance in her life. She told him about Grant Hayes, a great new guy she was seeing. Jason hoped that his little sister was embarking on a good relationship but knew the odds weren't in her favor. Her fractured family life and rocky high school experience had left her naïve, immature and vulnerable.

At the end of that month, Heidi returned from nearly two months of insurance training in Chicago. Laura greeted her friend with the news that she had a big surprise. When they got together at an Italian restaurant to celebrate Laura's twenty-third birthday on April 30, Heidi could see immediately that her friend was very excited. It went far beyond her regular perkiness; Laura seemed to hum and vibrate with high emotion.

Laura quickly blurted out: "I got married! Surprise!" She explained that she and Grant had exchanged vows in front of the justice of the peace in Raleigh earlier that very day.

Heidi was knocked off balance over the news—she didn't know Grant Hayes, and this all seemed so sudden, nearly surreal. She covered her shock with a smile and said, "Well, awesome."

It turned out that Grant, Laura's new husband, was a musician, who'd be performing at the restaurant that same night. Laura introduced Heidi to him out in the parking lot. Grant gave Heidi a hug, and she returned it while assessing the shorter, African-American man with a shaved head standing in front of her. Heidi thought that he looked familiar, but it took her a moment to realize that he was the same musician who'd been playing at the Blue Martini Bar and Lounge on South Wilmington Street, where she and Laura had gone together right before Heidi left for Chicago. She knew that Laura had spoken to Grant on his break between sets that night, but had no idea that there had been any further contact between the two of them.

She wasn't impressed; in fact, she was certain Laura could do better. But while her misgivings were immediate,

Heidi sincerely hoped that they were groundless and that her friend's newfound happiness would never end.

GRANT Ruffin Hayes III was born to Patsy and Grant Hayes Junior on April 30, 1979. He grew up with one sister, Grantina, whom everyone called Tina. According to his mother, Grant was a "sweet child—he was very docile." In high school, she said, her son was so charming "that all the girls liked him." Being able to play guitar added to his popularity, and even while still a teenager, he was good enough to perform on the Raleigh nightclub scene.

When he was eighteen, he married a ballerina named Emily Lubbers and moved down to Greenville, North Carolina. Grant said that she and her dancing were the inspiration for many of the songs he wrote. Emily attended school at East Carolina University and worked a job to support the couple. Grant was frustrated in his attempts to secure work that suited him. And that was a sticking point: Grant always seemed to think he was too good for any of the jobs he was qualified to get.

The relationship dissolved rather quickly. As it disintegrated, Grant fell into a deep funk and sought psychiatric treatment. He was prescribed medications for depression and bipolar disorder, including lithium. Then he moved back to Raleigh.

According to a close friend, the religious instruction Grant had received growing up remained apparent in his life. He regularly attended church, made prayer an essential part of every day and studied the Bible faithfully until

2003. But then, the friend said, Grant turned his religious fervor over to Tupac Shakur's music, learning all the lyrics of Tupac songs just as he once learned Bible verses. Grant began to spend most of his time talking to others by relating tales from the life of Tupac.

Soon after, he started drinking, smoking marijuana and experimenting with cocaine and heroin. Through this period, Grant still worked hard, made money, took his medication as prescribed, and seemingly maintained control over his mental illness. But after someone gave him 2C-E, a synthetic hallucinogen, Grant couldn't get enough of it. He was hooked on the intense visual hallucinations that many users said were more vivid than those experienced under the influence of LSD. Although the effects of each dose only lasted for six to ten hours, the drug tended to alter perception throughout the next day.

Grant snorted it regularly and, within weeks, his friend said, Grant was no longer capable of having a "normal, business-style conversation." He was consumed by delusions of grandeur and often made no sense at all. "It seemed he'd started a habit of believing the first thing that popped into his head. He'd continue trains of thought to nowhere and then start a new one in a split second. He had lost something—something in his mind. A part of him wasn't there anymore," his friend said.

ONE night in late 2006, as he performed at a venue, a twenty-two-year-old woman, Laura Ackerson, caught his eye. She attended a few more of his shows and once brought

Heidi with her to a performance before her friend went out of town. Right after that, Grant and Laura started dating. Laura was taken by the fact that she and Grant shared a birthday—it made their coming together seem like fate.

It was on their next birthday, April 30, 2007, that they exchanged vows before a justice of the peace. Laura turned twenty-three that day, Grant twenty-eight.

CHAPTER THREE

LAURA strongly believed in Grant's musical talent and thought that with a little help he could hone it into a remarkably successful music career. She actively marketed him to various venues and lined up bookings through Rare Breed Entertainment Agency, whose only client appeared to be Grant. She also encouraged him to keep working on the development of his natural artistic talent.

Grant, however, behaved like a man who wanted more than a supportive partner; he acted as if he wanted someone he could control at all times and in every way. In no time, Grant had taken charge of Laura's life. It was too easy for him to dominate and manipulate the younger, naïve woman with low self-esteem. He attempted to establish control over all her activities and associations.

The honeymoon was over. Among his more outrageous requests, he asked her to talk to his fans about their sex life and brag about his penis size. When she objected and was horrified at that prospect, he said he didn't understand why she had a problem with it. He said that it was obvious to everyone that she was "trash" because she was a white girl in a relationship with a black man.

Grant shocked Laura in a different way one evening a few weeks later at Jack Astor's Bar and Grill in Cary. Another musician rebuked him for arriving late for a gig and Grant pulled a knife on him. He told Laura he was justified because the guy had used the word "fuck" when talking to him.

Laura experienced other incidents that caused her to be fearful for her personal safety. From time to time, Grant slipped into what he described as his "blackouts" or "lost time." In the midst of those disengagements from reality, he acted odd and violent, and then he would fall suddenly into a restless sleep for many hours, twitching throughout as if he were engaged in an unceasing nightmare.

On one particularly bad occasion, Grant, fueled by cocaine, wrote a nonsensical autobiography that he posted on Myspace. After finishing that task, he pulled out an air pump BB gun and began shooting at Laura. The pings weren't causing any serious physical harm, but they were very painful.

She pleaded with him to stop but he just kept pulling the trigger and staring at her with empty, hawklike eyes as if she were prey waiting to be torn asunder. She held up a kitchen towel to block some of the BBs as she made her escape from the room. Laura was never certain if these episodes were all drug-induced or not.

He attempted to indoctrinate her in some of his peculiar beliefs. He told her he believed he was a "time traveler" and that "beings" from other planets followed him around and often talked to him. He thought that those same beings ran the United States. Not only did he believe a government collapse was imminent, he said, "The world will end on December 31, 2012," and he needed "to get enough cash to make it on one of those alien ships at the end of the planet." He believed that very rich, famous, necessary individuals would either be in an underground system of tunnels or on the ships while Armageddon raged across the earth. It sounded as if he had read a piece of Scientology literature and appropriated bits and pieces for his own personal religious doctrine.

Laura would have liked to have believed it was one big joke, but Grant seemed dead serious about his delusional belief structure. The more she learned about these ideas, the more disturbing it was to her. But she had grown more under his control once she was pregnant with his child. No matter how crazy he acted, no matter how nutty his beliefs sounded, he was the father of the baby she carried and she was totally dependent on him now. She had entered the relationship without a strong sense of self and Grant eroded what little she did have. She was stranded in a volatile relationship with none of the needed self-confidence to strike out on her own.

A few months after their wedding, Grant had also asked Laura to be in a polygamous relationship with him. When she refused, he went outside of the marriage and hooked up with a girl named Kristen that December, a mere seven months after his matrimonial ceremony with Laura.

Laura learned about the woman's existence when she was in the second trimester of her pregnancy. The grin on Grant's face while he talked to Kristen on the phone with Laura in the same room made it seem as if he was delighted to keep Laura's insecurity at the highest level possible. Knowing she could hear him, he asked Kristen to marry and run off with him. When Grant hung up from the call, Laura confronted him. He justified his behavior by pointing to her polygamy refusal. He then added that he wanted to have sex with Kristen because she had a "large butt." Although Grant obviously needed the company of adoring females, it seemed as if he had no respect for any woman.

Grant certainly didn't have any for Laura's close friend Heidi Schumacher—in fact, he despised her. He told Laura what he thought of that woman and insisted that she cut off contact with her, but the two women kept communicating despite Grant's disapproval. When he was at a band meeting, prepping for a show or performing, they'd get together somewhere for a cup of coffee or dinner.

Despite those efforts with Heidi, however, Laura would later admit, "I allowed myself to be alienated from my friends and family. Everyone I knew was either 'really dumb' or 'too fat' or 'not good enough to be around us,' according to Grant."

In her third trimester, Laura was once on the phone with Heidi, who could hear Grant yelling in the background, "Heidi is a bad influence on you! I forbid you from seeing her ever again."

When Laura tried to hang up the phone, Heidi begged, "Please don't, Laura."

"I have to," Laura said between sobs, and disconnected the call.

Worried about what might be happening at her friend's home, Heidi immediately hopped into her car and drove twenty minutes to check on Laura. As she arrived, Heidi saw a big black sedan pulling away with Grant in the passenger seat.

Laura opened the front door as Heidi approached. Laura was sobbing, her nose was bleeding and Heidi thought it appeared to be broken. One of Laura's eyes was swollen nearly shut, and the area around it was deep red. Heidi was certain that Laura would have a black eye by the next morning if not sooner. It didn't take a detective to reach the conclusion that Grant had physically assaulted Laura.

She suggested that the police should be called, but Laura said, "It's okay. It's okay. I'm not going to do anything. I'm not going to press charges."

"Laura, you need to go to the hospital. You're pregnant. You need to go to the hospital to make sure everything is all right."

"No, no, no. It's okay. We're going to get through this. He's never done this before but it's okay." Laura was shaking all over and crying, as she pleaded with Heidi, "Please. I don't want anybody to know."

"Just come out to my car and I'll drive you to the hospital," Heidi said.

Laura continued in her stubborn refusal. Heidi stayed with her for an hour and a half trying to break down her friend's resistance to seeking medical treatment but to no avail. She finally left after Laura's tears dried and she had calmed down. When Heidi saw her again a couple of days later, it was clear that Laura had tried to cover up her injuries with makeup, but the swelling and dark coloration were still quite obvious.

Laura's first child, Grant Ruffin Hayes IV, was born on May 2, 2008. Heidi visited Laura's home as soon as she returned from the hospital. With the birth of their grandson, Grant's parents completely embraced Laura as a member of the family. They often chided Grant to be as supportive of his wife as she was of him. Laura probably would have done well to rely on them a bit more, but she showed no inclination to turn to them about any of the problems she was having with Grant.

By the time little Grant was two months old, another conflict erupted—this time over immunizations for the baby. Grant said his son would absolutely not get shots. He repeatedly told Laura that the chances of an African-American boy getting autism were far greater than the rest of the population. Laura was in turmoil over the issue. She wanted the protection from childhood diseases for little Grant but she was afraid that her husband might be right. Again, this was a battle Grant won.

LAURA'S brother Jason met Grant Hayes for the first time when his nephew was about six months old. They had dinner together and hung out for a while, and Jason left thinking that they'd had a good visit.

Occasionally, after that evening, Jason would go with Laura to bars or clubs to see Grant perform. On one of his subsequent visits to their home, little Grant had been fussy for a while. Laura made sure he wasn't hungry or in need of a clean diaper, so then left him upstairs to cry, believing the old wives' tale that it would strengthen his lungs.

Grant grew progressively more agitated and angry as his infant son continued crying. He snapped at Laura, "Shut him up, whatever it takes."

Jason coaxed Grant outside to remove him from the situation, and talked him down into a calmer state of mind. Soon Grant acknowledged he was being too emotional, and matters settled down.

Not long afterward, Grant, Laura and the baby moved over to an apartment in the Camden Crest complex in North Raleigh, located very close to Jason's place of employment. He started coming to see his sister every week, either on his lunch break or when the work day was over. Usually when he arrived, Grant retreated to the back bedroom and never came out. The rare times he did emerge, it was only to go to the refrigerator and then back into hiding.

One day, Laura called Jason and asked if he could come and hang out at lunchtime. About an hour later, Jason arrived and knocked on the door. He could hear arguing and loud commands delivered by Grant to Laura. "He doesn't need to come around. You don't need to be hanging out with him. He's a bad influence."

While Grant yelled, baby Grant cried. Laura struggled to calm both of them down at once. And Grant continued ranting. "You don't need him in your life. I'm all that you need."

Jason stayed at the front door for about ten minutes, knocking again and again. He went around to the sliding glass door and tried to look inside. He couldn't see anything, but by that time all was quiet.

Jason left, but he kept trying to phone his sister all day. She finally returned his call the next day and said, "In order for us to see each other, it has to be private, when Grant isn't around. He doesn't like you."

Jason didn't like the situation, but he realized as long as Laura was in this relationship, she needed contact with family more than ever. Thereafter, the siblings continued to meet in secret, either when Jason came to Laura or when Laura met him at his work.

Grant continued his attempts to cut Laura off from all family and friends, from anyone who would provide her with support—the pattern of controlling spouses who desire to isolate their partners in order to make them more dependent and therefore more compliant.

DESPITE his desire to have Laura at home alone, however, Grant didn't seem to be capable of being alone himself. Whenever Laura left little Grant in his care for even the shortest amount of time, she always found other people with him when she returned. Even with his child present, Grant invited anyone and everyone into his home, from other musicians and groupies to pimps and drug dealers. Most worrisome to Laura was how Grant would pass little Grant around to total strangers. He even offered one convicted felon "godfather status" in order to solidify a business transaction.

One evening in the fall of 2008, Grant and Laura went out to dinner with their baby and eight of Grant's friends. They sat outside at a table, but within the first thirty minutes, Grant disappeared inside the restaurant and stayed gone for quite some time.

One of his friends went in to see what was up and found Grant in the men's room snorting and selling cocaine. When the friend returned to the table, he turned to Laura and said, "You should leave Grant and take your son." Knowing that Grant was an avid believer that immunizations caused autism, the friend added, "Get your boy immunized. He'll be fine. Don't worry."

IN February 2009, Grant Hayes's family staged what they called an "intervention" on Laura's behalf at their house. With Grant's mother, Patsy, and sister, Tina, gathered around, Grant's father told Laura that his son had "a crazy world-takeover plan. He wants to have fifty kids with different women of all races in order to build his empire," Grant Jr. said, adding that his son had told him he anticipated being about seventy years old before he achieved his goal. Her husband, they told her, believed this was the old way of building a business—like in the Bible.

Her father-in-law also warned Laura that Grant III "is the type of man who will pimp you if he needed to."

Suddenly, she saw the truth behind one of her husband's strange habits. He would always provide a "party favor" (aka a woman) to keep the host "company" at promotional parties for his new recordings or for a new artistic venture. Now she understood exactly what those phrases meant.

Her in-laws gave her the phone number for Grant's first wife, Emily. Emily's advice to Laura was: "Run—run as fast as you can."

When Laura walked out of the Hayes's home, she took little Grant and spent a couple of weeks with her friend Heidi Schumacher's parents. When Laura returned to Kinston, Grant's sister, Tina, took her to a magistrate to file assault charges against Grant. That same month, she contacted the Safe Alliance, an agency in Charlotte that ran a shelter for abused women and their children. She wanted to know if what she was experiencing was typical of abusive relationships. She wanted to know of any options she could use to correct the destructive path she traveled.

But Laura never followed through with any of it, fearing her little family would never recover—and she so yearned to provide her son with the cohesive, intact unit that she never had growing up.

She would come to deeply regret her naïveté at this point in her life.

CHAPTER FOUR

B^Y March 2009, life had grown ever scarier for Laura. Grant was spending more time with felons and drug abusers, and as a result his drinking and drug use escalated once again. One terrifying night, he ran into little Grant's bedroom raging and swinging a baseball bat. He told Laura that "the aliens were fucking with him." A hysterical, shrieking Laura threw herself between Grant and the baby to protect the little boy from his father. Then Grant rushed outside, still clutching the bat and running off crazed.

Throughout the chaos of Laura's disintegrating home life, Heidi and Laura managed to maintain their friendship, getting together as frequently as possible. One evening in late March, they were standing out in the parking lot of a Starbucks chatting when Grant pulled up and lit into Laura for continuing to see Heidi. Then he directed his comments to both women: "I am powerful enough and I have enough friends that I could have you both killed and no one will know what happened to you. So don't fuck with me."

Soon after that incident, Heidi obtained a concealed-carry permit. She wanted Laura to carry a gun, too, but Laura was very uncomfortable with firearms and wouldn't have one. Instead, Heidi bought her friend a knife with a rosewood handle, which Laura carried with her until she died.

Around that same time, when little Grant was still less than a year old, Laura found him sitting with his father watching a movie while a very explicit and realistic rape scene filled the screen. Laura was appalled and wanted to take her son out of the room. Grant refused to let him go and told her that little Grant was his son and her opinion was irrelevant. He knew what was best for his boy.

Shortly after those experiences, Laura suggested a temporary separation to Grant, saying she could go to her brother's house for a while. Grant went ballistic. "If you go stay with your brother, I will hunt you down, or my goon squad will hunt you down, and kill you. And Jason, too."

Nonetheless, Laura did broach the subject with her brother. After talking it over, however, they decided it was too much risk to Jason's young daughter, who lived with him part-time. Neither one of them wanted to put yet another person in danger.

After that, Jason stopped calling his sister so as not to further strain her relationship with Grant. He just waited for her to call him. They still talked every month, but now it had the undertones of an espionage assignation.

———————

AS time went by, Grant Hayes grew more frustrated with his trajectory as a professional musician in Raleigh. Some nights he played open-mike gigs, performing for hours for tips and coming home with no money after he paid his bar tab. He felt he needed a new audience to revitalize his foundering career.

He'd been playing on the college circuit with other performers but had been pushed out of that group. He later claimed that the reason for his ejection was that someone was trying to kill him because of his knowledge of or involvement in a murder. He expressed a desire to escape the heat to an acquaintance in the United States Virgin Islands, Joseph "Jose" Hardin, a music promoter/agent in St. John.

Jose thought Grant was a charismatic and creative musician who knew how to play a crowd. He smiled at individuals as he performed and had been described as a male Sade. Jose believed that getting an act like Grant's to St. John would be a real coup. He assured Grant that he could line up five to six gigs a week for him. On top of that, Jose said, "It's awesome here. No stress. No worries."

The smallest of the three main Caribbean islands—St. Thomas, St. John and St. Croix—that make up the USVI, St. John encompasses only twenty square miles and about 60 percent of that is under the purview of the US National Park Service. After a flight to Charlotte Amalie on the island of St. Thomas, reaching its smaller sister is easy on the Red Hook ferry. A fifteen-minute boat ride travels through breathtaking tiny cays, some lush and green, others covered with rocks, cactus and stunted trees.

St. John remained a lush and unspoiled paradise with pristine beaches and magnificent vistas around every corner. Any snapshot of Trunk Bay, with its underwater snorkeling trail, would strike most Americans as a familiar sight.

Grant thought about it and decided his folk-reggae music style would likely be popular in the islands—and it would be a way to get back at the guys who'd rejected him and prove himself. Little Grant was still small when Grant left him and Laura behind in Kinston while he went down to test the waters. In no time, he renamed himself Grant Haze and established a devoted following. Within one month, he had a girlfriend on St. John.

Jose knew Grant had what it took as a performer but he was further impressed by the extent of Grant's artistic abilities—"all he needed was a piece of paper and a pencil." Grant knew, too, how to capitalize on it. Every month, he came up with a new awesome business idea.

One successful plan was his souvenir T-shirts. Grant printed artwork he'd created on the shirts, then added the words "St. John, USVI" and they sold like crazy. Then, Jose said, Grant "manipulated other people to sell them for him, too," creating another stream of revenue as well as an effective promotional tool.

A crazier plan cooked up by Grant involved getting an elephant to give rides to tourists. Mark Gierth, a friend of Grant's on St. John who joined him in "chasing girls and imbibing pot and cocaine," said that he told Grant: "There are no elephants in the Caribbean; there must be a reason for that."

Still, Grant was enchanted with the idea until Mark reminded him, "Elephants poop—and it has to go somewhere. Do you want to shovel it?"

Mark said he often felt bad for Grant, who always seemed "two steps behind the guy who got the prize." For instance, Grant would become all teary-eyed when listening to "One Believer" by John Campbell. The song told the story of a man who dreamed of having his name in lights and prayed for someone who believed in him and opened the right door. Grant saw himself as that man—a lonely outcast whose career hadn't gone the way he wanted it to go. Grant grew bitter when talking about the success of others; it "made his heart race and his face change."

But according to Mark, Grant "was always a little short of what he needed," even though "he was always striving for success." Jose, on the other hand, came to believe that Grant's real problem was that he was very lazy and would back away from any real work.

Grant, however, could be very charming—so charming, Jose said, that "I knew he was manipulating me. . . . He'd say, 'I need you—only you can do this—you are special—you are awesome' . . . and I'd fall for it again and again."

WHILE Grant was in the islands, Laura told Heidi she wanted to leave him. She and little Grant again moved in with Heidi's parents. Heidi had long been dismayed by

Grant's controlling behavior and was quick with encouragement and an offer to help in any way she could.

Laura decided she wanted to take her son and stay up in Michigan with her father, Rodger Ackerson. Together, the two friends planned Laura's road trip, including an overnight stay at Heidi's grandparents' place in Ohio.

But just before it was time for Laura and little Grant to head north, Laura started feeling ill. Heidi took her to Planned Parenthood in Wake Forest, and Laura discovered that she was twelve weeks pregnant with a second child.

Laura shifted gears and decided not to leave Grant after all. Instead, she decided that she was going to tell him about their new baby and move down to the Virgin Islands to be with him, and to give their relationship one more chance.

Before leaving for the Caribbean, Laura told her brother Jason that she knew that Grant had begun another relationship on the island, but she added that he'd promised to stop seeing that woman immediately.

Their second son was born two months premature on St. Thomas on August 3, 2009. They named him Gentle Reign. Grant explained the name in a promotional interview for his website with Los Angeles publicist Hollace Dowdy. "In my maturity, I'm understanding what masculinity is. And it's gentle."

Not only did that line contradict his behavior, the interview was filled with information about an idyllic childhood complete with a gospel-music-star mother and a father who was a minister in a big Los Angeles church. It was all in direct contrast with previous statements he'd made onstage about abuse and alcoholism in his family life. Listening to Grant, it was impossible to know where truth ended and fantasy began.

UNFORTUNATELY, blissful island life on St. John did not seem to be in the cards for Laura Ackerson. She had to care for two little guys under the age of two, and the youngest one had been born with a serious health problem involving his kidney.

Mark Gierth, who lived with the couple on St. John for a while, said that Laura and Grant Hayes had frequent verbal squabbles, often over money issues and child care. Now that Laura was the mother of two, she wanted more financial stability and grew frustrated that Grant was hanging on to an empty dream. She still believed in Grant's talent but he wasn't making headway toward turning it into a reliable source of income. She wanted him to come back to reality and accept financial and emotional responsibility for their two children.

Even though Grant tried to hide it, Laura also knew that he was seeing another woman, but she didn't know if it was the same one he'd promised to give up when she came to the islands or if it was another woman altogether. She simply knew there was someone else, and she felt him slipping away. Grant blew off her concerns, telling her that it was part of his job to make women want to have sex with him so that he could pass them to the guys who tagged along as his unofficial entourage. He said that was why he was treated like a celebrity and why everyone wanted to pay for his expenses, from limos to dinners to clothing.

To make matters worse, Grant partied all the time, developed a heavy cocaine habit, and showed no signs of awareness or concern about any of Laura's needs. His daily drug and alcohol use made him incapable of caring for the children. That left all of the childhood duties and household tasks in Laura's hands—with one exception: he still managed to take out the trash. Typically, he was up most of the night, then slept into the afternoon. When he rose, he'd occasionally make a needed grocery store run. Then he'd eat dinner and go out to work and the pattern started again.

Whenever Grant was out doing drugs, he always told Laura he was with Jose, because Laura knew that Jose didn't like blow and wouldn't be around others who were using it. Many times, to reinforce his stories, Grant would trap Jose in a corner, pushing for confirmation, until Jose felt he had no choice but to lie for him.

The more Jose viewed Grant up close, the more troubled he became. He noticed that Grant's lyrics all seemed angry, filled with words like "rage" and "hate." He talked a lot onstage about his childhood with an alcoholic father who went to prison and beat him and his mother when he was at home. Jose wasn't sure if it was all an act or if there were truth in the dark story.

Grant told Jose that he was scared of black women because of past trauma and so was always with white women because he couldn't stand to look at a black woman's private parts. Jose never knew what to believe. He winced when he heard Grant threaten Laura and threaten to kill or take the children away from her. Jose saw Laura as a loving, caring woman who was supportive of Grant's career and put up with a lot of BS in the process.

Jose recognized that Grant's worldview was excessively self-absorbed. "He was in his own little world—it belonged to him. Everyone else who was there existed for his use."

Often, Grant brought other people home with him, and woke Laura at two thirty or three in the morning. One night, he opened his computer and started composing music and woke up the whole household. Laura was sweet to everyone but her irritation at Grant rose off her like steam from a boiling kettle. Still, she settled the boys back in bed and then asked if anyone was hungry. Of course, they all were. She fixed food and went back to bed, still obviously mad. Jose felt sorry for her but felt helpless in the shadow of Grant's overpowering, intolerant personality.

Jose came to view Grant as a perfect psychopath who lied and used people without mercy. He believed that Grant had a delusional personality and blamed others for his failures and essentially was a coward and lazy about real work. He saw that Grant could recognize and zero in on people who were caring, who would listen to his tales of woe and help him.

Gentle's physical problems became frightening—he needed special health care, including a surgical procedure to put a stent between his bladder and kidney. So Laura left Grant on St. John and moved back to North Carolina with her sons. She moved into a rental property in Kinston owned by Grant's parents that was located next door to their day care center. In exchange for her housing, she cleaned the center each night. Near the end of the year, to make additional money for expenses, Laura started a free-lance business called GoFish Graphic Designs, creating logos, layouts and print publications for other businesses.

THOUGH a great distance now separated them, Grant and Laura kept in close touch. He told her about a woman named Amanda who was feeding him and doing his laun-dry in exchange for guitar lessons. Grant described her as an investor who wanted to back his career.

When Grant met country music star Kenny Chesney on the island, he told Laura that Kenny had a huge crush on Amanda. "Maybe I should just pimp her—nah, I won't." Despite that denial, he detailed how if Kenny was in Aman-da's pocket and Amanda was in Grant's, then "I'm as good as famous."

When Laura sensed there was something more going on in his relationship, Grant complained about Amanda's "saggy breasts." He claimed that he was involved with her "only for the betterment of our family's situation." He continued talking about his strategy to take advantage of the woman's interest in him. "Amanda is generous as long as she doesn't feel you are taking advantage of her," Grant told Laura. In order to win her trust, he said, he some-times ate ramen noodles for dinner rather than accept Amanda's invitation to join her and her daughter Sha Elmer for meals "in order to come off in a humble manner."

On December 29, 2009, Laura sent Grant a desperate

e-mail. "Baby I can't go through this month of you with her. I feel like I'm dying on the inside just thinking about it and with you actually there, I think you may have a dead woman when you call—if not in body, in soul. This sharing has torn me from the inside out and I am here with your children and no family of my own. I'm sorry I took apart what you worked for. It was never intentional. I feel so up against a wall. I wish I could jump off a bridge sometimes and sometimes I wish I could just let you go. Either one would make the slaughter of my soul stop—how children complicate a situation incredibly. I can't share you . . . I want to concede, let her have you . . . I want my family and my man to want to be faithful only to me. I want a smile all the time. I want a bounce in my step."

BY January 2010, Grant was ready to leave St. John. Jose was there for him to the very end. Jose said that he packed Grant's bags while Grant snorted endless lines of cocaine. Then he drove Grant to Cruz Bay to catch the ferry to St. Thomas and the airport. It wasn't until that last night that Jose learned that Grant's legal name was Grant Hayes. Before then, he'd thought Grant Haze, Grant's stage name, was his name at birth.

Grant wasn't leaving USVI for his family in North Carolina, however—he was heading to New York City. Laura thought he was going there for a record deal. She had no idea that he was actually following Amanda Smith.

CHAPTER FIVE

AMANDA Perry Tucker was born seven years before Grant Hayes, on April 8, 1972. Her mother, Retha Faye, who was born in Taft, "The Friendliest Cotton Pickin' Town in Texas," had earlier had two daughters, Karen and Dorrie, with her first husband, and a son with her second husband, J. C. Tucker. After that, according to Amanda's daughter, Sha Elmer, her maternal grandmother worked at the Black and White Club in Farmington, a purported whorehouse, and for that reason had no idea who fathered her next child, Amanda.

Amanda's older half sister, Karen Berry, was already married and played a major role in raising the little girl, treating her just like one of her own children. Karen's son, Dalton, was only two years younger than his aunt, and the two became close growing up, often under the same roof.

Somewhere in Retha Faye's maze of husbands—family

legend said that she'd wed eight or nine times—she married a power plant employee. According to Sha, he was a "horrible, mean man" who created a miserable home environment for his young stepdaughter and constantly moved the family from one small town to another in New Mexico and Texas. Amanda coped with the unpleasantness and disruptions by retreating into a rich daydream life. She yearned to escape the confines of her insular, provincial life and make her mark on the world.

Amanda was fifteen when Retha Faye broke up with that husband, and the teenager returned to New Mexico with her mother. But Amanda was eager to leave her family home, and she took the first escape hatch available when she met Scott Elmer. She hadn't yet turned sixteen and Scott was twenty-one when they married in 1987. Their daughter Sha was born on June 7, 1989.

The marriage between Amanda and Scott was one constant squabble that ended in divorce when Sha was one year old. Amanda's desire to move to Texas permanently ignited a battle over their daughter, which Amanda eventually won. She starting dating, then married, attorney Ron Adamson. While they were together, Amanda finished high school and took a few classes at the junior college, but called it quits on the marriage after eight months. The relationship was over two years after it began.

Amanda and then-five-year-old Sha moved in with Amanda's sister, Karen Berry, in Lubbock, Texas. After a few months, Amanda found a place for just her and Sha, and she met a local children's-theater director. Through him, she became acquainted with the terminology of that world as she helped with touring productions of *Sleeping Beauty* and *Cinderella*. At the same time, Amanda was going to school in Levelland. The long drives for those two activities caused her to put fifty thousand miles on her car in one year.

It was too much. School was the first thing to go. Amanda stuck with theater until a friend introduced her to a wealthy entrepreneur named Nicky Smith. Born in 1958 to a multigenerational family of cotton farmers, Nicky was fourteen years older than Amanda. He was the owner-operator of Valley Ag-Electric, a wholesale manufacturer of irrigation systems and equipment located in Olton, Texas, just north of his birthplace in Lubbock. At one point, he had five separate dealerships for that enterprise. He also leased the farmland to tenant farmers; owned a company that embroidered jackets, T-shirts and hats; and made road signs for the state. He spent a lot of time traveling to other countries like Brazil and Egypt, teaching people there how to grow cotton. After dating for a year, the two married on March 19, 1998.

This life was a dramatic change from what Amanda and Sha had previously known. There were no more worries about finding the money for groceries and rent. Sha was in fourth grade when they moved into the home Nicky purchased near Austin on Inks Lake, situated in the scenic Texas Hill Country. The lake, a reservoir created by a dam on the Colorado River, offered a wealth of outdoor recreation, including swimming, camping, picnicking and fishing; plus, Inks Lake State Park was adjacent to the lake and added backpacking, golf and cliff jumping to the list of possible activities.

Nicky traveled five hours north most weeks to run Valley Ag-Electric and returned home for the weekends. Sha attended school in nearby Burnet. With freedom from economic worries, Amanda had time to pursue personal interests, and she discovered a passion for painting, particularly acrylic abstracts. With Nicky, everything felt so safe and secure.

But their all-too-fleeting happiness ended in one awful moment.

It was the beautiful lake setting, unfortunately, that caused the end of this idyllic period. Not realizing that Inks Lake had been partially drained to accommodate work on the dam, Nicky jumped in on Memorial Day in 2000— and landed in just six inches of water. He broke his neck and was paralyzed from the shoulders down in the mishap.

He had a week-long stay in an Austin hospital before he was transferred to Lubbock, where a surgeon was doing experimental treatment for spinal injuries. Pneumonia landed him in the Intensive Care Unit there, and following his recovery from that setback, he was moved down to a rehab facility in San Antonio and put on a ventilator. Amanda was dissatisfied with his care in San Antonio, and Nicky was flown up to a different rehab in Dallas.

There Nicky learned that his diaphragm was permanently paralyzed and his life now depended on the ventilator. To make matters even worse, his spinal cord was dying and would progress into his brain stem, leaving him incapable of doing anything but blinking his eyes. Nicky decided he wanted the ventilator removed, and he wanted to go home for his last days of life. He died of his injuries on October 11, 2000.

The settlement of the estate was contentious, but since Amanda didn't want any part of the business, issues were resolved when she sold her share to Nicky's brother and made a few trades with Nicky's adult children. She traded half of Nicky's retirement account for ownership of the children's half of the farmland.

Amanda was single again with a small daughter, but this time, she had a sizeable inheritance to cushion the blow. She had enjoyed participating in community theater and children's theater for years, and now she decided to try to build a professional career in acting. Amanda auditioned and was accepted to a two-year program geared toward film and television at a conservatory in New York City.

She settled her mother Retha Faye into the house where she and Nicky had lived, to help out her mom and to prevent the house from sitting vacant. She brought Sha with her, and enrolled the girl in a Catholic school in the city. But after about a year, Sha, who had gotten behind in her studies, begged her mother to let her go stay with Aunt Karen in Texas, and Amanda agreed. Sha also lived part of the time with her father, Scott Elmer, in Farmville, New Mexico, where she started high school.

Back in Austin, Retha Faye fell and broke her leg, which set off a multitude of further health complications, so Amanda moved her other sister, Dorrie, into the house to care for their mother while she finished her studies in New York.

After getting her film and television degree, Amanda knew she had to go to Los Angeles—that's where the work that she wanted to do was centered. She sold the Ink Lakes home and everything in New York and moved her mother into a little house in LA.

She scored some small parts out there. Among her credits were television shows like *The O.C.*, *The Sopranos*, *Dexter*, *Twins*, *Zoey 101*, *According to Jim* and *Century City*, along with the Nicole Kidman movie, *The Stepford Wives*. Every role, however, was very minor and usually did not make the list of credits. Soon, Amanda realized she was going nowhere. Although she was only in her early thirties, her age was already a barrier for a woman trying to break into the business.

So Amanda went back to Texas with her mom and got her real estate license. Neither woman was happy, though, and soon Retha Faye moved in with Karen, and Amanda returned to New York.

In New York, Amanda finished a cosmetology education she'd begun in Texas and began managing a salon day spa on the upper east side of Manhattan but felt she was wasting her life in that position. In January 2007, she vacationed in the United States Virgin Islands and fell in love with St. John. After her fourteen-day getaway turned into a six-week stay, Amanda decided to relocate there. She returned to New York, sold her car, sublet her apartment, put some items in storage and sent a small shipment down to the island.

When she arrived, Amanda worked as a bartender before becoming a gallery director for the Artists' Association of St. John, an organization formed in the 1990s with help from the Artists Association of Nantucket. When Amanda stepped into her position, there were 152 members, most of whom were full-time residents on the island. Each was given sixteen square feet to display their work. The featured artists each month got a whole wall dedicated to their art. The first exhibit of the gallery under Amanda's watch was in August 2007. Amanda also had plans for daily art classes in subjects from oil painting and watercolor to pottery, sculpture, photography and jewelry making.

She told the *St. John Tradewinds* newspaper that she wanted to expand the membership to hobbyists. "I'd really like to get more people to come out and join the association. You don't have to be a professional artist to join. There are a lot of people out there with talent who don't see it for themselves." She added a word to the aspiring artists: "Don't judge yourself. It's important to keep your channel open and just have fun. Every person is unique and there is no comparing one to the other because everything is so different."

Amanda also noticed that there was no place on the island to buy what she needed to continue her own painting, so she decided to redesign an unused portion of the gallery space as Pirate's Paradise Art Supply. Originally configured as two rooms and a hallway, a boyfriend and his cousin helped Amanda transform it into one large room with slat walls painted bright white. She stocked the space with a large selection of quality brushes, acrylics, watercolors, oils, canvas rolls and prestretched canvasses and paper. She also placed special orders for any unusual items the artists needed. The shop opened in November 2007. Among the featured works for the gallery in December that year were paintings by Amanda Smith.

In early 2008, Amanda took a trip to New Mexico to visit her teenage daughter, Sha, who was then living with her dad, and ended up bringing Sha back with her to St. John. There, Sha finished her junior year and started her senior year of high school before dropping out. Amanda was not happy with Sha's decision to terminate her education and the conflict escalated into a physical altercation. After that, Sha returned to her father in New Mexico and got her GED, and she later rejoined her mother in USVI.

Upon Sha's return to St. John, Amanda taught her daughter the business side of running the art-supply store and Sha became the manager of Pirate's Paradise. Sha reveled in the energy of the island—unable to describe it but definitely feeling it every day.

AMANDA was out on a date when she first saw Grant Haze performing at the Parrot Club. She didn't see him again for another six months. In the midst of all the beauty and tranquility, another relationship ended for Amanda and she grew lonely and depressed. Then, one night, she saw Grant Haze again. They talked and he gave her one of his CDs. Amanda felt their connection was instant and electric. As a ploy to get to know him better, Amanda asked him to teach her how to play the guitar and Grant agreed. She told

Sha about the lessons and described her teacher as a performer who sounded like Darius Rucker, the lead singer and rhythm guitarist for the Grammy Award–winning group Hootie & the Blowfish.

She invited Grant to accompany her to a group dinner with a bunch of friends where it was her turn to cook that week. He soon started hanging out with her friends. The first time he kissed her, Amanda kicked him out of her home and avoided him for a week. She felt he was moving too fast and her own feelings for him were getting out of control. The ice thawed quickly, and soon Amanda could not see enough of him.

Those close to Grant saw Amanda as a "starry-eyed groupie," said Mark Gierth. Many were appalled that he was cheating on Laura, who was still on the island with their two infant sons, but who thought he was using Amanda for her money and contacts.

From the start, even before they started dating, Amanda displayed signs of extreme jealousy. Any time another woman approached Grant, Amanda's body language grew hostile and she sent venomous glares in her direction—a business problem for someone building a fan base.

It was no surprise that Jose took an instant dislike to Amanda. He snapped at her once and Grant came down on him hard, threatening to kill Jose if he ever spoke to Amanda again.

Sha met Grant Hayes when he came into Pirate's Paradise looking for a sketch pad for a project he was doing for a local school. Sha knew Grant was teaching her mother to play the guitar. She had no idea, however, that the two of them were in a romantic relationship when she and her mother went to New York in October 2009 for a two-week visit. At the time, one of Amanda's former boyfriends on the island was acting a bit crazy over their breakup—stalking and harassing Amanda. In a small place like St. John, there didn't seem to be any way to avoid him, and his actions were causing increasing discomfort. Add to that Sha's desire to move back to the city and renew her education, and the vacation turned into a relocation-planning trip.

They returned to USVI to prepare for the two of them to move back to New York. Sha finally learned the truth about what was going on between her mother and Grant on Thanksgiving Day 2009.

On New Year's Eve, Amanda and Sha flew back to New York and settled into an apartment in Manhattan. Grant and Amanda kept in touch with frequent phone calls. In retrospect, a lot of what he said to her at that time seemed geared to impress and to secure an invitation to join her in New York. Grant said that he once had an opportunity to go to New York but hadn't acted on it. Amanda told him that New York was probably a good place for his music career. He'd told her that he'd toured a lot, including with folk-rock singer Jack Johnson. Grant said that he'd made quite a name for himself in North Carolina in the music business. He claimed to have dated Norah Jones. He told Amanda that he had once worked as a stockbroker and made over a million dollars. He said that he had sponsored several families in association with a Bible study course.

One night, he got what he wanted when he told her he'd

had to go to the cops about Amanda's ex-boyfriend, who Grant said was now stalking and threatening him. The cops told him that it was probably time for him to leave the island, Grant claimed.

On January 16, 2010, with a plane ticket purchased by Amanda, Grant arrived in New York. Amanda didn't inform her daughter that Grant was coming. Sha thought he'd just showed up on their doorstep carrying two suitcases.

CHAPTER SIX

IN the first month after his arrival in New York, Grant Hayes wrote a song about Laura Ackerson called "Broomstick Rider." The lyrics were full of hate and threats of violence. He recorded it in the apartment in the presence of Amanda Smith and her daughter, Sha Elmer, who said she didn't see the red flag flying. She simply believed it was Grant's way of blowing off steam and getting the poisonous feelings out of his system.

WHEN Grant asked to take little Grant back to New York with him in February to take part in a supposed photo shoot for a BabyGap commercial, Laura was reluctant to let her son, not even two years old, go with his father. Her friend Heidi Schumacher also strongly warned against it. "If you do, you'll never get him back," she said.

But Grant wore Laura down by insisting that their son would only spend three days with him up there and then he'd bring the boy back. Laura caved to Grant's pressure yet again, and once she did, that time was stretched to ten days.

When little Grant arrived on February 18, Sha thought he would be visiting for two weeks. She believed that Laura asked Grant to keep the little boy longer than the original plan because she was having difficulty raising two boys on her own.

In mid-March, Grant suddenly stopped sending Laura child support money. She called her brother Jason and said, "Grant kidnapped little Grant. He's in another state and I don't have the money to travel there. And I don't know what I can do legally."

"I wish I had legal advice for you, but I don't," Jason said. "Make sure you stay in contact with Grant Junior as much as possible."

Laura went to see Dr. Joanna Wolicki-Shannon at East Cove Psychiatric Services in Kinston. She wanted answers for Grant's behavior and to see if she could get a name for his problem. After that appointment, Laura began describing Grant as a "sociopath." At this point, Grant was still referring to Amanda as his "investor" and insisting that he was only sleeping with her to benefit their children and their family. Laura didn't know if she should accept this behavior or not, but she felt she needed to learn the root of it first. She knew intuitively that going along with his plan was wrong, but she'd been so battered down by his belittling and by his dire predictions for the fate of their children that she just couldn't walk away.

On March 29, 2010, Laura's pro se (without an attorney) request for the return of little Grant was served on Grant. He sent her a plane ticket—one that Amanda had purchased—writing, "You can come up to New York, you can bring little Grant home, but you'd have to drop the lawsuit in Lenoir County." When Laura refused to agree, he canceled her flight. She now had no doubts about Grant's intentions.

Events proceeded at a reckless speed after that. Grant contacted attorney Brad Hill in North Carolina and told him Laura had used his checking account in Kinston to pay for a subscription to a website called Sugar Daddies where she was prostituting herself and that he had contacted the FBI. Although Laura later admitted to some immature sexual posting on the Internet, calling it "prostitution" was an over-the-top characterization. According to Amanda, Hill told Grant that the courts would view any of Laura's alleged solicitation on the Internet just as harshly as they would his cohabitation with Amanda.

On April 1, Grant sent a message to fellow musician Nick Hagelin. "I'm marrying an actress from that movie *Stepford Wives*." He invited him to come up to New York and take part in his weekly Sunday evening variety show at a Bleecker Street venue. Grant had high hopes for his future, writing, "All I need is someone to get signed and discovered there and my show blows up."

Amanda said that Grant started planning an elaborate wedding, and she said, "Can't we just get married? Does it have to be something crazy?"

Later that month, instead of bringing little Grant home

to Laura as he'd promised, Grant took his almost-two-year-old son with him on a trip to Las Vegas, accompanied by Amanda, Sha and Paul Hutchins, a man he introduced as a former manager. Grant and Amanda were married in Vegas on April 10.

Grant had always treated Sha, then twenty, as if she were a dumb kid who didn't know what was going on. His new stepdaughter, however, was more aware than he knew. She made that clear in Vegas. "Grant, if you ever mistreat my mom," she told him, "I *will* deal with you."

Laura was stunned when Grant sent her a photograph of his Las Vegas wedding along with a message that he and Laura had never really been married because he hadn't signed the paperwork.

She rummaged around in her papers and finally found their certificate of marriage. Laura stared dumbfounded at the piece of paper. She called Heidi and said, "I can't believe it. He never signed the marriage certificate. I can't believe it." Without his signature, the document was not legally binding. She never had been Grant's wife. She had two sons with him but no tie that binds.

Laura's sister, Jennifer Mae Cross, chatted online with her on April 29. She asked Laura how she was doing, adding, "G4 (little Grant) is beautiful."

Laura answered the question, "Terrible but wonderful, too!" Then she responded to the compliment about her son, "Thank you. His dad and I just broke up and he got married right away and little G is in New York with them and we are in the middle of this ugly custody battle. . . . His lady is a movie star. Sigh . . . LOL."

Jennifer sent her number to Laura so that they could continue the conversation on the telephone.

AT the end of April 2010, Grant, Amanda and little Grant came down to Kinston, North Carolina, driving overnight so that little Grant could sleep through the trip. Grant wanted to celebrate his son's second birthday at his parents' house. He told his mother that she could invite Laura if she promised "not to make a scene." Laura was thrilled to see her oldest son at the party but disappointed that she was not allowed any one-on-one time with him outside of the home.

Grant had filed an ex parte motion telling Judge Les Turner that Laura was an unfit mother. "Ex parte" refers to the fact that the other party—in this case, Laura—did not appear before the judge. Grant alleged that Laura purchased a Craigslist ad looking for someone to live with her at no cost. In arguing this point, Grant's attorney inferred that Laura was willing to trade sex for housing. Grant also claimed that Laura was having trouble parenting the children and controlling the temper tantrums of the youngest child—which, he said, was why little Grant went to New York City with Grant. Without any opportunity to appear, object or fight for her boys, the court accepted him at his word at the time, awarding Grant full temporary emergency custody of the children.

Amanda did not tell her daughter, Sha, about Grant's disparagement of Laura's parenting abilities. Instead, she explained that the custody change had come about because of Gentle's need for kidney surgery.

Amanda, Grant and little Grant returned to New York City for two weeks before leaving to move to North Carolina. Amanda paid cash for their Raleigh apartment deposit, furniture and a car.

ON June 15, 2010, Laura was served the emergency ex parte custody motion. Worst of all, when she received the document, law enforcement immediately removed Gentle from her car and turned him over to Grant. Amanda later said that Gentle cried his heart out on the drive back to Raleigh.

Two days later, paperwork in hand, Laura met with attorney John Sargeant. When Laura finally got her day in court for a return hearing on June 25, Judge Beth Heath had to decide whether to keep the emergency order in effect or to put some other arrangement in place. Laura did not look very stable to the judge. She had no permanent place to live and didn't have a job. Offsetting that was Laura's allegation that Grant was a substance abuser.

The attorneys met with the judge in chambers and reached an agreement. The children would remain with Grant during the week but would be with Laura on the weekends. They would make the exchange at a public place in Wilson—about halfway between their two residences.

Grant had complained that Laura wanted to delay Gentle's surgical procedure because she wanted a second opinion. Laura's attorney, however, said that it was Grant who had pushed to get another doctor involved because he wanted to pursue a holistic cure that did not involve surgery. In the agreement, Gentle's operation would go through as indicated by the original physician.

Gentle's medical situation was one of the reasons that Laura was willing to go along with Grant having the boys during the week, since Gentle's medical care provider was in Cary, much closer to Grant's Raleigh apartment. The other reason Laura agreed was the nature of their employment. Laura was about to start a job that required her to work during the week and, as a musician, most of Grant's work was on the weekends. Since she'd only seen her son little Grant once since February 14 and hadn't seen Gentle for more than a week, Laura viewed the agreement as a blessing.

The judge also ordered a full psychological review of Grant, Laura and the boys because of the dueling charges about the issue of character and behavior. Additionally, Grant would be the one responsible for covering the upfront cost of the evaluation. The judge recommended a doctor named Ginger Calloway for this job.

A handwritten consent agreement put everything in place. Provisions were made for telephone communication allowing for reasonable contact when the boys were with the other party, no more than twice a day and fifteen minutes or less in duration between the hours of ten A.M. and eight P.M. Other conditions were that neither party would get a passport for the children or remove them from the state of North Carolina while the order was in effect. After

it was typed and signed by the judge on June 29, a copy
was officially filed.

Little Grant's visitation with his mother began immediately. Laura and her friend Heidi Schumacher took him
straight from the courthouse to Laura's apartment. Gentle's
was delayed for a few weeks to give him time for surgery
and recovery, but Laura was there at the hospital throughout the operation. She and Amanda had a positive interaction there. Amanda assured her, "Things will get better as
time goes on."

"You still don't know Grant," Laura said. As far as Laura
could see, Grant hadn't changed "a single step in his game"
and was running the same plays on Amanda that he had
run previously on her.

The meeting place established for the exchange of the
children was the Sheetz gas station and convenience store
near the intersection of Interstate 95 and US 264 in Wilson, about halfway between Raleigh and Kinston. Occasionally, Laura and Grant met up for the exchange at a
Monkey Joe's in Raleigh, a franchise for kids featuring
inflatable slides, jumps and obstacle courses for the under-
twelve set with a mini-monkey zone for safe toddler play.
The general manager there was Lauren Harris, a longtime
friend of Grant's, who never made little Grant and Gentle
pay the seven-dollar entry fee. According to Lauren, Grant
brought the boys into Monkey Joe's nearly every day she
worked. He played along with his children as if he were a
kid, too.

Laura filled her weekends with the boys with trips to

the playground and to nature parks. They did arts and crafts projects together. One night of each visit was pizza night—together they'd build little pizzas and pop them in the oven.

GRANT had a lot of complaints about the new court order arrangement. In a Facebook message to his friend Crystal Wiggins, he wrote: "I'm very happy, stressed from the whole custody arrangement and what it is doing to my boys. Their mom is a woman scorned and, well, making life for me as difficult as possible. My wife is going to New York to clean out our place [and] put it on the market."

When Crystal responded with regret that things did not work out with his wife, Grant fired back: "My wife? I was never married to my kid's mother. My wife now is awesome." He continued grousing that the custody arrangement made it impossible for him to leave the state and his rent in New York had been paid up front for a year.

CHAPTER SEVEN

LAURA got busy getting her house in order. She moved from the Hayes's rental home to her own place on North Heritage Street, within walking distance of just about everything in downtown Kinston. The building was a renovated warehouse with shops and a beauty salon. Most important for a single woman, her second-floor apartment was very secure—a key was needed to enter the building and a remote to enter the garage.

She set up a bedroom for the boys. Once Gentle moved out of his crib, he used a white wood toddler bed, and little Grant slept in one that looked like a sporty blue car. On the table between them was a photograph of Laura and Grant. She put that there, she said, because she wanted the boys to know they were loved by both Mommy and Daddy. Toys tucked around every room of the apartment gave the entire space a whimsical air. Every week before the boys visited, Laura went to a toy-rental store to make sure little Grant and Gentle always had something new for their play.

Laura got a job at HealtHabit Natural Foods, a health food store on North Queen Street, and started taking classes at the community college, studying early childhood development. Ultimately, she wanted either to be a teacher or to open a holistic day care center with organic food and classes for the kids. Then she told Heidi she was ready to do battle for full custody of her kids.

In one of their regular Tuesday night conversations, Heidi Schumacher assured Laura, "I will be there for you if you chose to fight. You'll be fighting all your life for them. Do you want to be a lioness or a lamb?"

"I'm going to be a lioness and I'm going to fight every step of the way," Laura told her friend.

Heidi, who was in the process of obtaining her master's degree in criminal justice, knew the value of documentation and told Laura, "Go get a tape recorder immediately and record every conversation with Grant. And keep a log of any contact you have with Grant and with the boys—write down the food you give them so he can't claim you fed them something that made them sick."

"Yeah, and when I feed them and when I change their diapers," Laura agreed.

"Every little thing you do with those boys."

"I'm going to get them back, no matter how long it takes."

"Good for you," Heidi encouraged.

Because Laura feared that Grant had hacked into her e-mail account, she and Heidi set up a secret communication link through an address known only to the two of them. Laura used it for safe storage, forwarding any information relevant to the custody case, whether it was e-mails between her and Grant or messages from her attorney, the psychologist or anyone else involved in her fight for her kids.

Laura started attending Grace Fellowship Church on a regular basis. She also went to "house church," a smaller gathering in other people's homes to study and worship.

By late summer, she'd added a Monday night one-on-one Bible study with Barbara Patty, an older church member who'd become a mentor to her. At one of their first get-togethers, Barbara said, "Laura, I don't know how you take your babies back every Sunday night and leave them for the week. I don't know how you do it as a mother. I don't understand. I'm not sure that I might not take my children and leave."

"Oh," Laura said, "if I did, he'd kill us."

It was a reflection of Laura's new assessment of Grant also seen on July 4 in a message to Alison Gunson, a woman in England who had posted about a sociopath-victims support group on Facebook. "I recently got OUT of a relationship with one but we have two children together," Laura wrote, asking if Alison knew of any resources to help her get him diagnosed. "My kids are at risk here and I need all the help I can get."

ON August 11, 2010, Laura started her phone call log to record her observations and make note of patterns as well as to record anything negative or abnormal. "Prior to starting this log, I have observed several things when talking to my boys via Grant's cell phone. . . . Most times, the volume in the house is very loud, making it hard to hear either Gentle or Grant. This is due to the TV, restaurant noises, or Grant's music. When Amanda answers, it is usually quiet."

THAT summer, Sha was still living in her mother's New York City apartment. At Amanda's request, she packed up everything belonging to her mother and Grant. Amanda flew up to New York to meet the movers who would load everything into a U-Haul she'd rented up there. One of the pieces of furniture on board was an English castle antique that Amanda had inherited from her deceased husband, Nicky Smith. It was an elaborate specimen with a green granite–topped wet bar, flanked by two cabinets and drawers. A large decorative topper made the piece taller than the height of a typical contemporary ceiling.

Amanda and Sha drove the truck down to North Carolina. After a night's sleep at the apartment, they and Grant unloaded the contents at a storage facility in Raleigh.

During that visit, Laura's and Grant's parents gathered at the apartment to celebrate Gentle's first birthday. Apparently, something Sha did set Laura off. She later called the girl and said, "Stop raising my children. They have a mother and father and it's not your job to raise them."

Amanda was furious at Laura. She told her, "Never call my daughter again."

The conflict between Laura and Amanda didn't end

there. When Laura was concerned that Gentle might have croup, she sent Grant an e-mail containing information she had found online. Laura was careful to couch her words with an abundant use of "if" and "if necessary."

Nonetheless, the message prompted a strong reaction in Amanda, who called Laura and said, "You are psycho-crazy. You don't have anything better to do with your time than research crap on the Internet." She went on to tell Laura that the kids "didn't have a virus, they had a cold." She accused Laura of always bringing the kids back home ill because she took them to the water park and let them stay wet all day long. When Amanda hung up on Laura, Laura called her back and told her what she did was inappropriate. "You are still new to the situation."

Amanda shot back, "I am responsible for your kids now because you are psycho-crazy."

Laura was "shaken by Amanda's call." She was certain that Grant had painted her as wacko and had convinced Amanda that she needed to help him protect the kids from their mother.

FOR some inexplicable reason and despite the fact that the judge designated Dr. Calloway for the evaluation, Grant and Amanda had first contacted Dr. Kristen Winns, a female psychologist in Raleigh, for a custody consultation. Little Grant came along on the visit and Dr. Winns was alarmed at how Grant was willing to rage about the boy's mother with him sitting right there listening to every word spoken.

In August, Grant, using Amanda's money, finally made the first down payment of five thousand dollars to Dr. Ginger Calloway. First, she spoke with the two attorneys, who informed her of the questions their clients hoped would be addressed through the process.

On Grant's side, there were questions about Laura's psychological state—he stated that she was either mentally unstable or mentally ill. He also claimed that she had a negative impact on the children and was attempting to alienate them from their father.

From Laura's attorney, Calloway received questions about Grant's credibility and his manipulative behavior. Concerns were also raised about the numerous threats he'd made about taking the children from their mother.

The next step, on August 26, was a meeting with both Grant and Laura together to determine their issues and evaluate their interactions with one another. In that session, Grant said that he and Amanda wanted full custody and stated that Laura should have supervised visitation only. Laura, on the other hand, said that she thought both parents needed to be involved with the children in an established parenting-access plan.

Grant said, "I think Laura will go away as soon as she sees there is no payday. This is all an act."

During that initial appointment, Calloway noted that Laura was quick to criticize Grant with "barbed or sharp comments."

On September 9, Laura returned to Calloway's office for a further interview and psychological testing. When asked about an early, very short-term breakup in November of 2008, she said that she'd left Grant and gone to her brother's home in Youngsville, North Carolina, because Grant had insisted on anal sex. On another occasion, she said that Grant beat her up and threw her out. From Laura's testing, Calloway concluded: "Laura engaged in a considerable amount of denial. In short, she was highly defensive, making interpretation of her MMPI"—Minnesota Multiphasic Personality Inventory, a standard psychological assessment tool—"difficult." However, she noted, "this was not true with the Rorschach. On the later measure, she was highly engaged, provided ample number of responses for interpretation and provided a rich, elaborate record."

On the fifteenth, Calloway met with Grant. When she asked him about the short separation in November of 2008, he contradicted Laura's versions of the events, saying that he kicked Laura out because she was soliciting men through the Internet for pay. From the testing, Calloway saw that "Grant was extremely negative, at times paranoid, about Laura, her character and her alleged actions." She met with him again on September 28. Grant referred to every day with Laura as negative and described her as controlling and accused her of flip-flopping on stories. He claimed that he'd reported Laura to the FBI for online prostitution because he was afraid that, if she were prosecuted, his bank account would be affected.

After those meetings, both parties were given forms to fill out about themselves and their children and were requested to fill out a lengthy questionnaire detailing their parenting histories.

———————

EARLIER that month, on September 10, when the boys came to her home for the weekend, Laura noticed that little Grant was in tears and fretful. She worried about the return of a bladder infection he'd had previously and had him tested, but no bacteria was present. She wondered what could be going on with the little guy. "I'm afraid to approach the subject with Grant and Amanda. They act as if I don't exist. . . . It is so discouraging to deal with them with my children. I encourage the boys to love their Dad and Amanda. I wish I had a picture of both of them for the boys' room. It would be less of an oddity than Mama and Daddy's picture."

During the month of September, Laura did a lot of fretting in her phone log about difficulties with talking to her boys on the phone when they were at Grant's apartment. "Amanda was teaching the boys new words like 'iguana.' It was good to hear the interaction," but, she said it pulled the children's focus away from talking with her. She noted that video chats would be a better way to capture and sustain their attention. On another day, she complained that the boys were eating dinner when she called at her agreed time. She wished that Grant and Amanda would help arrange more compatible times for the calls. "Even if I try to speak to them, I get zero response." On another occasion, she was trying to talk to the boys but could clearly hear Sha in the background playing with them making "I'm gonna getcha" taunts. She was happy that the boys were having a good time but she wished "that Grant III would value and encourage my times with the boys. . . . He's gotten Amanda so worked up about me that now instead of giving me reports on the kids, she looks at me with disdain."

The following weekend was a remarkable improvement. Laura noted in her journal that "Amanda and I were able to talk joyfully about Grant IV and Gentle."

But the skies darkened again on Friday, September 24. After the exchange of the kids, Grant sent Laura a text saying that he would "pick the boys up tomorrow, Saturday, September 25, at 2:01 P.M."

Laura didn't know what to do. No matter how she handled the demand, it would be wrong. She could anger Grant and his family by saying no or she could violate the court order by saying yes, and thus eroding the whole structure that had been put in place. Unable to decide, she simply did not respond at all.

The afternoon Grant had said he would get the boys, Laura looked down at the McDonald's restaurant behind her apartment building and saw Grant sitting there in his car at 1:18. She called him and said that while she appreciated that he was waiting until the time he'd given her, she was not going to violate the court order.

Grant told her that the lawyers had already worked the situation out. The court order said that if he was in Kinston, he could pick the boys up there.

Laura reviewed the court order. There was no mention at all about Kinston being an alternate exchange point. She then checked her e-mail and voice mail messages to make sure there was nothing from her attorney. She called Grant back and told him that, while she understood his logic, she would be bringing the boys to Wilson on Sunday. He hung up on her.

Around four that afternoon, Grant's mother, Patsy Hayes, called, but her number came up on Laura's cell as an "unavailable number," so she didn't answer it. She did listen to the voice message from Patsy, pleading with her to bring the boys to her house. She even invited Laura to stay for dinner with them.

But Laura declined, and on Sunday, she took the boys to Sheetz as usual. She was greeted there by Amanda and Sha. Amanda was "visibly angry" and shaking. Her tone was curt. Defeated, Laura wrote in her journal. "This weekend was terrible as far as Grant III is concerned. So I lose until we get to court, I hope."

CHAPTER EIGHT

LAURA Ackerson wrote to her sister Jennifer again in September to update her on the situation, telling her that the horror story she'd told her on the phone had "improved by the thousands of percentages."

Jennifer asked, "So are the boys with you most of the time?"

"Not yet," Laura responded. She explained that the ex parte order wouldn't be lifted until the psychological evaluation was complete and they appeared again in front of the judge. "Grant has been dragging his feet on it forever now."

On the seventeenth, Laura and Jennifer had an online chat. Laura told her sister that "I am attracted to someone but I know that my 'picker' is still out of balance. I want to give myself some time to 'get to know' me. . . . When I was with Grant, everything was about him and I had zero of my own identity."

Later in the conversation, she said, "Grant is a sociopath. Being with one changes your mind about relationships in a big way. . . . And he does everything with a smile. Passive Aggressive is an understatement."

THE next step in Dr. Ginger Calloway's analysis was visits to the individual homes to observe and videotape the parent and children together as well as look for any problems regarding the safety or well-being of the children. In Laura's apartment, nothing was amiss in the physical home environment. At Grant's place, the only concern was a missing screen in the window of the boys' bedroom. However, observing the interaction between parent and children, she noted dramatically different emotional settings.

Laura was very sweet with the kids and, as a result, the boys were very low-key most of the time. When little Grant made an aggressive move toward Gentle, Laura intervened and stopped it immediately. During that session, she provided them both with healthy snacks.

In Grant's house, the boys' play was more violent. They slammed toy cars into each other's legs hard enough to leave bruises.

ON October 8, 2010, a friend sent a short "Sup?" to Grant on Facebook. Grant was still fuming about the situation with the kids and Laura. "Two boys, nasty custody battle with Laura's crazy ass . . . pregnant wife. . . . Just got back from LA recording with some heavy cats out there."

LEARNING that her mother was pregnant and feeling very ill in her first trimester, Sha moved down to live in Grant and Amanda's apartment to help out. The new intensive view she got of Grant was disturbing. She learned about his bizarre beliefs concerning the aliens that were following him and running the government and his sense that he'd been chosen by them for both persecution and salvation. Sha had often mocked her mother's "very Buddhist/earth-child belief system, believing in God more as a higher power of Karma," but still she thought Grant's odd religious/political philosophy would be considered peculiar even by Amanda's standards. But when Sha asked her about it, she learned that her mother took it in stride. Amanda told her, "Looking at it from his perspective, I can see how it makes sense to him." Sha knew her mother could be a bit out there, but that was still hard to believe.

A chain of seven e-mails between Laura and Amanda Hayes began on Sunday, October 24, after the two women had an unpleasant encounter when Laura dropped off the boys. Laura wrote, "I understand that you were upset today because I was fifteen minutes late. I am sorry for the inconvenience. . . . I would like to address the attitude you have toward me in front of my children, though I understand that Grant III has probably told you I am the worst person in the world. . . . Please understand something from my side of the fence. . . . I am the mother of two sweet boys who didn't ask to be put through this mess. The LAST thing they need to see is the person they spend their week with upset at their mommy. If you could please contain yourself in front of them, it would be appreciated."

Six days later, Amanda responded, "I'm not sure what you're asking about at all. If there were ill feelings over the exchange last Sunday, they were not on this side of the family."

Laura wrote back the next day. "Very strategic response. . . . I'm talking about the time you yelled over Grant IV's head, 'You started this!' outside Grant III's parent's house, for instance. I'm talking about the obvious attitude you had toward me after I followed the court order and 'made' you guys follow it, too. I'm talking about the consistent, openly disrespectful attitude that you have toward me [and] that you show in front of Grant IV and Gentle. I know you care about them, so please understand. I am their mommy. . . . But if you have something you would like to express to me, I don't mind a bit as long as they are out of earshot."

On Friday, October 29, Laura met Grant, Amanda and the two boys at Sheetz. Laura asked, "Grant could you stay right here so Amanda and I can talk out of the kids' view for a second?"

When the women had stepped away from the car, Laura asked, "Did you receive my e-mail?"

"You just made us late last weekend and we would have appreciated being told. Would you just let us know when you have plans to be late? We have never been late more than five minutes even because I am very, very, very anal about being late. I guarantee that I've been late. And the day that we were late—the rainy day—we were six minutes late. . . . I would just as soon we would never speak again."

Afterward, Laura wrote in her journal: "I don't know why she wants my kids so badly. She definitely does not seem to have their needs placed in front of her own."

ON November 1, 2010, Grant send a Facebook message to an old friend telling her how glad he was to have found her there since he'd been looking everywhere else for her without any luck. He told her about living for a year in the United States Virgin Islands, where his second child was born. He then asked what she'd been doing. She responded with a brief update on her life including her job change, and then she asked, "How's Laura?"

Grant wrote: "Fuck Laura. We split up in the Virgin Islands, I'm surprised you remember her name, no one else did. Figured out she was just using me, Sugar Daddy Grant. She got two kids outta of me, but I love them both." He followed that with a brief comment describing the custody sharing.

ON November 3, Amanda made an attempt to smooth the waters with an invitation to Laura to join them for Thanksgiving dinner. "Maybe you can make a dish, a pie or the turkey if you'd like. You can cook here if you want to come up early. I think the boys would enjoy that. . . . They don't have to know 'this' was happening."

Laura responded the same day. "Thank you, but . . . until this is actually over, I can't come to your home again. I would love to spend as much time as possible with the boys . . . but allowing Grant yet another opportunity to accuse me of ludicrous things would go against common sense."

GRANT delayed making any payment to the psychological evaluator for a month or two after the order. He made two separate payments of five thousand dollars to Dr. Calloway but balked at paying anything additional at that time.

As requested by the psychologist, however, Laura did all that was requested of her in a prompt fashion. She answered every question in her parental history report at great length, turning in a document more than eighty pages long. In her comments, she wrote that she was most concerned with little Grant's aggressiveness toward her and Gentle, as well as his use of profanity and the fact that he called himself a "a bad boy."

Grant, on the other hand, dragged his feet on his paperwork. When he did send some to Calloway, he expressed concerns about little Grant's anger after phone calls with Laura.

"Both parents feel attached to Grant IV. Although Laura described specific ways in which she noted how the attachment developed, Grant's description was in more general terms and he seemed confused as he described his own attachment to his own father."

In response to the question of whether or not they

contributed to the problems with the other parent, Laura wrote "yes" and explained. "The problem of lack of common values . . . became serious when I realized I was trapped. I'd gotten rid of everything I owned. Grant III now owned our car and Grant III and I had spent all of my savings and then some. After it was gone the 'real Grant' came out. He started openly snorting coke and telling me about kissing other women instead of being the doting Prince Charming he'd been previously.

". . . Grant III thinks it's okay to sleep with people to manipulate them into doing what he wants and encouraged that behavior in me. I didn't think that was acceptable. . . . Grant has a larger than life perspective. He thinks he should have servants and that he should have the best of everything at all times. . . . I contributed how? I really didn't believe he thought this behavior was okay. I was so shocked that I thought he wasn't serious when he asked if I would consider being a 'bottom bitch' and help him pick up strippers to run through Vegas. I thought he was testing me."

ON Monday, November 15, Laura wrote to Amanda and Grant requesting to pick up the boys on Thursday evening at seven. Otherwise, if she stuck to the Friday exchange, she could only do it at six thirty in the morning because of an appointment with Dr. Ginger Calloway. They refused to cooperate.

That obstruction set off a chain of bitter messages from Grant declaring Amanda's superiority in mothering and accusations from Laura that Grant was ridiculous and childish. Laura accused Grant of obstructing the process ordered by the court because he did not want to appear before the judge again and Grant blaming everyone but himself for any delays in compliance.

By the time December 2010 rolled around, Amanda's once comfortable inheritance was nothing but a memory. One piece after another of Amanda's jewelry was pawned—a diamond necklace, a Rolex watch, the engagement and wedding rings from her marriage to Nicky and more. Pawn tickets for ten thousand dollars, five thousand dollars, three thousand dollars piled up as her treasures dwindled and the money evaporated in Grant's pocket. Grant even took a trip to New York supposedly to get the best possible price when he sold a green-and-yellow diamond that Nicky had brought back from Brazil for Amanda.

Beginning that month, their credit cards, one by one, were maxed out to cover expenses. Still, Grant did not alter his habits—he still spent three to four nonworking nights a week at bars. His pitiful earnings covered his bar tabs but not much more. Amanda was not in a position to work outside of the home to supplement their income—she had the full-time job of caring for Grant's children five days a week with little or no help from her husband. Still she ran up expenditures, financing his projects and long trips to Los Angeles so he could pursue his pie-in-the-sky plans to start his own record label.

CUSTODY cases are nearly always problematic and lengthy. On December 9, 2010, Laura's attorney, John Sargeant, filed a motion alleging that Grant was in contempt of court for not cooperating with or paying in full for the evaluation. Sargeant asked the judge to return the children to Laura because of this behavior. After several court conferences, Grant's attorney, Brad Hill, withdrew from the case at Christmastime, and Grant hired William "Ford" Coley to represent him instead.

Coley and Sargeant met before the judge, who ordered that Grant and Laura would split the remaining costs, approximately five thousand dollars. They were ordered to make payments in February and April. Laura paid the full twenty-five hundred dollars she owed immediately, but Grant did not.

The boys' future remained an open question as the calendar flipped to 2011.

CHAPTER NINE

O N January 2, 2011, Grant Hayes wrote to an old carousing buddy asking him to remove any photos of him from his Facebook page. "I still got a long way to go with this court shit and I know Laura's spinning everything."

The next afternoon at three thirty, Laura Ackerson wrote to request to speak to her boys, and said that she'd been trying to reach them since noon. Two and a half hours later, Grant responded and Laura asked if she could have a video chat with them. After nine that night, Grant wrote back, complaining about her desire to talk to the kids, even though daily conversations with their mother were ordered with the court. "We don't bother you when you have the boys. . . . I'd rather not infringe on *their* time with you. . . . It is good to miss and be missed." He went on to claim that the boys didn't want to talk on the phone and that he would not force them to do so. He ranted on for a bit, accusing her of playing head games with little Grant and claiming that she encouraged the boy to "antagonize Daddy."

Laura fired back, "Wow, Grant. I guess I will never stop being simply in shock about how far you stretch the truth. . . . I'm not going to stop calling Grant IV or Gentle."

Grant listed more of his hostile perceptions of her. He alleged that her reckless behavior had made Gentle sick. He accused her of needing a scapegoat to have someone to fight with and blame for all the problems in her life. He ended with a mocking prayer to the universe to send Laura "a sweet, handsome, Christian man."

Laura went on the defense about allowing the boys to play in the snow and blaming him for their son's illness. "You criticize me constantly, taking a GRAIN of truth and building a pearl of crap around it. . . . I have put up with your need to degrade and manipulate people to feel better about yourself for several years against my better judgment." She wrapped up her message with a request that he help out financially with health insurance for the children. She reminded him that the judge would view that as a positive contribution to the boys' welfare.

Grant refused, saying that the insurance cost more than it was worth and all his money was being spent on the custody case, rent, food, toys, clothing and medical bills. "And you want me held in contempt of court for not having more money to pay Calloway? I grew up poor in Kinston and it sucks. My kids will not live that way. This is their only childhood. Grant will be three soon. His whole life has been mommy and daddy fighting. . . . You got some real stuff you need to deal with. You got a raw deal when you were their age and you are trying your damnedest to make sure your kids get one, too. That's bad karma, Laura. . . . I was weak and let you intimidate me, exploit my guilt and hold my failed marriage over my head. . . . One of my biggest mistakes was not showing your hateful, twisted, childish spirit to the door sooner." He went on to shred Laura's character to bits with allegations of promiscuous and crude behavior.

Laura's response to his lengthy tirade was brief and to the point: "I am literally LAUGHING right now. Thanks! I'm done, Grant, DNR [Do Not Resuscitate]."

But when Grant questioned what she wrote and accused her of creating drama, Laura wrote again asking if he believed his own lies and begged him to stop spreading them. She ended with: "Grant, I've spent too long in conversations like this. Go talk to your wife."

Grant wouldn't let it go. He poked at her with every stick he could find. Despite Laura's expressed desire to terminate the conversation, she kept responding like a cornered animal.

The acrimonious exchange finally came to an end when Laura wrote that his messages and attitudes were proof of why a psychological evaluation was necessary and urged him to turn in the required paperwork. "E-mail me about our boys, not our case, not our past, not your conquests. Bye."

ON February 12, 2011, Grant was still trying to repair his online image. He wrote to musician Frankie Goodrich via Facebook, pleading for his help to get rid of any images that showed him under the influence or engaged in any illegal or questionable activity that the courts might view as unacceptable or inappropriate. He said that he had serious problems with the custody case and the IRS was on his back for his 2009 earnings.

Five days later, another friend complimented him for the photo of his family on Facebook saying that his kids were beautiful but "this clearly isn't the wife we met, right?"

Grant responded to her, referring to Laura as a "hanger on" and said he met Amanda in St. John. He complained again about the custody battle: "We been in court for a year, it's hard on everybody. She's just gold diggin' and thinks these kids are her ticket."

On February 7, 2011, at Grant's urging, Sha moved out of her mother's apartment and into another unit at the opposite end of the complex.

A few days later, Heidi Schumacher brought Laura and Oksana Samarsky together at Reader's Corner on Hillsborough Street in Raleigh. Heidi thought Oksana was a fantastic artist and Laura was a marketing whiz. "I thought they would hit it off and they could help each other," Heidi said.

Laura brought the boys with her, and as the women talked, Gentle and Grant crawled all over her. Oksana thought the bubbly mother made a good first impression.

As Heidi predicted, the two became very quick friends. Oksana felt a bit like Laura's side project but was grateful for the other woman's belief in her talent and willingness to help her succeed. They e-mailed and phoned for the most part—occasional face-to-face meetings did happen, but only when the two women could juggle often conflicting schedules of school and work demands and within the confines of Laura's first priority, her boys.

The casual and flexible relationship worked well for both women until everything went horribly wrong.

CHAPTER TEN

DR. Ginger Calloway next wanted to evaluate how the Hayes children reacted when a parent left and came back. At the child trauma center, they set up the scenario. First the parent played with the child in a playroom. Then, a stranger went in and talked to the parent and child together for about two minutes. At that point, the parent left, but returned again in two to five minutes. Then the stranger left and parent and child played together again. After that, the child was left alone for a few minutes before the parent came back in again.

When Laura Ackerson arrived with the boys, Gentle was asleep. He was left in Heidi Schumacher's care in the waiting room while Laura and little Grant went into the playroom. Mother and son interacted well together. When Laura left the room, little Grant kept asking, "Where's Mommy?" When she returned, he gave a sigh of pleasure.

When Gentle first woke up in that strange place, he screamed. When he was left with the stranger in the playroom, he seemed unsure of what to do. He went to the door and rested his head on it. Then, he started to wail and couldn't be comforted by the stranger. Because of his distress, Laura was brought back in right away. Laura easily calmed him and seemed attuned to his needs.

On a later day, Grant Hayes repeated the scenario. When his father returned to the room after an absence, little Grant showed no reaction. He continued playing with the cars and then noticed that his dad was getting blocks out of a box. He said, "Put more, Daddy."

Grant said, "More what?"

"More blocks."

The session with Gentle started playfully, with Grant mimicking Gentle. The boy then explored the room and had little interaction with his father. When Grant said his name, Gentle ignored him. Grant urged him to come look at one toy after another. Gentle would look at the toys then take them to another part of the room and play by himself. When the stranger came into the room, Gentle sat down by his dad's feet.

When Grant left the room, Gentle cried. But when his father returned, they did not have a reunion. Grant immediately went to the toys for a distraction. When he left the boy alone, Gentle whimpered. With his father gone, Gentle continued to stand near the door, making those pitiful noises. The stranger came in and was able to soothe him for a little bit. When Gentle's whimpering began anew, the stranger tried to engage his interest in toys. When Grant came back into the room, Gentle tried to escape.

ON the first day of March 2011, Laura chastised Grant via a string of text messages asking him to demonstrate a modicum of respect for her phone time with the boys.

Grant asked what she wanted him to do and Laura wrote: "Something other than what you are now. The few times that your group have called here, I have kept it quiet and non-distracting. Not only is it rude to constantly have the TV on when I'm trying to talk with Grant and Gentle, but it makes you guys look bad to anyone who hears the recording of the call. Could you please give it a rest and work with me here? WE have two children. Not you. WE. I will always be their mom and its best if they have a healthy relationship with me. Could you encourage that please?"

Laura did not seem to blame Amanda for these problems. A few days after her exchange with Grant, she sent Amanda a thank-you note expressing appreciation for all that Amanda did in the day-to-day caring for the children. Although she didn't mention it in the correspondence, Amanda's presence in the household made Laura feel more comfortable than she would have if the boys were in Grant's care alone.

LATER that month, at HealtHabit, Laura helped a customer named Chevon Mathes, an African-American woman with a full, attractive smile, broad face, high cheekbones and a soft voice. The two women chatted, and they discovered that they shared a conceptual vision. Both independently wanted to start an advertising company selling noncompeting ads on placemats or menus at diners and cafés. Chevon had business sense and a sales instinct and Laura had graphic design skills. It was like two halves of a whole. They exchanged phone numbers that day. Later they talked on the phone and met face-to-face, both growing more excited about the possibility with each encounter. They shaped their dreams into a start-up called Fork & Spoon and started looking for customers. In addition to her job at the shop, Laura continued with her freelance work as GoFish Graphic Designs while she worked on building a new business with Chevon.

Laura and Chevon had two types of sales calls to make. One group was the restaurant owners whom they had to solicit to use the free menus or placemats with ads for other businesses. The others were those companies buying the ads to make the freebies possible. Soon, Laura quit her part-time job at the health food store. Their business started in Kinston in March and by the time July 2011 arrived, they'd expanded to Wilson, with Laura making pitches there and in Goldsboro while Chevon tried to get sales by telephone since she did not own a car.

Chevon spent time working with Laura in her two-bedroom apartment and soon became aware of the ongoing custody battle and Laura's conflicts with Grant.

MEANWHILE, back in March, Grant had filed a social-services complaint against Laura because of bruises on the boys. The caseworker was confused about why Grant also told him that Laura had sexually transmitted diseases, since it was not relevant to his original allegations. The agency investigated and discharged the case as groundless.

Laura assumed that Grant had filed the report in the first place because the evaluation was not going as he'd hoped. Laura told her lawyer, John Sargeant, that she was afraid that Grant's actions indicated he was getting desperate, and she was concerned he might try to run off with the children or do something bad to her. Sargeant urged Laura not to take any unnecessary risks, and to always meet Grant in a public place. He told her that if Grant ran with the boys, in all likelihood she would be awarded full custody—but she'd have to go through a lot of trouble to find him and get her children back.

In mid-March, Grant wrote again to the friend he'd griped to in February, and his bitterness appeared to have escalated. After answering questions about his music, he complained: "My x started a ridiculous custody dispute over our two sons. I mistakenly came down to NC to answer the hearing and the court ordered I couldn't leave the state with my boys even though I paid $40,000 to get into my place in New York City. Down the drain." He said that he couldn't get gigs in Raleigh and that they were living off their savings and having to pay eighty-five thousand dollars to attorneys, evaluators and psychologists.

"We've gone from having financial security to allow my wife and I to stay home all day, to selling jewelry just to keep the lawyers on the case and the lights on." He said that he'd considered gigs in St. Lucia and Hawaii but he hated to be away from his little boys and his pregnant wife. "I'm dedicated to the arts, been full-time earning a living with my guitar since I was 19 years old."

He told her his dream was to be a songwriter. "I love to write songs and don't do anything 99%. I go all the way."

THAT April, Sha went up to Amanda and Grant's apartment and found her mother sitting on the bathroom floor bawling. Amanda said she felt trapped. She had no options and her money had all "gone down the drain." Seven months pregnant, and all she could do was wail. "I don't want to be a single mother at forty but there's no way he can ever take care of me or these kids. He doesn't need to have these boys if I'm not here," she told her daughter.

Grant did nothing to dispel this concern. In May, despite his wife's advanced state of pregnancy and her imminent due date of May 31, Grant left Amanda to take care of his children on her own and flew to Hawaii. He stayed with his friend Lauren Harris's fiancé while he was in the islands. Amanda thought he had booked a few gigs, but according to Lauren, Grant just went out looking for the possibility of work.

Grant was still in Hawaii on Mother's Day. Sha and her new boyfriend, Matt Guddat, a man more than twelve years her senior, took Amanda out to brunch that day. It was the first time Amanda and Matt had met.

Others were more sensitive to Amanda's needs in her

current state. Her in-laws transported the boys for her on one occasion. Laura, too, volunteered to pick up the boys in Raleigh during Grant's absence. Grant obviously didn't understand or subscribe to the notion that the needs and desires of his partner were as important as his own. He continued to display the same self-obsessed, callous characteristics in this relationship as he had in the past.

CHAPTER ELEVEN

O N May 17, 2011, Dr. Ginger Calloway sent her final
report to both attorneys as well as a sealed copy to the
judge, which would not be opened until it was properly
presented in the courtroom. Laura Ackerson met with
attorney John Sargeant the next day to review the fifty-
nine-page document.

In the report, Calloway noted that Grant Hayes and
Laura both had chaotic personal histories. Both had had
trouble with relationships, including the one with each
other, which was volatile and destructive.

Calloway noted that she found no evidence that Laura
was mentally ill, and no support of Grant's claims that his
ex was "sick" or that she "poisoned the children's minds."
However, Calloway wrote, Laura "is defensive and comes
across as tense and stiff during interviews. She has not
learned to successfully balance appropriate self-disclosure

and a need to be private. . . . Her tenseness, reserve and careful manner could lead others to mistrust her and to question the accuracy of her reports. Her uncertainty and lack of self-assurance caused her to appear to be vacillating or 'flip-flopping' as Grant describes her. This is an accurate and perceptive comment about her. . . . She is less mature than other adults and is easily overwhelmed, relative to other adults. She is a chronically vulnerable or fragile person with a poorly developed sense of self that she defends in impulsive emotional ways at times. . . . When she is overwhelmed she can and has shown poor judgment at times and she will act impulsively without consideration for consequences."

About Grant, Calloway wrote: "His rambling and tangential thinking included excessive negative commenting about Laura" and noted that his anger toward Laura and his inappropriate "characterizations of her make him appear to have a determined agenda."

Calloway continued: "It is concerning when Grant goes on the attack against Laura and portrays her in a highly negative and morally depraved ways. His upbringing in what he describes as fundamentalist family where guilt was used freely for control is likely the source of his rage at Laura.

"He also fails to understand the impact . . . of his angry rantings about Laura . . . in front of the children. This is very worrisome for parenting and for what he is willing to communicate. . . . It is disturbing that his intense rage serves as an anchor for his disturbed thinking.

"Grant and Amanda were unequivocal about wanting

to leave the area while, at the same time, they said they planned to buy a house in Raleigh. Both have said repeatedly that they want to travel out of the country and to far-flung places like Hawaii, Europe, Sweden, India or China. Grant says he would like to get a boat and sail to Greece and 'live before I get too old.' He said he 'wanted his kids to be citizens of the world and not just the U.S.' Amanda reports they wanted to move to Nashville, Tennessee, because Grant is a songwriter . . . 'As a family it is important for us to travel with him. It wouldn't be fair if me and the baby get to travel and they don't.'

"With these kinds of expressed wishes of Grant and Amanda to move away, it is obvious that they do not want Laura included in the children's lives. This is very concerning because in essence, they want to obliterate her."

In the analysis, Calloway stated: "There are several areas which are highly significant with regards to findings from this evaluation that are necessary for the court to have. These concern the disruption of the children's relationship with their primary caregiver, their mother, an understanding of the parents' separate pathology, the chaotic and destructive nature of their conflict. Grant's misinterpretations that are passed on as totally accurate and factual to authority figures who can pass judgment on Laura and Laura's underdevelopment that causes her to become defensive rather easily are significant findings. It is critical that the court be informed regarding the insensitivity of Grant and Amanda and the paternal grandparents regarding the children's deep need for an unalterable bond with Laura . . . and Grant's stated opinion that he should have total control through legal and physical custody of the children with supervised visitation only for Laura."

She summed up: "The most significant finding to emerge from this evaluation is the description to the relationship with their primary caregiver, their mother. For a variety of reasons both children spent the majority of their time with their mother during the critical age periods for attachment formation . . . Laura was primarily the individual immediately available to both the children when they cried, to rock them or otherwise assist them to sleep and the parent most immediately available to meet the needs of hunger, discomfort, wet, dirty, upset, pain, pleasure, joy, light, competence."

Calloway noted, "When taken to New York City in February 2010, Grant IV was abruptly removed from his primary caregiver at 21 months of age. . . . Gentle who was nursing at the time, was abruptly removed from Laura's care at roughly ten months of age. About two weeks after the transition to Grant's home, Gentle underwent surgery. The importance to Gentle of his father's absence as a routine caregiver from roughly two months of age to roughly ten months of age is critical in terms of attachment relationships and in terms of his transition to his father's home. His father simply was not present for the attachment process to occur. Hence, he was a virtual stranger to Gentle and therefore, not someone Gentle could rely on when he was transitioned to Grant, Amanda and Sha."

In the next section, Dr. Calloway made a number of recommendations, starting with the need for a guardian ad litem for the boys and consultation with a therapist as a follow-up with them. She also wanted little Grant to start preschool immediately and Gentle as soon as possible. She asked the court to mandate drug screens for both parents to determine that the children were safe until the guardian ad litem deemed them unnecessary. In doing so, she validated a request Laura had made in her parenting-history document, where Laura stated, "Because Grant III has been regularly partaking of drugs over the last twelve years of his life, I believe that he will continue to after our court case is over. I request that we do any testing possible. I also request that there be a system for following up on these tests after the court date is over."

The current visitation arrangement, Calloway wrote, was "totally inappropriate for the age of the children." She recommended split custody, a two-three-two plan. The children would be with one party for two days, the other for three days, then they would return to the first party for two days. The pattern would then start again with the second parent going first, creating an alternating week scenario.

For Laura, Calloway believed she should obtain a coach or parent substitute as a sounding board to help her with her insecurity, her sense of inadequacy and her anxiety—someone who could help her learn how to develop social networks and help train her in assertiveness. Also recommended was that she interact with a group of other single moms.

For Grant, Calloway suggested the same, but in his case, a coach who was trained in attachment theory and how to provide a better sense of reassurance and comfort to his children. In addition, she noted that he needed education on the significance of different developmental points. Then she wrote: "It is recommended that Grant be referred to a psychiatrist for evaluation regarding the question of a mood disorder or other possible explanations for the illogical, disturbed thinking he exhibits." She went on to say that Grant needed a psychiatrist "knowledgeable about addiction and poly-substance abuse" because it appeared that Grant had "used multiple illegal drugs to self-medicate for an underlying mood or thought disorder."

LAURA was ecstatic over the report. Sure, there were things she needed to address, but she had actually been hoping the evaluation would provide guidance on her most-needed areas for self-improvement. She took each point seriously and applied herself to reconciling her deficiencies as a parent. She felt the report vindicated a lot of things in her custody argument, and confirmed some of the allegations about Grant's lack of parenting ability with the boys. As she told her friend and business partner, Chevon Mathes, "I got the psych eval back and I'm not the crazy one."

GRANT was still in Hawaii when Amanda first thought she was going into labor. Her Braxton Hicks contractions felt so much like the real thing that Sha rushed her mother to the hospital. They were there until two in the morning, when the doctor determined that it was all just a false alarm. That night, Amanda bought a plane ticket for Grant, and he flew back the next day.

ON May 23, 2011, the custody attorneys had a conference with the judge and a trial date was set for August 15. Laura's optimism rose even higher when John Sargeant assured her that the least the judge would do would be to comply with Dr. Calloway's recommendation of shared custody, but that the court could take it further—the possibility that she would be awarded full custody of her sons was a realistic outcome.

Grant understood the tone of the report, too, and its consequences. He clearly knew he was going to have to give up at least some of his control over the boys, and thus, over Laura. His hostility about this new state of affairs seeped through his contacts with the mother of his children. The dark undertones of their interactions troubled her. Laura told her friend Heidi Schumacher, "If anything happens to me, even if I commit suicide or if I go missing or if I get into a car accident, know that Grant did it."

ON May 24, 2011, Grant wrote to a fellow musician, Ashton, telling him that he had a "baby girl coming in a week so I've decided to take some time off until late August." He then pitched him on his portrait special for the month of June. All he needed was a photograph and he'd deliver an 18" × 24" charcoal for $250. He referred him to his website for examples.

The performer congratulated him and said he had one coming, too, according to his ex.

Grant fired back, "What!!! Is she crazy?"

"What you mean by that?" Ashton asked.

"My x Laura was crazy and I didn't know it until it was too late. . . . She's still putting me through hell."

In addition to the portraits, Grant was scrambling for money in every way he knew how. His latest scheme—creating art for iPhone covers—was in the prototype phase. He specialized in drawings of dead rap musicians. He desperately wanted to get his special designs into the Apple Store—anything to keep him and Amanda afloat now that her savings were gone.

CHAPTER TWELVE

BUSY with complications in their lives, Laura Ackerson and Oksana Samarsky hadn't touched base for a while by June 2011. Oksana's work and class studies had gotten knocked off track by a medical crisis that required her to make two visits to the emergency room. Laura—torn between the additional classes she was now taking at the community college, the custody case, her two boys and trying to turn her fledgling businesses into successes—could relate.

Oksana replied to Laura's e-mail sent a few days earlier: "Hi, are you there? I'm sorry it took me a few days to reply to your last e-mail."

Laura had good news to report: "Should have my boys back in August and then some huge project"—i.e., her court case—"can come to a close."

Oksana had good news, too. She told Laura she'd sold two small canvases for a thousand dollars on Facebook.

Laura cheered her friend's news and suggested ways to expand her sales—even going so far as to volunteer to help set up the online infrastructure that Oksana needed to get more consistent sales. Oksana offered to pay her a commission.

Laura said, "Eh. I don't need a percentage for it."

"But you are helping!"

"Then send me a painting. Sign it, too?"

GRANT Hayes could be very reasonable and polite to Laura when he wanted something from her, and in early June he did. He asked her to keep the kids for a week, since Amanda was past her due date and about to give birth any moment, and caring for the boys was too demanding for her at this time. Laura was happy to comply. She switched up her work schedule and Chevon picked up the slack. The meetings with clients and potential clients that Laura had scheduled that week were all covered by Chevon using Laura's car.

Amanda was additionally relieved to be free of that responsibility, because she suddenly had a new emotional burden to handle as well: on Sha's twenty-second birthday— June 7, 2011—Amanda's mother, Retha Faye Ryan Abernathy, passed away in her sleep at her Kirtland, New Mexico, home. She was seventy years old.

Sha and her boyfriend, Matt, had invited Amanda and Grant to join them for dinner to celebrate Sha's birthday, and they kept the date despite Retha Faye's death so that Sha could comfort Amanda. Grant met Matt for the first time, but it was a brief encounter. He dropped his wife at their table and announced he had to leave for an appointment in Morrisville. He exhibited no concern about Amanda's loss.

Two days later, on June 9, Amanda gave birth, by cesarean section, to Lillian Ann Love Hayes—nine days past her due date. The next day, Laura brought Gentle and little Grant into the hospital to meet their new half sister.

THE economic situation in Grant and Amanda's household had reached a critical point. There was no money coming in but plenty of it rolling out the door. No small economies would resolve their dilemma. They were not capable of placing a deposit on a cheaper apartment. They had to take action before they were evicted and left stranded on the street with three children.

Grant's parents owned a number of rental properties in Kinston but they were currently all occupied—some by other family members. The only option that remained was moving in and living with Patsy and Grant in their small house. The prospect of going back home had to seem like abject failure and it was not a feeling that Grant had the emotional strength to take in stride.

WHEN Grant didn't need anything from Laura, things got ugly fast. On Wednesday, June 15, Laura met her kids at Monkey Joe's to spend some extra time with them. She hugged them tight to say good-bye and the kids started to cry. They blubbered about not wanting to leave her, and

Laura tried to comfort them with sweet words and kisses. Grant grew impatient with the emotional display. He jerked the children out of her arms and tossed them into the car while they cried. He told Laura that there would not be a midweek visit again.

Laura was distraught. She could not believe that Grant would be so rough and unfeeling to their boys and did not understand Grant's attitude that it was best for them to leave her in an abrupt fashion.

That night she wrote to him: "I appreciate you allowing me to see our boys during your ordered time. Thank you. If you allow it in the future, could we please plan it so that you're not 'waiting an additional hour and a half for me.' Or so I can say goodbye to my boys without being rushed. Thanks. Why don't you use it as three hours of free time to take your wife out or do something for yourself. . . . I would like this to be a mutually beneficial thing—not just you 'doing me a favor.'"

On June 20, Laura wrote again requesting another midweek visit, and that instigated another angry exchange of messages. Grant accused her of negligence or worse, claiming the boys always came back sick after being with her. Then they argued about financial issues. Laura accused Grant of using Amanda. "You were trying to convince Amanda that I was an evil, money-hungry woman out to 'get you' so that you could garner her sympathy and move to a quick emergency wedding, allowing you total access to her money in case she were to wise up. . . . What does it benefit you to have someone so 'crazy' in your past? Does it give you good stories? Or is it just good to manipulate and get sympathy with?" Laura mentioned that an earlier girlfriend of Grant's had "bought it. Amanda's buying it now. How far does the gravy train go? . . . Will I still be the enemy when you're done with Amanda? Why don't you put your energy into writing a sitcom about someone with Borderline Personality Disorder and get rich off your own back instead of trying to take advantage of women like Amanda?"

After that exchange, Grant denied Laura her requested midweek visit and accused her of using the boys as tools of manipulation. Then, he climbed on his high horse and claimed everything he was doing was for the sake of the two kids.

Laura ended her participation in the conversation by writing, "Grant, this is a power play for you. I'm not participating. . . . I guess I'll have to wait until August when I ask for a different order. Thank you for being difficult once again."

LAURA called her brother Jason at the end of June, but Jason was in line at the DMV and had to end the call abruptly. As she hung up, Laura said, "I love you."

Laura and Jason never spoke again.

ON June 28, 2011, Laura met with her attorney, John Sargeant. He was impressed by how far she'd come with her personal development since they'd first met a year ago. Back then, her lack of self-confidence and her doubts about herself were apparent. Now, she was more poised and her career success was a point of pride. They discussed possible witnesses for the August hearing. Laura was eager for the date to arrive.

John Sargeant never saw his client again.

ON Friday, July 8, 2011, Laura picked up the boys a few hours earlier than usual. They had a lovely weekend. They played at home and at the bounce house at the park-and-play and did some shopping together. On Sunday morning, they went to a different church than usual so she could see whether they liked the Children's Church. Laura was very pleased with their behavior. The proud mother wrote in her journal that little Grant "had a good weekend and four-day week. He watched fireworks and learned about space, compasses and how popsicles are really made. The boys got along really well and we used the system star charts that improve our interactions greatly."

On Monday the eleventh, Laura swapped e-mails with a former boyfriend, James Harrison, telling him that she'd been in court with Grant for the past year. "I've heard that your twenties are the hardest compared with the rest of adulthood and I can definitely say mine have been rough but good." She went on to express optimism about rebuilding her life, growing her business and being a single mother.

CHAPTER THIRTEEN

LAURA Ackerson spent most of Tuesday, July 12, 2011, with Chevon Mathes. The friends and business partners met at Laura's apartment to work on their game plan for the next day. Then they went out to shop for a car for Chevon and run other errands. They returned to get more work done, and Chevon left for home about four o'clock that afternoon.

Earlier, while Chevon was still there, Laura also chatted with Oksana Samarsky, the artist whom she was helping to assemble a portfolio. Oksana asked how the custody case was going, and Laura wrote, "It's going. I joined a group online of ladies in a similar situation—people who had to deal with assholes. LOL. And my situation is so, so, so, so good comparatively." The two talked about tentative plans for the next day, when Laura hoped to visit her boys in

Raleigh. They wanted to get together to talk about using Oksana's artwork on cell phone covers and T-shirts.

"It might still be up in the air," Laura typed. "I don't know if I'll see you or not. I have to figure out how to see my kids first and see how that goes."

Oksana understood, saying that depending on the time she might not be able to make it herself because her study group would be meeting that evening.

"I'll get back to you when I know when," Laura said.

GRANT Hayes sent a response to Laura's earlier message that night at 9:25: "If you want to try the midweek thing again, you can come up tomorrow. Let me know so I can make arrangements with Lauren [Harris, the manager at Monkey Joe's]. I might not be able to stay the whole time because I have packing to do."

Laura accepted his offer and asked how much time she'd have with them so that there would be no chance of an "overemotional goodbye."

Grant blasted back that the decision to leave the last midweek visit was because the place was closing, not because of what he wanted. The kids, he said, were losing interest in the place anyway. He wrapped up by mocking her need for a prolonged good-bye.

Laura said the best thing would be to have a beginning and end time set in advance that included five to ten minutes for the transition. That, however, started another argument, which Laura brought to an end with a qualified apology, wrapping it up by writing: "It is the most frustrating thing I know of to deal with a parent partner who doesn't view love in the same light that I do."

AT ten that night, Grant Hayes wrote to Mark Gierth, a music promoter and his friend from St. John, telling him that he and Amanda wouldn't be down in the United States Virgin Islands until late August because of "a court date for child support and shit. Nobody is going to give a black guy custody over a white girl and North Carolina ain't gonna let me share custody unless I stay here and I just can't make a living here. I'm just gonna let Laura keep the boys." His plans after that, he said, were to move to St. Thomas with his wife and baby girl. He then asked about the number of days per week he'd be needed to perform if he returned to St. John.

Mark wrote back indicating that he'd be flying down over the weekend himself and really wouldn't know with any certainty until he was there.

Grant asked about a mutual acquaintance and whether or not she was still working in St. Thomas, because he was going to need to find a job for his wife, too.

Mark wrote, "I will need people . . . could fill gap till she finds something she really digs."

CHAPTER FOURTEEN

O N Wednesday, July 13, 2011, Laura headed out for her
sales calls. Building security cameras showed her walking out the black door of the entrance to her unit and down
the stairs at 8:10 A.M. She wore a black sleeveless shirt and
brown Capri pants and carried a brown Liz Claiborne purse
and a black leather bag. It turned into an excellent day for
business. Laura made successful presentations at Nash
Street Grille, World Seafood, the Creamery Family Restaurant's corporate office, Pup's Steakhouse and Anthony's
Italian Restaurant.

She called Chevon after her first appointment to crow
about her success.

Chevon urged her on. "You go, girl!"

Laura seemed to be nailing a sale every place she went.
She called back several times to announce, "Hey! I got
another one."

Her success made her run a bit behind schedule. At 12:56 she sent a text message to Grant: "I can't be there until after my last appointment in Wilson. When do you think they will be up?"

A few minutes after that, Laura wrote to Heidi Schumacher, who was on her way to a job interview in Charlotte, and told her that she was thinking about an idea for starting a new magazine in a big city. She asked Heidi to pick up any local or regional magazines she saw in Charlotte to see what was currently available. She moved on to her frustration with Grant and the upcoming custody hearing in August. "Do you think I should call on his ex-wife? I need to round up a few witnesses."

Then she wrote to her church friend and mentor, Barbara Patty, thanking her for all she got from their Monday night Bible study and asking Barbara if she would be a witness at the hearing.

She called Randy Jenkins at Bill's Grill, five miles southeast of Wilson, to let him know she wouldn't be on time for their two o'clock appointment. When she arrived at three, they sat at the front of the restaurant and discussed menus and getting area businesses to advertise on them.

Randy was interrupted from time to time to fix orders for customers. But when he sat down across the table from Laura, he found her very persuasive, professional and pleasant to deal with—in no time, he signed a contract.

They talked briefly about their children as they wrapped up the meeting. Laura was excited to learn that Randy had nine children. Randy was struck by Laura's enthusiasm for and pride in her kids. As she was leaving, she mentioned having another appointment in Raleigh. Randy explained the quickest way to get there, but told her, "It's a bad time to leave because of the heavy traffic right now. You might want to reschedule."

"No," she said with a smile, "I really have to go to this appointment." Laura was obviously very upbeat and excited when she shifted gears and headed to Raleigh.

At 4:08, Grant sent Laura a text message: "Would you like to keep the boys for the week until Sunday the twenty-fourth?" At 4:12, she responded: "Okay. I'm leaving Wilson now. I'll call when I get past the traffic. Where will you be in an hour or so?"

Oksana received a call from Laura at 4:19 P.M., but she was in her study group at the time, so she let it go to voice mail. After she was finished there, she listened to the message:

"Hey, lady. It's Laura. I am heading into Raleigh. I'll be there in about an hour but—um—I'm gonna go visit with my boys. Don't know what's gonna happen as far as that's concerned. So—uh—I'll just give you a call when I'm done. And I just wanted to let you know, too, I don't know if I'll be able to see you before seven, but just wanted to find out if you're gonna be available after that at any point. Give me a call. I'll talk to you later. Bye."

Oksana never spoke to Laura again.

CHEVON knew about Laura's planned meeting with Oksana, but not that Laura planned to stop at Grant and Amanda's apartment. Laura had said she'd phone Chevon as soon as she got back home in Kinston, probably around nine that night.

But Chevon never got that call.

SHORTLY after she left the message for Oksana, Laura arrived at the apartment complex where Grant and Amanda Hayes lived, to pick up her boys for the weekend.

No one else ever saw her again after she walked through their door.

CHAPTER FIFTEEN

JUST after two A.M. on Thursday, July 14, 2011, Grant Hayes entered the Brier Creek Wal-Mart, grabbed an empty cart and made his way to the hardware department. He studied the aisle with power saws and blades for a bit before going off to look for assistance. He asked the assistant manager, Susan Dufur, "What's the longest blade that will fit in a jigsaw?" he asked.

Susan went back to the aisle with him and showed it to him.

"What about those longer ones?" he asked, pointing to a blade hanging farther down the row.

"No," she said, "that won't fit a jigsaw. It's for a reciprocating saw." She explained that on a reciprocating saw the blade goes in and out to cut objects like drywall and used longer, sturdier blades for that purpose; but a jigsaw worked on a flat surface to cut, so its blades are shorter and thinner.

Grant asked about the reciprocating saws but then balked at the price. Susan left him to his decision and went back to her work. Eventually, Grant dropped a box with a reciprocating saw into his cart along with a couple of blades.

He approached Susan again and asked where he could find large industrial trash bags. She escorted him to that spot, and then he wanted plastic tarps. She pointed him to the aisle. After picking up those up, Grant returned to Susan inquiring about goggles. After picking out a pair, he headed to the front counter and checked out.

IN Kinston, Chevon Mathes woke up on Thursday morning wondering why Laura hadn't called the night before as she'd said she would. When she telephoned Laura, her call went straight to voice mail. Now Chevon was concerned. She knew that Laura never turned off her phone and always had it near her in case the kids ever tried to call.

She kept trying to get an answer from Laura's cell without success. Worried, she walked up to Laura's apartment complex. Since it was gated and locked, she knew she wouldn't be able to get inside but she could see into the garage from the outside. She was even more dismayed when she saw that Laura's car wasn't parked there.

EIGHTY miles away in Raleigh, Amanda Hayes called her daughter, Sha Elmer, and asked her to pick up little Grant and Gentle and take them out somewhere. Sha said, "I'll get over when I can—I might be able to leave in half an hour."

"No, I need you now," Amanda said and reminded her of the urgency of their move to Kinston.

Sha arrived around ten and took the kids to Monkey Joe's. Lauren Harris, the manager, gave the boys iced tea and pizza. By three o'clock, little Grant and Gentle were getting into trouble for hitting other kids, and Sha could tell that the boys were getting tired and needed their naps. But when she called her mother, Amanda said, "We need about two more hours. We're looking for a moving truck."

Sha and the boys left Monkey Joe's at four o'clock and went to Lynnwood Grill, where a friend of hers worked. She ordered brownies and ice cream for the kids. When she brought them home, Amanda put them down for a nap.

Amanda told Sha that her vacuum cleaner was broken and she needed to borrow Sha's. Sha—who had recently moved in with her boyfriend, Matt Guddat, on the other side of Raleigh—balked at driving across town and back in rush hour traffic, but Amanda insisted that she needed it right away. She also wanted Sha to pick up some food for them on her return trip. Sha huffed out a sigh. To complicate matters, the vacuum actually belonged to Matt—not her. She called and got Matt's permission before begrudgingly battling through heavy rush hour traffic and grabbing meals from Wendy's on her return trip.

As she neared the apartment, Sha called and asked her mom to send Grant down to the parking lot to help her carry everything upstairs. It was nearly six when Sha walked into the apartment and handed over the food. Grant followed right behind her with the yellow vacuum. Sha hugged her mom, and Amanda said, "I love you so much. Thank you." For the few minutes Sha was there, Grant was busy snapping photos of the sofa and love seat to post on Craigslist for sale.

AT 4:08 A.M. on Friday, July 15, Grant sent an e-mail to Laura, exactly like the message he texted to her on Wednesday. "Would you like to keep the boys for a week until Sunday the twenty-fourth?"

A little later that morning, Amanda called Sha and told her that the move to Kinston was on for the next day and that they sure could use her help. She mentioned that they had to get a trailer hitch put on their Durango to haul a rental trailer to transport their belongings. "Can Matt install one for us tomorrow morning?"

Initially, Matt was willing, but after a barrage of questions from Amanda and Grant about his experience, Matt reconsidered. He thought about the difficulty of getting use of the lift at work on his day off and obtaining the needed parts. He finally said, "Tell them I've never installed a hitch on that year Durango. I think they'd be better off getting Raleigh Hitch or U-Haul to install one for them."

JUST after noon on Friday, July 15, Chevon sent Laura an e-mail with a subject line that read, "You okay?" In the body of the message, she wrote: "Hey, been trying to call you since yesterday. Let me know that you're okay. Did you lose your phone? A sister's getting worried."

AROUND that same time, Grant was back shopping at Wal-Mart, where he paid cash for three black and three red duffle bags. Minutes before two P.M., Grant sent a message to Laura's e-mail complaining about not being able to reach her on her cell. "This is not cool," he wrote. He griped about Laura's attorney going away on vacation for a week, and then reverted to his problems reaching her: "You're not holding up your end of things and that's REAL fucked up. . . . We're trying to reach a settlement and then go dark on me after agreeing to shall I say 'certain terms.' Yes, REAL FUCKED UP. I'm moving my family to Kinston, yet again to accommodate you, not our kids, but you." He reiterated that he needed her to keep the kids this coming week. Then he warned: "DO NOT try to talk to me about anything at the exchange today. I have NOTHING more to say to you until I hear from your attorney . . ."

He then got on her case about leaving a bag of the kids' clothes at the house when she was bugging him about returning clothes. He ended with another subtle dig: "I will ask my mom to braid little Grant's hair this week while you have them, he needs it."

At three thirty that afternoon, the usual established time for them to exchange the boys for the weekend, Grant strapped little Grant and Gentle into car seats in his Durango and made the drive down to the Sheetz in Wilson. At about four thirty that afternoon, he entered the convenience store and purchased a pack of American Spirit menthol cigarettes, then exited through the back door.

A few minutes later, Grant came back inside through the front door and made another purchase, then went back outside once more. At 4:58, he came in again, this time holding Gentle with little Grant walking by his side. After a visit to the restroom, all three walked out and stood around in the shade of one of the covered tables.

Grant smoked a cigarette and talked on the phone. At 5:16, he went inside for the fourth time, using the side door, and bought drinks for the kids. Four minutes later, he was back at the tables. They got in the car and pulled out of the parking lot at 5:46 P.M. Five minutes into the drive, Grant called Laura. Immediately after that he phoned his mother.

AROUND seven thirty that night, Amanda called Sha again and said, "We're not moving tomorrow. We're thinking about going to Texas."

"I want to go with you. I haven't seen Aunt Karen and my cousins for a long time," Sha said.

That idea angered Amanda. "Stop being selfish. I just lost my mother and gave birth to a new daughter. I need my big sister." She added that no one out there had ever met Grant and it was about time they did.

In the background, Sha heard Grant loudly complaining that Laura hadn't come to get the kids even though he'd waited for her at Sheetz for an hour.

Amanda continued, "So I won't need you. I have to go now—Grant just came in with the boys."

———

GRANT shopped at Wal-Mart again Saturday morning, July 16, 2011. At 6:56 A.M., he bought a 120-quart cooler and three bags of ice. After loading them into the Durango, he went back inside and returned three of the six duffle bags he'd purchased the day before. Then he bought a seventy-five-quart cooler, and made a stop at the in-store McDonald's.

At 10:59 A.M., Grant walked into a U-Haul facility in Raleigh. He did not look the least bit worried, hurried or alarmed. Under the name Grant Haze, he rented a trailer for $159. He also bought boxes, a sofa cover, a lock and a ball mount and ball for his Durango to enable him to haul the trailer for an additional charge of $102.70.

That night, pulling the rental behind his car, he made a trip to the Target a mile from his apartment. At 8:10, he purchased two Igloo MaxCold wheeled coolers, one seventy-five quarts, the other fifty quarts. He put them into the trailer and went back into the store, where he bought a toilet brush and paper towels.

THAT Saturday night at midnight, Amanda, Grant and the three children set out for Texas—a journey of twelve hundred miles, an arduous undertaking with three little kids on board. About eight hours later, the Durango pulled into a Motel 6 in Montgomery, Alabama, not quite halfway through their cross-country trek. Amanda paid $44.24 in cash for a room and registered as Amanda Smith. She and Grant grabbed a few hours of sleep before heading west to Texas.

CHEVON waited and fretted all Friday and Saturday and into Sunday, July 17. She labeled an e-mail "worried" and sent it off to Laura. "L, I've been calling you since Thursday, sent you an e-mail and went by your house. If I don't hear from you by tomorrow, I am calling the cops. So please get in contact with me because I am really worried about you. If you lost your phone again," she wrote inserting her number, "or just come to my house so that I know you're good. You're scaring me."

ON Sunday in Richmond, Texas, Amanda's sister, Karen Berry, told her son, Dalton, to mow the path down to the johnboat they had tied up at the edge of Oyster Creek. She told him his aunt Amanda was on her way and her husband wanted to take his boys fishing while they were there.

That day, Grant exchanged messages with a friend he hadn't seen in a while. She complimented his kids and asked it the woman in the photos with them was a different wife than the one she'd met in the Virgin Islands. Grant wrote back, "I wasn't married to their mom. She was just a hanger-on. I had to do like Mimi and shake her off. I met Amanda in St. John."

———————

ALL day Sunday, Sha called her mother, alternating her calls between Amanda's and Grant's cell phone numbers. Most times, she was sent straight to voice mail or got no answer at all. Once Amanda actually answered but she said she was busy and would call her back. The call never came.

Sha called her aunt Karen and asked if she knew where her mother was. Karen had no idea where they were on the journey, but told Sha they were keeping the phones off to save the batteries.

Around five on Monday morning, July 18, 2011, Karen awoke to a knocking on the front door—Amanda and her family had arrived. Karen fixed breakfast for them all, then Grant and Amanda went to bed while Karen stayed up playing with the children.

CHAPTER SIXTEEN

EARLY Monday morning, July 18, 2011, Sha Elmer called her aunt Karen Berry to ask her if her mother had gotten there yet. "Yes," Karen said, "she's here with Grant and the three kids." She said that they arrived just a little while ago when her son Shelton was still sleeping, and before her other son Dalton came home at five thirty that morning.

She also told her niece that they'd brought the valued antique that Amanda inherited from Nicky to her place for safekeeping. Sha was irked that her mother had done that without speaking to her first. The piece had been left with her in New York and she had been the one to transport it down to North Carolina the previous October. Sha had been promised the unique piece of furniture for quite some time.

BY that morning, Chevon Mathes was certain something was seriously wrong. She called Grant's mother, Patsy Hayes, and asked, "Do you know if Laura picked up her kids up on Friday?"

"No," Patsy said. "I'll find out and give you a call back."

Less than fifteen minutes later, Chevon's phone rang and Patsy said, "Oh, I forgot. Grant asked me to go by Laura's on Friday because she hadn't picked up the kids."

Chevon headed out her door and went straight to the Kinston police station. She walked in and filed a missing persons report. She told the police about the custody battle Laura Ackerson was having with Grant Hayes, said she was worried about the possibility of foul play and turned over a photograph of Laura.

Chevon went over to Laura's apartment building and asked the manager if she would go into the missing woman's residence to see if Laura was there. Chevon also described Laura's business notebooks and requested that the manager bring them out if she saw them.

Then Chevon spoke to the Wilson Police Department, as well as the police department in Raleigh. She told them all that she was very concerned about her friend because of the many comments Laura had made about Grant and her fear of him.

Kinston police's Commander Jennifer Canady handed over the missing persons file to Detective James Gwartney to investigate. He first went to HealtHabit to talk to

Chevon at about one thirty that afternoon. She turned Laura's notebooks over to him, verifying that they were in her missing friend's handwriting. One page had the appointments she'd set for Wednesday, July 13.

The detective contacted two of the businesses to verify that Laura had been there and then went to the RadioShack where Chevon said Laura had gotten her prepaid cell phone. They connected him to the service provider T-Mobile.

While Gwartney talked to that company, Detective Melissa Whittaker overheard him mention Laura's name. When he disconnected from the call, Whittaker said, "I'm familiar with Laura Ackerson." She'd investigated an alleged case of child abuse involving her. Grant Hayes had claimed Laura was abusing their kids, but no charges were ever brought because nothing he said was substantiated.

CHAPTER SEVENTEEN

AFTER he woke up Monday, July 18, 2011, in Richmond, Texas, Grant Hayes asked Amanda's nephew Dalton Berry, "How deep is the creek?"

"In some places it gets really deep—some areas up to thirteen feet. It varies depending on what part of the creek."

"Are there alligators in the creek?"

"Yes, there are."

"How long's that creek?"

"It heads a couple of miles upstream. Downstream, it goes about half a mile to a dam and then dumps into another creek."

MEANWHILE, in Raleigh, North Carolina, Heidi Schumacher rose that morning oblivious to Chevon's concerns about Laura. Heidi and Laura had had their weekly telephone chat the previous Tuesday. She hadn't received any e-mails from Laura since then, but that wasn't unusual. Heidi remained blissful in her ignorance until her phone started to ring.

First, she got a call from Laura's former supervisor, Mike Rivera. As soon as she hung up, the phone rang again. It was Chevon. After talking to her, Heidi fell to her knees and bawled. She knew Laura wasn't missing—she knew it was much worse. She went to another friend's house and sat on her front porch for twelve hours wrapped in her misery as she tried to absorb the horrible reality.

IN Kinston, Detective James Gwartney placed a call to Grant Hayes and left a voice mail. Grant returned the call later when the detective was back at HealtHabit speaking to Chevon. Grant left a voice mail saying he got a message from his mom that Laura Ackerson was missing.

Gwartney called Grant back while he was driving from the health food store to the police station. "Mr. Hayes, this is a missing persons case and I'm trying to track down Laura's last known location."

Grant said, "I haven't seen her since the evening of Wednesday the thirteenth. She came to my apartment to pick up the boys to take them to Monkey Joe's."

"Did you have any other communication with her?"

"We usually e-mail a couple of times a week on Mondays and Tuesdays. I can forward them to you. And I called her that Wednesday around three. She said she was in Wilson.

Then I talked to her later and she said she was on Glenwood Avenue but I don't know if she was on that road in Raleigh or Wilson. But she said she was coming to pick up the boys and take them to Monkey Joe's."

Grant then told him about the custody case between him and Laura that was going through the courts. "It's ongoing and heated at times."

"When did she bring the boys back?"

"Sometime between nine and nine thirty that night, but she must not have gone to Monkey Joe's because when they got back, the kids were all sweaty and hadn't eaten. My wife Amanda had to take them to Chick-fil-A to get something to eat."

"When did Laura leave your place?"

"About ten o'clock that night."

When Gwartney asked if Grant could forward the e-mail to him right away, Grant said, "I can't do it right away because I'm in the boonies and have bad reception. I'll have to get closer to Raleigh for a decent Wi-Fi signal." Grant certainly was out in the sticks, but he was in Texas, more than twelve hundred miles away from Raleigh.

"I didn't realize Raleigh had boonies," Gwartney joked.

"I'm driving—on my way to Kinston," Grant lied.

"What was Laura wearing?"

"She had heels on but I don't remember the clothes she was wearing because I wasn't really checking her out, if you know what I mean."

"I need you to come see me in Kinston so we can sit down and talk. I need to get a written statement from you about Laura's last day's activities."

"I'll tell you what," Grant said, "I'll e-mail a statement to you when I forward those other e-mails."

"Who was at your apartment when Laura came over?"

"Me and Amanda and the boys were there. But Amanda took them into the other room and they didn't know she was there at first. Me and Laura were going to talk about me signing an agreement for her to keep the boys."

"Did Laura usually pick them up at your apartment?"

"Nah, we always met in public places like Monkey Joe's if not at the Sheetz in Wilson to avoid ugliness."

"Did she always pick them up on Wednesdays?"

"No, Fridays, not usually in the middle of the week. But Amanda and me are going to meet her family in New Jersey." As Amanda did not have any known family in that state, one can only assume that Grant was attempting to direct law enforcement away from their real vicinity.

"What happened last Friday? Did Laura get the boys then?"

"I went to Sheetz but she never came. I waited for quite a while and called my mom in Kinston and ask her to go by Laura's apartment and see why she didn't come pick up the kids. I left Laura some pretty nasty e-mails while I was waiting for her at Sheetz."

When Gwartney asked about where he lived in Raleigh, Grant said, "We're in the process of moving to my mom's house in Kinston." He then spoke off the phone to someone else. "Watch him. The last time, he pulled the cat's tail." Then to the detective he said, "Hold on for a second. I need to walk away, my boys are near me."

"I really want to speak with you in person. Would you meet me in Kinston for an interview?"

Grant agreed and said, "In the meantime, I'm going to go ahead and try to e-mail you these conversations."

Gwartney assumed that Grant would be on his way shortly. But the detective did not receive the e-mails, and saw no sign of Grant.

Grant called back later and said, "I'm still trying to send those e-mails but I keep getting an error message."

Gwartney called Raleigh and told them that Laura Ackerson had last been seen in their city.

BARBARA Patty was expecting Laura at her house on Monday evening for their weekly Bible study and prayer get-together. Usually Laura sent her a text on Monday afternoon to make sure that they were still on for that night. When Barbara didn't get a message, she sent one to Laura, but never got a response.

Later she got a call from the house church leader, Rob MacArthur. He said that he'd heard from Heidi Schumacher, wanting to know if he'd talked to Laura. He hadn't, and wanted to check with Barbara.

THAT evening, sitting in the living room in Richmond, Texas, Amanda said, "We're worried 'cause we brought the kids across the state line and there was a court order in the custody battle saying we can't do that."

"From what I know," Karen said, "and I don't really know anything, but when there's a court order and you take them across state lines then I'm pretty sure they would consider it kidnapping, even if he is the parent."

"What would happen?" Amanda asked.

"Well, they would arrest Grant and Child Protective Services would probably take the kids."

"I do not want to go to jail," Grant said.

CHAPTER EIGHTEEN

JUST after two A.M. on Tuesday, July 19, 2011, Karen Berry's younger son, Shelton Berry, left his house with some friends to go to Denny's. He got back two hours later and found Grant and Amanda sitting on the tailgate of his truck. Shelton asked for a cigarette.

Amanda gave him one and said that they'd unloaded the piece of furniture from the U-Haul. Shelton joined them on the tailgate, where they had a couple of beers and talked.

Amanda asked, "Do alligators eat people?"

"Yeah, they're alligators," Shelton said.

"Where are most of them?"

"Well, you need to go further down the creek where there aren't any houses. But if you want to see lots of them, you need to go to the Brazos River."

"You hunt them?" Grant asked.

"Yeah. You hang a chicken from a hook in a tree. The alligator jumps up to get it and it gets caught. You lower it down and shoot it in the soft spot on the top of its head."

Amanda knew that Shelton operated a business rounding up problem feral hogs for a fee, so she asked, "What about the hogs? Will they eat people?"

"Yes, they will. They're carnivores," Shelton said, thinking these were city folk scared of the wildlife.

Then the conversation turned to the beach and shark fishing. Grant said, "I'd like to catch some sharks to take back to my dad in North Carolina. Where are they?"

"All over, but mainly we fish for them in Matagorda, past Baytown. Takes about an hour, hour and a half to get there."

"Would you take me?"

"If I get time before you go, but I have to work and all."

BACK in Raleigh, Heidi Schumacher went to her computer early Tuesday morning and loaded up a month's worth of e-mails from the last of May to the end of June on a CD and a flash drive. She drove down to Kinston and left the CD with Detective James Gwartney, who explained to her that the Raleigh police, led by Detective Jerry Faulk, were now running an investigation into Laura's disappearance. When she returned to Raleigh, she gave the flash drive to Faulk and told him she thought Laura had been murdered.

———————

LATER that morning, Amanda approached her sister Karen in the kitchen and said, "I need to speak to you alone—it's serious."

"Can I get a cup of coffee first?"

"Sure," Amanda said, but then continued, "I hurt Laura and I hurt her bad."

Karen looked at her little sister's face, seeking answers but afraid to find them.

Amanda said, "Laura is dead."

The two sisters went outside to the swing. Amanda pointed over to Grant who was in the yard, "Could Grant come over with us?"

"He's your husband," Karen said. "If you want him to come over, it's up to you."

Amanda asked, "Is there any property that has a big hole in it?"

Grant followed up with, "Does your well have a big hole in it?"

"No, it doesn't," Karen said. "It's not that kind of well." Karen was confused by the progress of the conversation. She kept waiting for Amanda to explain her comment about hurting Laura—she sensed something was very wrong. "If this is bad," she said, "really bad, it's best to tell the truth. I know an attorney you can go talk to if you need to talk to an attorney."

Grant and Amanda kept asking a bewildered Karen about deep places, and finally she said, "There's a septic tank in the back."

But as Karen and Amanda headed that way, suspicion smacked up against Karen's denial. "I don't think this is a good idea. One day this house might belong to one of my kids—it's not a good idea at all," she said and headed back to the house.

Grant told Karen he needed some acid, and asked if there was a Home Depot nearby. Karen gave him directions and let Amanda borrow a vehicle to drive there.

At 9:37 that morning, Amanda Hayes walked to a drive-up ATM in a strip shopping center and made a withdrawal. A little after ten, in that same shopping center, Grant entered the Home Depot wearing a dark shirt and pants. Employee Raymond Boyer had been at work for about an hour when another associate pointed him in Grant's direction saying that the customer needed assistance.

As Raymond approached, Grant said, "I have an odor I'm trying to get rid of."

The two talked for a while about available products. When Raymond inquired about the nature of the problem, Grant said, "I'm here visiting relatives and one of the sons captured a wild hog and put it in a pen. He's released it now and I volunteered to clean the area up."

"None of the odor removers we sell here at Home Depot would do that job. They'll only mask it for a bit but that's it." Raymond explained that he'd raised a son and daughter who were both in the Future Farmers of America, and "the way we used to do it is, a couple of times a week, we would go in and dig the dirt out of the pens and replace it with new soil. That's the only way I know to get rid of that odor. Do you have a shovel to do that?"

"No. I need something to take care of that odor," Grant insisted. "Do you have any kind of acid?"

"Well, we've got muriatic acid but that's not going to do the job," Raymond said.

Nonetheless, Grant was adamant. He wanted to see the muriatic acid. It was kept in the open garden area of the store because it was most commonly used by bricklayers, swimming pool people, and contractors who needed to clean concrete. Raymond led Grant out to it but then spent about fifteen minutes trying to talk him out of buying any. "It's not going to do the job for you—it's not going to remove the odor."

Finally, Raymond gave up and helped Grant load four boxes into his basket. "You ought to get some gloves—black neoprene or other chemical gloves."

Grant purchased the recommended gloves, a thirty-two-gallon plastic trash can, and the muriatic acid for a total expenditure of $69.49.

DALTON Berry got up while Grant and Amanda were gone and saw the dresser sitting out in the front yard wrapped in a gray U-Haul wrapper. When he noticed ants were getting all over it, he and a friend moved it up onto the porch.

SHA Elmer talked to her mother that morning. Amanda needed her to go over to the apartment to meet a man who wanted to look at, and possibly purchase, the furniture they'd listed on Craigslist. Sha walked in and was surprised to notice that the home reeked of bleach.

It was notable, because bleach fumes had always tended to give her and her mother migraines, so Amanda always cleaned with white vinegar instead. Sha called her mother and told her about the smell. She also mentioned a huge bleach stain by the front door.

"Oh, that was the boys. They kicked over a bucket of bleach that Grant was about to take out and dump on the parking lot."

"But, Mom, I thought . . ."

Amanda cut her off. "Just air the place out and call me if you sell the furniture."

Sha opened the sliding glass door to the balcony as well as a window in each bedroom. She spotted a damp towel lying on the stain and picked it up and put it in the linen closet on top of the washing machine.

As a young, single woman, Sha was smart enough to know that being alone, meeting a stranger she didn't know in a far-from-public spot was a risky proposition. For her protection, she plucked a couple of knives from the block in the kitchen and placed one in the top drawer of each of the nightstands on either side of Amanda and Grant's bed.

She laughed at herself when she looked down from the balcony and saw the man arrive—it was someone she knew, a musician named John Williams, who frequently performed at the bar across the street from where she worked.

After looking over the pieces for sale, John got on the phone with Grant and negotiated a price for the sofa and love seat. He gave Sha a deposit of $350 in cash and then left to grab some lunch and wait for the arrival of friend, David Soto, who had a van spacious enough to move the furniture.

Sha called her mother and told her that she had half of the money and was waiting for John's return.

"Take it to the bank and deposit it," Amanda ordered.

"As soon as I get the other half, I'll go straight to the bank and make a deposit," she assured her mother.

"No," Amanda insisted, "I need you to deposit that money right now."

Sha grumbled to herself but did as she was instructed. When she returned, she roamed around the apartment while she waited for John's return, but she never noticed anything amiss besides the bleachy smell.

DETECTIVE James Gwartney went to Laura's bank, BB&T, that same Tuesday, July 19, and asked if there had been any activity on her account.

A bank officer checked and said, "Not since the tenth of this month."

On that ominous note, Gwartney drove to Raleigh and briefed the homicide unit there. They put out a BOLO (Be On the Lookout) for Laura Ackerson and her vehicle through the National Crime Information Center (NCIC) system.

When Gwartney returned to Kinston, he; his supervisor, Commander Canady; and State Bureau of Investigation (SBI) Special Agent Lolita Chapman, met with the manager of Laura's apartment complex and learned that her lease had both of her boys listed as residents. Then they did a walk-through of Laura's place, looking for any signs of the missing woman and collecting anything that might point to her whereabouts.

Canady secured Laura's laptop from a desk in Laura's bedroom and what at first appeared to be a planner on the bedside table. When they flipped through it, they realized it was more like a diary. The last entry was on July 12 and it was quickly apparent that Laura had been having problems with Grant Hayes. Her notations about interactions with others, including her children, were also very detailed.

There was a planner page for July 11 lying on the dining table. The plants all appeared dead as if it had been a while since they'd been watered. The chances that something bad had happened to Laura seemed increasingly likely.

The detective assisted the Raleigh Police Department in obtaining a search warrant.

THAT evening, just after five thirty, Amanda's niece, Kandice Rowland, stopped by her mother's house after work to see Amanda. Because Kandice was due to deliver her first baby in two months and Lily was then just over a month old, the women spent an hour in conversation about being pregnant, giving birth and taking care of an infant. Kandice handed Amanda a check for $425 in payment for a loan her aunt had previously made to her.

Amanda said, "We need money for the trip back—could you pay me in cash instead?"

"I don't have it on me but I could get some from the

ATM tonight and write a check for the rest," Kandice offered.

Then Grant and Amanda went outside. Amanda came back in a few minutes later to get bottles of water and to borrow a pair of black sweats and a thermal T-shirt from her sister Karen. She said, "We're going to take the boat out and go fishing. Will you be here for a while?"

"No," Kandice said, "if you're going across the street, I'll head on home."

The two hugged and said good-bye.

Kandice went to the ATM and withdrew $300. She came back to her mother's house and dropped off the cash and a new check for $125. After chatting a little with her mother, Kandice left at about nine that night.

Karen was impatiently waiting for Grant and Amanda to return. She saw the couple take something out of the U-Haul but was too busy watching the children to notice what it was. She was running late to pick up one of her sons from work at ten o'clock but she hadn't wanted to go and leave the kids alone. She left as soon as Amanda entered the house.

CHAPTER NINETEEN

RALEIGH Detective Sergeant Robert Latour entered the investigation when Kinston Detective James Gwartney briefed his department on July 19, 2011. Latour interviewed a distressed, soft-spoken Chevon Mathes, but wasn't able to work more on the case until eleven P.M. that night.

Meanwhile, Raleigh Intelligence Center (RIC) sent Laura Ackerson's last known address in the Raleigh area to Sergeant Dana Suggs. Suggs requested that patrol officers check out the parking lots in the surrounding area, and about thirty minutes later, he got a call back with the news that Laura's 2006 white Ford Focus four-door sedan had been spotted near her old apartment complex.

Suggs called Latour, as did Detective Steve Previtali, another homicide investigator, and all three rushed to the scene. When Latour arrived, he noted that the wheels of the car were turned to the left and the car was locked up tight. The officers stood by while they waited for detectives and techs to complete their examination of the vehicle.

Detective Amanda Salmon, who was in charge of the homicide unit that summer, organized a canvas of the apartment complex. She divided it up into areas of responsibility, and she and five other detectives knocked on doors and asked questions of the tenants and personnel.

At two A.M., Latour called Chevon Mathes because she had a spare key to the vehicle. Sergeant Jackson of the Kinston police retrieved the key and sped to the parking lot in Raleigh, arriving at three A.M.

Meanwhile, Certified Crime Scene Investigator Tracy Tremmlet of the City/County Bureau of Identification arrived on the scene to begin the documentation and exterior survey of the vehicle. With a camera, a video camera and a 360-degree camera to take panoramic shots, she circled the car, documenting it from every angle from a distance and then from close up. She spotted a gray hair on the exterior driver's door and secured it as evidence.

Using a magnetic wand, she applied a combination of a magnetic powder and volcanic ash on all the exterior car door handles and any other spot that looked likely for fingerprints, but she found none. Tremmlet then pulled out a clean swab and distilled water and rubbed the surfaces for possible touch DNA. Each swab went in a box, which was placed inside an envelope.

With the arrival of the key, she processed the interior, starting with close-up shots and moving on to the fingerprint search and found one on the right rear passenger door, another on the interior of the driver's door, one on a cup and two more on a take-out tray. She also took a touch DNA sample from the lock button.

She moved to the interior portion of the trunk, where she found an unknown substance. She used phenolphthalein to do a field test for the presence of blood. It did not, however, turn hot pink in reaction, meaning the result was negative.

CHAPTER TWENTY

ON the morning of Wednesday, July 20, 2011, Grant and Amanda Hayes were packing up to leave Texas. Amanda drove her nephew Shelton's truck with its magnetic sign bearing the name "Critter Catchers" in big arched lettering and a message below that read: "Wildlife Control. Feral Hog Removal." She went first to an ATM at Waterside Market and made another withdrawal of cash, then shopped at Wal-Mart.

On the way back, she went to the cul-de-sac at the end of Skinner Lane. There she got out and lowered the tailgate on Shelton's truck. She hauled out the boxes that held the muriatic acid that Grant had purchased the day before and set them one by one next to a cluster of trees. Then she drove away.

While she was gone, Grant started cleaning the four coolers they'd brought with them. Dalton pitched in and helped. Dalton thought they looked brand-new except for one black mark on the inside of one of them. While they worked, Dalton overheard Grant tell someone on the other end of his phone, "I don't need an alibi. I was with my family." Grant left two of the coolers behind since they weren't bringing the U-Haul back and didn't have room for them in the car. That wasn't all they discarded. One of Amanda's old suitcases was dumped in a trash bin, and Grant told Shelton, "I'm leaving the machete. I don't need it. I was going to use it fishing or alligator hunting." He added that he had to get back, since he wasn't supposed to bring the kids across state lines.

Meanwhile, Karen had pulled Amanda aside to talk to her sister privately. She sat Amanda down next to her just like she used to do when Amanda was a child. She looked her straight in the eye. "I'm going to ask you this one time and one time only and I want the truth and I'll never ask you any questions again. Are you covering for Grant?"

Amanda raised her head and looked straight in Karen's eyes. She nodded her head up and down.

Grant and Amanda packed up their family, returned the trailer and traveled east back to North Carolina. After they left, Dalton spotted the machete lying on rocks beside the driveway. Karen told him to leave it alone. She used a rag to pick it up and stow it in the garage, along with the rags Grant had used to clean out the coolers.

Karen felt an immense sense of relief with the departure of her little sister and her family. Despite all she had heard, she still wasn't able to accept that it was all true. Then her children, responding to their mother's concerns, researched on the computer and fed her information from news stories about Laura's disappearance. With that knowledge, Karen's denial began to erode. Now, she was scared. Every time the phone rang, she was terrified that she was about to hear that Amanda and the children had been found dead on the side of a road somewhere.

THAT same Wednesday morning back in Raleigh, North Carolina, Detective Mark Quagliarello knocked on the door of Sha Elmer's apartment. He heard a dog barking but no other response. He knocked again, waited and turned to walk away. Finally, the door opened and Sha asked what he wanted.

After he introduced himself, Sha said, "Are my mother and the kids all right?"

"I'm here looking for a missing person, Laura Ackerson," Detective Quagilarello said. "I'm trying to get information about her, Grant and Amanda Hayes." He asked for her assistance locating her mother and Grant and requested that she come to the police station with him. Sha agreed, and she called her boyfriend, Matt Guddat, from the back of the detective's car.

After answering their questions, Sha accompanied Quagliarello to Grant and Amanda's apartment for the execution of the official search warrant. Detective Latour brought the paperwork. He noticed that, aside from a large bleach stain to the inside right of the door, the place was neat, but the potted plants appeared to be dying from a lack of water.

Detective Previtali assigned personnel to different rooms. Quagliarello searched the boys' bedroom but found nothing of evidentiary value.

Detective Salmon, after finishing the survey of the area where Laura's car was found, joined the team at the Hayeses' apartment. She noted that the large bleach spot on the carpet next to the tile of the front entrance began two feet from the front door and continued for three or four feet along the wall, extending out from it one and a half to two feet.

Senior Agent Shannon Quick with the Raleigh/Wake City-County Bureau of Identification photographed the entire apartment. In Grant and Amanda's bedroom, all the bedding had been stuffed into a closet except for the mattress cover, which was still in place on the bed with two reddish brown spots on its surface.

Salmon searched the area labeled as the master bedroom and connecting bath on the floor plan. It was not being used for its intended purpose; instead, it seemed more of a general storage area. The space was filled with a changing table, office furniture, electronics and materials, musical instruments and art supplies.

In a briefcase, she found a receipt from the Apple Store in Crabtree Valley Mall, stamped at 8:45 P.M. on the day after Laura was last seen, for the purchase of a MagSafe power adapter for $79—a total of $84.33 including tax, paid in cash. When they later obtained the shop's video, it showed Grant, accompanied by little Grant and Gentle, making that purchase.

Then Salmon went to the kitchen area to review a handwritten document with writing from two separate individuals, discovered by Detective Previtali in a stack of miscellaneous papers on the counter. One of the people contributing to the note was later confirmed to be Laura Ackerson. It read:

"I, Laura J. Ackerson, for the sum of $25,000 agree not to pursue custody of the two minor children, Grant and Gentle Hayes. I am not surrendering parental rights but I do consent to leaving them in the sole custody of their father for now. Further, I agree to drop all pending litigation against their father in the Lenoir County Family Court."

A different hand penned an added statement:

"By notifying counsel John Sargeant of our arrangements, less monetary considerations, I understand I'll be able to see my kids when I want at the discretion of their father."

The paper was initially dated "6/13/11." The six was marked through and a seven added in its place. The initials "LA" were next to the revision. It ended with the signature "Laura Ackerson."

Sergeant Brian Hall aided in the search, too. He noted that the foyer was relatively clean, the only anomaly being the bleachlike stain on the carpet bordering the linoleum by the entry. He found the hall bathroom remarkably clean—practically sterile—with a distinctive odor of cleaning solution in the air. There was no shower curtain or rod and no floor mats.

After Sergeant Hall finished up in there, Agent Quick entered the room wearing orange goggles and carrying a mini BlueMax alternative light source. She was looking for telltale indications of blood but found none. However, the presence of soap and shampoo on the rim of the tub told her that, despite the immaculate state of the room, it had been used as a functioning bath.

After leaving the apartment itself, Sergeant Hall researched the situation with the apartment Dumpsters and learned that the most recent pickup had been on July 15 and the next one wasn't scheduled until the twenty-ninth. He drove out to the trash center and asked the employees if they'd noticed anything unusual. They said that they looked for hazardous materials or currency when the refuse was dumped and felt certain that they would have noticed a body or a lot of blood by the smell if not by the sight of it. They provided him with the video that showed a couple of employees working the load when it came in that day. Hall also found out about a discouraging fact: with forty to forty-five trucks coming in each day, the trash from that apartment would now be underneath ten feet of newer trash.

ACROSS town, Matt Guddat was very concerned about his girlfriend being hauled off by law enforcement. He called Sha's mother and left a message asking her to call as soon as possible. Amanda sent a text with her sister's phone number. Matt called Karen Berry's cell and Amanda picked right up. "Sha has been picked up by the police."

"Huh," Amanda said. "That's strange."

Matt asked, "What do I need to do for her?"

"Well, we're getting ready to leave Texas. We'll be back soon."

DETECTIVE Latour drove back to Kinston to get the files on the missing persons case from Detective Gwartney. While he was there, he went by Laura's apartment in the renovated old warehouse building. He secured Laura's BB&T checkbook, hair from her hairbrush and a tape from the video camera in the complex showing Laura leaving on the morning of July 13. Latour then went to Star Day Care Center, where Patsy Hayes, Grant's mother, worked, and interviewed her before returning to Raleigh at 7:15 on the evening of July 20.

THAT day, Grant Hayes, while en route from Texas to North Carolina, had a conversation with Lauren Harris and continued the lies about his location. He told her that his boys were with him in Kinston and they were going to a candlelight vigil for their mother at a church there.

THE police brought Sha back to the station and Matt picked her up. The next time they wanted Sha to come in to talk, she was very uncomfortable. Matt offered to go with her for moral support and he ended up being questioned, too.

———

THE media caught the scent of a hot, developing story. ABC News interviewed Patsy Hayes about her missing daughter-in-law. Speaking of her grandsons, she said, "They get over things a lot faster and they could probably not be affected by things as much as adults are. You know, because they are small and they're very resilient so they probably figure they're just staying with Dad now."

CHAPTER TWENTY-ONE

ON Thursday, July 21, 2011, Detective Robert Latour and another detective went to the restaurants where Laura had scheduled visits on the Wednesday she disappeared. On the way, they also stopped by the Sheetz in Wilson where Laura and Grant usually exchanged the boys. They requested the videotape from the previous Friday but learned it had already been shipped to the corporate office. They filed a request for a copy.

Then they went to Bill's Grill and met with owner Randy Jenkins. He didn't initially recognize the photo of Laura. They checked the carry-out trays used by that restaurant but they were not a match for the one found in Laura's car.

When Latour returned to Raleigh, he began a review of the diary he received from the Kinston police and quickly noted the tumultuous nature of the relationship between Laura and Grant. He also viewed the video from Laura's apartment, which captured her leaving on the morning of July 13. He circulated the last known description of Laura's clothing to the investigators.

ON the road from Texas back to North Carolina, Grant Hayes did not see for a couple of days the promising message sent to him by Lainie Panos on July 21. Lainie was marketing the cell phone covers with Grant's artistic designs. A top designer in New York was very excited about his covers featuring deceased rap legends Tupac and Biggie and had passed one along to singer-actress Vanessa Williams. Even more enticing, Lainie received an invitation to a party that P. Diddy, a contemporary rap artist and producer, was attending. She needed a Biggie cover to give to him. She asked Grant to please call her the next day.

WHEN Detective Latour got to his desk on July 22, he had a message from Randy Jenkins waiting for him. Randy said that, although he hadn't recognized Laura in the photo they'd shown him, he was mistaken. "Laura's hair was different when I saw her than what she wore in the photograph and her face looked a little fatter in person." Randy said his wife saw a missing persons story on the news and called him to see it. That's when he realized that Laura was actually the girl who'd come to see him on the thirteenth.

Latour then called U-Haul's corporate headquarters in Phoenix, Arizona. They confirmed that Grant Haze had rented a trailer in Raleigh on July 16, and had returned it on July 20 to a location in Katy, Texas, near Houston. Latour called that location and talked to Rhonda Holiday, who verified that Grant had brought the trailer back but said that it had already been rented out to another party that morning. Latour was pretty frustrated about the timing.

Rhonda called back in a short while, though, to tell the detective she'd been mistaken. The trailer in question was still on her lot. The exterior had been cleaned but it was now secured for law enforcement. A relieved Latour reached out to the local Harris County Sheriff's Office, which agreed to send deputies to the U-Haul location and bring the trailer to their storage facility for safekeeping.

OUT in Texas, John T. Schneider, an environmental investigator for the Fort Bend County Attorney's office, headed out on his routine chore of collecting the tapes of photos from the motion-activated deer-trail cameras installed by the county at spots known for illegal dumping. He visited each site for a pickup as often as every other day but definitely at least once a week.

The cameras took photos whenever something moved in front of the sensor, took a minute to reset, then snapped another photo, repeating for as long as it caught movement in the vicinity of the lens. He arrived at the dead end of Skinner Lane, where a camera had been positioned since 2008.

On July 22, 2011, he reviewed those shots, going through a long series of joggers, coyotes and turnarounds before finding anything of interest. He pulled off the series in question for a closer look. Seeing the corrosive emblem on the side of the boxes being unloaded from a pickup truck by a woman, he went back in person to the location the next day and found three cardboard containers a little ways off the road, concealed from view by some logs.

That same day, Officer Kevin Crocker and other members of the Raleigh Police Department Fugitive Task Force headed down to Kinston to look for two persons of interest: Grant and Amanda Hayes. Crocker and crew went to the home of Grant's parents, Grant II and Patsy Hayes, and set up covert surveillance. Other team members scanned the area. One of them spotted Grant III's white Durango at a nearby law office.

A while later, that vehicle pulled up to the older Hayeses' home with Amanda Hayes behind the wheel, Grant in the passenger's seat and three kids inside. Amanda went inside with the children while Grant made multiple trips carrying a pink tote bag, several grocery sacks and two large blue coolers with white tops—one with wheels.

Crocker and the others kept an eye on the house until lead investigator Jerry Faulk and another detective arrived with search warrants for the Durango, for Grant's and Amanda's cell phones, and one allowing them to fingerprint and photograph the couple. When the detectives knocked on the door, Grant answered and introduced himself, speaking briefly. They found Amanda in the kitchen with the three children. Since Grant's parents had gone out earlier, a neighbor was recruited to watch the children until someone returned. A tow truck hauled the car back to Raleigh. Law enforcement brought the couple back to the house after midnight. Throughout it all, Grant seemed relaxed and composed.

THAT same day, Detective Mark Quagilarello thought about William B. Umstead State Park, nearly six thousand wooded acres filled with hiking and bridle trails, campgrounds and three man-made fishing lakes, nestled between the bustle of Raleigh, Durham, Cary and the Research Triangle Park. In the past, many have gone into that near wilderness and grown disoriented and gotten lost. The investigator sent a team of searchers to look for any sign of Laura Ackerson there.

At the same time, Detective Amanda Salmon was busy talking to several of Laura's friends, obtaining a video from Monkey Joe's and interviewing the manager, Lauren Harris. She also initiated another search into Laura's bank accounts for any activity since July 13.

At four thirty that afternoon, Detectives Robert Latour and Dexter Gill set out on the eighteen-plus-hour drive to Katy, Texas. They traveled down 85 South through Atlanta and Montgomery. They paused at a rest stop in Alabama, where they caught two hours of sleep in the car. Then they were off again, taking Interstate 10 through Louisiana and then "drove forever in Texas" until they reached Katy at four forty-five P.M. on Saturday, July 23. They shoveled down dinner and fell into bed at a local hotel.

BACK in Raleigh, Grant was feeling the heat. When a friend wrote at 7:23 on the evening of July 23 to congratulate him on his new baby and say he was taken aback by the news about Laura, Grant was ready with a question. "Can you remember any details from stories she might have told you about her past? . . . Any little thing would help."

A few minutes later, he contacted a woman who had been helping with the distribution of promotional copies of the cell phone covers and asked her to send some cases to Lainie Panos. "This thing with Laura is very serious. They trashed our house and took our car. Pray for us and pray for her, too. . . . I may be up for the fight of my life and I'm really scared. Black guy. White girl. Custody fight. WTF? . . . It's a nightmare."

A few minutes later, Grant wrote to another friend: "We don't have our phones, our house has been trashed and they took our car last night. Pray that Laura shows up in good health."

Right after that, Grant sent a message to yet another acquaintance. "Y'all keep us in your prayers for real." He went on to explain the situation as he had with the earlier friend and ended the message with: "It's bad movie, man."

That guy apparently hadn't heard the news and asked for the identity of the "they" who'd trashed the place and taken his stuff. Grant explained it was law enforcement looking for the mother of his boys. "They said 'missing person' but the warrants said 'homicide.'"

He then had an exchange with Lainie Panos about the cell phone covers he wanted to get into Apple Stores nationwide. After talking about that, he switched gears.

"I don't know if you've heard but Laura's gone missing and the police took all my shit. . . . I've got three little babies and they took my car, too." He authorized her to make business deals on his behalf and wrote: "My attention is on this very serious matter . . . until Laura shows up. . . . It's not a joke and somebody is playing a very serious game with my life right now."

Lainie offered her support and the use of her Gmail account, and displayed a little bit of paranoia as she did so. "Brother, take care. I don't know what's up but get me word and I am here in any way. Peace, love, erase. Get to me. Somehow. Whatever you need."

The next morning, Grant was still distressed. He wrote to a female friend asking a lot of questions. "Did Laura ever say anything to you about running off? Leaving town or wanting a new life? . . . We really need to help the cops find her."

She suggested he contact some of Laura's friends but couldn't remember any of their names. "I keep thinking she is somewhere close watching this play out." She added that Laura could have gotten a false ID and fled anywhere.

Grant wrote about his distress about comments on websites and added, "She told all of her friends I was a monster. . . . I think Laura took off, too. This is a real mess."

The woman tried to reassure him. "The news report I saw said . . . that Laura was unstable and you were given full custody. I have never seen anything negative about you."

CHAPTER TWENTY-TWO

WHILE Grant Hayes was fretting about the current turn of events, the investigators from North Carolina contacted the Fort Bend County Sheriff's Office in Texas and requested the assistance of a couple of deputies. They arranged to meet the deputies in the rural outskirts of Richmond at Beland Park and, together, they went to Karen Berry's home on Skinner Lane.

A three-plank wooden fence with pieces of the bottom board missing ran across the front of the house by the road. Detective Dexter Gill and one of the deputies approached the front door and knocked. The other two hung back just off the porch. Karen answered, appearing somber and worried. They introduced themselves and said they wanted to ask her some questions. She invited them in.

Gill and Detective Robert Latour went inside. Gill said, "I know Grant and Amanda have recently made a trip to your residence and brought a U-Haul trailer with them. It was an unplanned visit that seems a little unusual. Grant has children by another lady by the name of Laura Ackerson who is currently missing in Raleigh. I just wanted to speak to you to see whether or not you have any knowledge of that and to find out how the trip went."

Karen, looking visibly distressed, said, "I'll answer your questions. I'll tell you everything I know. But can I pray first?"

"Of course," Gill said.

Karen prayed aloud to the Lord to give her the strength to say what she needed to say. Latour and Gill started the interview with Karen together. In response to their question about who lived in the house, she told them that her two sons, Dalton and Shelton, were there. Her husband, Stanley, a truck driver, was away at the time. Her older son and two daughters no longer lived at home.

After establishing that Amanda and her family had visited and gone, Gill asked, "Is Laura here?"

Karen sobbed out loud. "I'm afraid she is. You need to look across the street." After a pause, she added, "I can't stand the thought of standing in court and facing my sister afterwards, but I have to do what's right." She revealed her concerns about Oyster Creek across the street from her house, and Gill went outside to speak to the Fort Bend County deputies who responded to the scene with them.

They made a call for additional personnel. More deputies and detectives from the sheriff's office as well as the dive team from the Richmond Fire Department were on the way.

The Raleigh detectives walked over to look at the creek
and then came back across the street to examine the property. Latour saw the dresser/wet bar that had been brought
from Raleigh sitting on the front porch of Karen's home.
At the rear of the house, on a broken-down deck that didn't
appear safe to use, were old weathered wooden chairs and
a cooler. They spotted another ice chest in the grass beside
it. Lots of trash was scattered in overflowing bins around
the backyard. It was a very rural area, so there was no garbage collection. Trash had to be burned, but the drought
had called a halt to open fires. From one of the trash bins,
they secured a khaki green suitcase as possible evidence.

Behind the house was a garage in a state of disrepair, a
defunct old general store that the family now used for
storage and as a hog pen area. For use in his feral-hog
hunting, Shelton had dogs in a pen on the opposite side of
the property. Karen pointed out a spot in the hog area
where the dirt looked different from the rest. Karen then
directed them to the garage, where she had jammed Grant's
machete, with its two-foot-long blade and standard handle,
down between the studs in the wall. She also pointed out
that in that same spot they would find the rags that Grant
used to clean out two coolers before they left. They also
pulled out a bottle of advance enzyme treatment from the
same location. Karen said she didn't know where it had
come from. Deputies secured those materials for forensic
analysis.

After surveying the property, Latour asked Karen and
her two sons to go to the sheriff's office to give their statements. He then searched Shelton's truck, an F-150 parked

in front of the house. Finding nothing of evidentiary value in or on the Critter Catchers vehicle, Latour released it so that Shelton could use it for work.

After checking on the items for processing, Latour left Gill in charge and went across the street to watch the divers at work, walking down the fifty-foot-long mowed path to the water.

Gill checked out the septic tank to see if that needed to be searched as well. He found old lumber and other miscellaneous materials piled on the lid. It appeared as if they'd all been stacked up there for quite some time.

BEFORE beginning the search of Oyster Creek, the Richmond Fire Department contacted the Gulf Coast Water Authority. That agency ordered the closing of dams upstream to reduce the flow of water.

Crime Scene Investigators Kim Oreskovich and Jack Clark arrived at the scene at three fifteen that afternoon, hauling a trailer to transport the Berrys' johnboat to a secure location for forensic examination. The boat was wrapped in a tarp before being loaded onto the bed.

Oreskovich and Clark were joined in the fire department's flat-bottom recovery boat by an armed officer ready to fire on any alligator that menaced the team. When they hit the outer perimeter of the designated search area, they spotted two white objects floating up against a massive patch of lily pads.

Oreskovich and Clark dipped a sheet under the water, slid it beneath the objects, and scooped them up. Holding the four corners of the sheet, they carefully lifted it out of the water and into the boat.

They had recovered two portions of a human torso, without limbs, severed at the navel.

Without attempting to judge possible relevance, they continued to gather up anything they could find in the vicinity of the remains: trash, plastic, containers, bottles and even fish eggs. By the time they had finished that task, the thick vegetation encompassing their boat prevented any further progress in the direction they had been going. They headed back the opposite way and, thirty yards from the first discovery, they found part of a leg.

When they arrived at a point directly across from the Berry home, they pulled into shore and Oreskovich placed the wrapped body parts on another sheet spread on the ground. She took a series of photographs and examined the cut ends to determine the nature of the tool markings.

She was walking up to the street when Detective Gill approached her and asked, "Could the cuts have been made with a machete?"

They walked down to the evidence to see if the marks on the largest bone from the leg could have been made with that implement. Oreskovich then met with the death investigator for the Galveston County Medical Examiner's Office, who ordered an autopsy and had the remains transported to his office.

Oreskovich began processing evidence that same day. She found a single hair and a small piece of vegetation in one of the coolers. She applied the blood reagent BlueStar to the inside of the johnboat. It illuminated, indicating the possible presence of blood. Further testing would need to be conducted to determine if it was human and to rule out any reactions from detergents or other substances. She also got a glow on the exterior of the boat. Using a Sharpie, she drew an outline around it to make the exact spot obvious for lab analysis.

She processed a hair found on wire fencing and another from the U-Haul. She catalogued the four pairs of women's panties found in the seized piece of luggage. She swabbed, sprayed, dusted and collected any samples she could find— from the trailer to the johnboat to found items that might matter but could possibly have no relevance at all. After the collection was completed, she had 110 items, which she turned over to Detective Gill.

Once it was too dark for the divers to work, Detective Latour joined Gill, who had returned to the Berrys' backyard with Fort Bend County detectives. The Berry family couldn't spend the night in the home because it was still part of the active investigation, so they were supervised as they retrieved personal possessions they needed. Before leaving the premises, Latour searched through those items before sending them on their way. Investigators left the residence at nine P.M., leaving a deputy positioned in front of the house all night long.

THE discovery of body parts in the depths of Oyster Creek in Texas pushed the Raleigh, North Carolina, investigation in a different direction—transforming it from a suspicious missing persons case to an obvious homicide of an individual strongly suspected to be Laura Ackerson. Detective Amanda Salmon obtained a search warrant to secure DNA from little Grant and Gentle to compare with what was found half a country away.

Sergeant Brian Hall called Heidi Schumacher to get a description of the tattoo Laura had on her foot in case they found that appendage in the creek. He telephoned later that day to ask if Laura had recently had a car accident, because of minor damage found on the right rear side panel of her car. Heidi was not aware of any vehicular mishap.

ON Monday, July 25, 2011, Detective Latour spoke to the local justice of the peace, who bore the responsibility for releasing bodies after autopsy. Then he made the ninety-minute drive to the Galveston County Medical Examiner's Office in Texas City. On the way, Latour called Dr. Deborah Radisch, the medical examiner back in North Carolina, to inform her that the case was now officially a homicide. He described the condition of the remains and asked for any special requests she wanted him to make of her counterpart in Texas. Latour wanted to be certain that he collected the correct bones and tissue for her analysis.

Latour observed as Assistant Medical Examiner Dr. Nobby Mambo performed the autopsy on the two-piece torso. The upper portion had been cut near the neck and below the ribs as well as at both shoulders. The lower half was cut at the hip joints. Portions of cut bone and hair were transferred to the Fort Bend County Sheriff's Office to remain secure until it was time to transport them back across the country.

Meanwhile, the Houston Police Department dive team had returned to the scene to assist in the search. Latour arrived back at the creek just in time to see the divers recover a human head at 3:09 that afternoon.

Karen Berry agreed to another interview, but this time she wanted to meet at her attorney's office. After that, Latour also spoke with Karen's daughter, Kandice Rowland.

He started wondering about the possibility that Grant or Amanda had also disposed of potential evidence at a nearby Dumpster. He contacted the South Grand at Pecan Grove Apartments down the street from Karen's house, off of Skinner Lane, but unfortunately, their trash containers were emptied often—every Monday, Wednesday and Friday. At the end of that long day, he and Detective Gill met with Fort Bend County detectives to review the status of the case.

Detectives always need a strong argument to justify the expense of long distance travel, so Gill and Latour had high hopes of finding pivotal information when they'd set out on that long journey to Texas. The significance of their findings, however, far exceeded their expectations. They now knew what happened to Laura Ackerson's body, had determined the two people who were definitely responsible and had gathered a massive amount of crucial physical evidence. There were still some details for law enforcement to nail down to wrap up the case, but now the burden of securing justice shifted to the medical examiner and the prosecutors.

CHAPTER TWENTY-THREE

BACK in Raleigh on Monday, July 25, 2011, Agent Michael Galloway with the Raleigh/Wake City-County Bureau of Identification stepped into the case at the request of the Raleigh Police Department. He went to their secure garage, where they had towed in Grant's Dodge Durango for processing. Galloway shot a 360-degree series of the exterior and moved to the interior. He applied volcanic powder with a brush and transferred found fingerprints to a card. That task was made more difficult because, although some of the surfaces were smooth, much of the interior was cloth, a difficult material for fingerprints to adhere and be lifted.

He sprayed luminol inside, looking for blood. He got the telltale glow on the seat and floor mats on the driver's side, and also on the right front door, the right seat belt latch, and the left second row and third row seats. Secondary confirmation tests using the three-part phenolphthalein process, however, had negative results. Detectives Zeke Morse and Thomas Oullette searched the vehicle when Galloway had completed his tasks. They seized the child custody review, which had been jammed down between the center console and the passenger's bucket seat.

Then, Galloway, Oullette and Morse went to SecurCare Self Storage on Glenwood Avenue, where Galloway took photographs of the unit rented by Grant and Amanda. At seven thirty that evening, the three detectives reported to the couple's apartment, where Galloway shot photos and pulled the molding away from the bathtub and toilet to see if any blood had seeped behind it. He sprayed luminol and several areas fluoresced, but again, confirmatory tests were negative. (The problem with both luminol and BlueStar is that they not only react to the iron in blood, but to anything with iron or other metals in it like pennies, mayonnaise or bleach.) He sprayed in the east side bedroom and bath, the living room, the foyer area beside the front door and on a mop on the balcony. All were negative.

That evening, John Williams called the police to report a spot that he thought could be a bloodstain on the covering under the couch he'd just bought from Grant Hayes. Detective Quagilarello went over to take a look and agreed that it looked suspicious. He brought in Agent Mike Galloway from the Raleigh/Wake City-County Bureau of Identification, who conducted a presumptive test on the spot, but the results were negative—it was not blood.

John then pointed to the arm on one side that had more

play in it than the other one did. He was concerned that it might have been damaged in an altercation.

OFFICER Kevin Crocker and his Raleigh Police Department Fugitive Task Force returned to Grant and Patsy Hayes's home in Kinston to keep watch—the news from Texas made Grant and Amanda likely murder suspects. Grant remained in the house most of the time, coming out occasionally for a cigarette. After the eleven o'clock news aired with news of the imminent arrest of him and his wife, Grant's trips outside to smoke became more frequent and his behavior seemed more nervous and unsettled.

In the early morning hours of July 25, detectives arrived and took the couple into custody. That evening Raleigh Detectives Thomas Ouellette and Zeke Morse conducted a search of Grant and Patsy's home. In the master bedroom, Ouellette found a yellow envelope sitting upright in a chair. It contained $571 in currency and a personal check for $125 written on the account of Kandice Rowland to Amanda Hayes. In that room, he also found writing on a used envelope that appeared to be notes in preparation for a press conference. It read:

1) *Grant Hayes—introduce Amanda, Father of Laura Ackerson's children Grant and Gentle Hayes*
2) *Like I told my mom, I was supposed to meet her 7/15/11. I called my mom to get in touch with her and she couldn't*

3) *If anyone has seen Laura, please call the police department and Laura: Grant and Gentle ask for you. If
you're listening to this broadcast, please call us.*
4) *I've spoken to Detective as soon as I learned of this
situation*

The detective also took possession of a men's chain
necklace, a small necklace with a palm tree pendant, a pair
of pearl earrings, a bracelet, matching diamond wedding
rings, a woman's watch, a small handwritten note, the two
coolers Crocker had seen going into the house and an RBC
Visa check card in Grant Hayes's name with a Post-it note
bearing the PIN adhered to it.

In the home office, Morse gathered up the computer,
its power cord and a notebook with a note about the children, dated July 24, 2011, that read:

*I, Grant Hayes, leave Gentle, Grant and Lily Hayes in
the sole custody of Grant and Patsy Hayes.*

It was signed by both Grant and Amanda. Below that
the name of a Raleigh pediatrics office was written along
with two telephone numbers.

ON July 26, while divers were continuing their arduous task
under the hot Texas sun, Grant and Amanda Hayes appeared before District Judge Jacqueline Brewer in Raleigh,
North Carolina. Even though the body parts found halfway
across the country had not yet been officially declared as

the remains of Laura Ackerson, the judge ordered both held without bond on first degree murder charges and appointed public defenders to represent them. She set their next court appearance for August 16.

Across town, CCBI Agent Michael Galloway and Raleigh Police Detective Amanda Salmon went to Glen Burney Trail in response to a report of possible drops of blood leading from the parking lot, down a sidewalk and a flight of stairs to the door of an apartment. When phenolphthalein was applied, the suspicious red drops did test positive for blood. Excitement over that find faded quickly when the innocent explanation was discovered—a man living in that unit had cut his hand and run inside to clean it up and bandage it.

IN Texas, John Schneider had run down the partial license plate for the vehicle seen dumping the muriatic acid at the end of Skinner Lane and had received two possible matches. One was for a much older truck registered to an address down in McAllen, more than three hundred miles away. The other was co-owned by Shelton Berry and Kandice Rowland, with an address on Skinner Lane.

Having heard about the body parts found on the creek beside Skinner Lane on the news and recognizing the address in the story as the same one listed on the registration of the truck in question, John went online to do a little digging. He found the booking photo for Amanda Hayes and compared it to the pictures he'd retrieved from the deer camera. "The hair, the tank top, everything matched," John said. He contacted Fort Bend County Detective Brad Wichard and turned copies over to him for use in the homicide investigation. Pursuit of the dumping offense went on hold awaiting the outcome of the murder trial.

DETECTIVE Robert Latour returned to the Galveston County Medical Examiner's Office that day to observe the autopsy on the newly discovered head. Its condition was deeply disturbing. The skin from the face had slid down, collecting near the jaw, exposing huge portions of the facial bones.

After the procedure was complete, Latour waited for the arrival of Forensic Odontologist Paul Stimson. Latour provided a copy of Laura's dental records to the doctor and remained there until he had the results.

Stimson took x-rays of the skull with all the teeth in place. Then he examined it thoroughly, using Laura's dental records and film. He compared the actual bone structure of the mouth, the alignment of the teeth and the pulp chambers. He applied iodine dye to make all the non-metallic fillings stand out readily. He prepared a report itemizing all of the similarities and explaining any dissimilarity caused by additional dental work or pre- or postmortem injury. In the end, he concluded, the skull did belong to Laura Ackerson. The stage was set to find justice for the mother of Grant Hayes's two little boys.

CHAPTER TWENTY-FOUR

BEFORE Grant Hayes's arrest, it seemed the only people who talked about his talent as a musician sang his praises. Now, the tide had turned. Writing for the *Houston Press*, Craig Malison said that serial killer Charles Manson had more musical talent. "Haze's songs range from mediocre, inoffensive Starbucks fare to the kind of music occupying forces blare through tank-mounted PA systems to wear down ruthless dictators in order to get them to leave their surrounded palaces."

SHA Elmer didn't know what to think about the avalanching events when she went to her mother's apartment after Amanda's and Grant's arrests. She picked up all of the children's belongings so as to deliver them to the elder Hayeses' home, where little Grant, Gentle and Lily were now staying.

It was during that visit to the apartment that she first noticed the condition of the hallway bathroom.

It was the only bath except for the en suite connected to the master bedroom. It was used by guests, and since it was the closest to the children's room, it was also where they'd brushed their teeth and had their baths. Now, it was empty of everything but bare fixtures—no potty chairs, no bath toys. The shower curtains, liner and rod were gone, too. The toilet seat cover and the floor mats weren't there either. Sha assumed the police had taken them and wondered why.

She went through the stack of papers on the kitchen counter with no particular purpose in mind. When she found the manual for the reciprocating saw, she was aghast. She'd heard the news from Texas and now she suspected she knew the tool that had been used. She took the manual to the Raleigh police.

ON Wednesday, July 27, Detective Robert Latour picked up videos from the U-Haul and the Home Depot in Katy, talked with Dalton Berry and then drove to Skinner Lane to help Karen Berry hang "No Trespassing" signs around the property in an attempt to keep the media from trampling all over the place.

The next day, Latour contacted Shelton Berry and asked for another meeting. Shelton, however, was away on a hunting trip, so he conducted that interview by phone.

Detective Previtali and Detective Melissa Goodwin flew

into Texas to help bring evidence back to North Carolina. On Friday, July 29, Latour visited Home Depot again, this time to try to get photographic identification from the employees there. He also purchased some dry ice to safely move the bone and tissue samples to North Carolina.

BACK in Raleigh, Detectives Michael Galloway and Brian Hall went to Raleigh Solid Waste Services Department on Corporation Parkway. In a cordoned-off, sheltered area, Galloway photographed the garbage that had been dumped from the apartment complex where Grant and Amanda lived. After getting big-picture shots, he stood by, photographing individual items that law enforcement pulled out for further investigation.

Hall dug into the mess and sorted through bag by bag, piece by piece. He saw the yellow-and-black vacuum that had belonged to Grant and Amanda as well as the black shower curtain with white liner from the hall bath. He also recovered a scrub brush found near the vacuum, the bath mats, a toilet brush, an empty gallon-and-a-half bleach container, several towels, gloves, a respirator, clothing, shoes and lots of packaging including some for a prepaid cell phone. He and Galloway collected and delivered those materials, and more, to CCI for latent print processing.

VERY early on Saturday July 30, Detective Robert Latour and Dexter Gill hitched the U-Haul trailer to the back of their police car. Previtali and Goodwin climbed into a rented truck packed with other pieces of evidence. The four detectives set off in their mini-caravan for the long journey back to North Carolina at five forty-five A.M. They finally reached their destination on July 31 at one forty-five in the morning.

CHAPTER TWENTY-FIVE

O N Tuesday, August 2, 2011, Senior Agent Shannon Quick returned to Grant and Amanda Hayes's apartment. She took additional photographs and cut out the bleached section of carpeting in the foyer and hall.

In the bathroom, she removed the quarter round at the base of the molding on the floor, and applied luminol to check for blood again. She got a positive purple area and used cotton-swabbed samples to test again with phenolphthalein, but got a negative result. She also found the telltale color on a small spot in the linen closet that was too small to risk further testing. She took a sample of the stain and packaged the swab to take to the lab.

She collected the shower head, the sink and bath faucets and the caulk behind them, as well as the plugs, drains and overflows with hair and debris caught inside them. To get the P trap, she went to the apartment in the floor below, cut a hole through the ceiling and collected it along with four vials of water from it.

THREE days later, a grand jury delivered indictments against both Grant and Amanda Hayes for the first degree murder of Laura Jean Ackerson.

Outside of the courtroom, Detective Robert Latour consulted with an anthropologist in Texas who had examined Laura's teeth for possible acid damage. That professional believed that acid had at some time eroded the enamel. The medical examiner had already requested Forensic Odontologist Stimson to examine the tooth in question and offer his opinion to confirm or discredit that possibility. Stimson was in the area on Tuesday, August 9, and paid them a visit.

"This is one of the teeth in question that I want you to look at," the medical examiner said, handing Stimson the maxillary left incisor and a small 100X magnifying glass. Stimson stepped over to the window for better light. He noticed that the natural protective barrier produced by saliva on teeth—the slime layer—was missing, and discovered an area of slight erosion. Although there was no way to identify the precise substance in question, the damage could have been caused by muriatic acid.

ON Thursday, August 11, the Gulf Coast Water Authority in Texas was performing routine cleaning of the water gates under bridges to keep the water flowing. At the gate located three-tenths of a mile from the Berry property, they found what looked like part of a human body in the midst of fallen brush and trash. The Fort Bend County Sheriff's Office arrived on the scene and verified that it was a portion of a leg, and secured it. Another piece of Laura's remains joined the rest.

WITH all the necessary steps taken, Detective Latour called Laura's brother Jason and her father, Rodger Ackerson, about bringing her body back to North Carolina. Once all the arrangements were made, Fort Bend County Detective Brad Wichard went to the medical examiner's office and observed as the body parts were placed in a Ziegler case and the top screwed down. He followed behind the official vehicle that carried the metal transport casket to the airport in Houston. Wichard watched the remains of Laura Ackerson being loaded onto a Continental jet for the return trip home to North Carolina.

Latour went to the Raleigh-Durham International Airport, where he was escorted down to the tarmac. From that post, he watched the jet land and taxi. He took custody of Laura's body at 4:56 P.M., when he signed the paperwork with Continental Airlines. Assisted by a company employee, he checked to make sure that the evidence seals were still intact and that no one had tampered with the Ziegler case. He kept a close eye as the wooden box holding the casket was transferred from the plane to a Brown-Wynne Funeral Home van. He made certain that the vehicle remained in his sight all the way to the medical examiner's office in

Chapel Hill. There he found a note written sideways across lined paper: "Please place remains of Ackerson in this cooler. Lock when done."

Laura Ackerson was back in the area where she'd lived, loved and died.

THE next morning, Chief Medical Examiner Dr. Deborah Radisch slid out the metal shipping box containing Laura Ackerson's remains. Inside she found another box sealed with evidence tape. Opening that, she saw a black body bag, which held several white bags of body parts.

The remaining tissue on the bones was decomposed—soft, gray and discolored. First, she and her staff x-rayed all of the material. Then she examined each piece she had received, noting: "Two pieces of torso show relatively shallow cuts, many of them with a rectangular shape and indented sides. . . . Postmortem radiographs . . . of bones with soft tissue show no foreign materials. However, cartilage is detected in a mass of moderately to severely decomposed soft tissue and muscle and gentle removal of this following thawing of the tissue yields the hyoid bone and the crushed, partially ossified thyroid cartilage." (That ossification was considered a natural part of the aging process.)

She added that strangulation could have possibly caused the damage to Laura's throat tissues, but "decomposition makes determination of what happened more difficult than making the determination on the dismemberment."

CHAPTER TWENTY-SIX

THE week after Thanksgiving 2011, Jim Freeman, Grant Hayes's court-appointed attorney, presented the court with a motion and a letter handwritten by his client. In it, Grant asked Superior Court Judge Donald Stephens to appoint him a new public defender. Freeman told the court that there was "good cause" for this action but, ethically, he could not reveal anything more. He was replaced by Mike Klinkosum.

The state requested handwriting exemplars from both Grant and Amanda Hayes. In North Carolina, they could not be legally compelled to do so; nonetheless, both separately agreed to comply.

SHORTLY after her mother's arrest, Sha Elmer went to Farmville, New Mexico, to live with her father. It was a rough, chaotic time for her. Her whole world had disintegrated almost overnight. After a few months, she got her thoughts and emotions under enough control that she recognized an obligation and responsibility to her half sister, Lily, and returned to North Carolina.

Thinking that it would help her to get custody of Lily, Sha jumped into a marriage with Matt Guddat on April 20, 2012. In many ways, Sha was cut adrift by her mother's arrest. She had spent her life looking up to her mother. She had seen Amanda as "an invincible war goddess who made something of her life despite lousy beginnings." Sha had wanted to be just like her. Now, when she tried to get custody of her half sister, Grant Hayes wrote to family services and told them that Sha was crazy and addicted to drugs. To make matters worse, Sha's connection to the crime made getting employment difficult—she was damaged goods by association. When she went to the grocery store, she was hounded by people who told her that she should be ashamed. Before long, she gave up, leaving her inappropriate marriage and returning to her father's home.

Sha wasn't the only one harassed in the aftermath of Grant and Amanda's brutal crime. Grant's mother, Patsy, had run a day care for many years, but after her son's arrest, two-thirds of the children stopped coming. In a short time, the endeavor was no longer viable. She lost her business and was now the caregiver for her three grandchildren, a challenging responsibility under the chaotic circumstances.

ON July 3, 2012, thirteen lounge chairs were donated by one of Laura's friends to the Fairfield Sprayground in Kinston in memory of Laura and in honor of little Grant and Gentle. It is a spot where Laura brought little Grant and Gentle quite often, and Grant's parents continue to make regular trips there with the children to play.

DR. Deborah Radisch, the chief medical examiner for the state of North Carolina, released the final autopsy report on September 6, 2012. Although it was clear that Laura had a sharp-instrument injury to her neck as well as other damage that suggested strangulation, exactly how Laura died was uncertain. "The cause of death is best described as undetermined, homicidal violence."

GRANT Hayes requested a new attorney again in November 2012. He claimed that Mike Klinkosum, his attorney at the time, had not done what he had asked. Klinkosum reported that he had an ethical conflict. Grant told the judge that he wanted a black attorney from Durham. Judge Stephens granted his wish for new counsel, but told him it was the last time he would do so. He appointed Jeff Cutler, a white attorney from Raleigh, to the case.

ON March 1, 2013, Grant and Amanda Hayes sat at the same table with their separate attorneys for an appearance before Judge Donald Stephens. Both of them appeared paler from their time in lockup, but aside from that the differences were striking. Grant seemed to have put on some weight, his demeanor was relaxed and at times he looked indifferent to the proceedings. Amanda, on the other hand, appeared gaunt and maintained a tense, rigid posture throughout. The state requested that the two defendants be tried together, citing efficiency and cost savings for the taxpayers.

At that time, neither defense team objected to that arrangement. Judge Stephens said, "At this point, I think the state's position is appropriate. Frankly, I think that the interest of justice would be best served if both persons charged with the same offense be charged at the same time by the same jury."

The trial date was set for May 20, 2013.

A month later, on April 8, everything changed. Rosemary Godwin, an attorney on Amanda's defense, filed several motions. In one, she requested that her client sit at a separate table during the trial, since Grant Hayes had written her a threatening letter. In another, the lawyer alleged that Amanda had an alibi for the time Laura was killed, and that she'd helped dispose of the body under coercion from Grant—she'd feared for her life, as well as for Lily's, Sha's and the two boys' lives. Grant Hayes's attorney told WRAL News that these motions called into serious question whether the two could be tried together. The judge set a new hearing on the matter for April 22.

On that date, Grant's legal team requested that the joint trial be severed under the current circumstances. "Based on the filings of Amanda Hayes and her attorneys, it is now apparent that we have antagonistic defenses based on the reading of the motions. Clearly, they are going to attempt to make him look bad. That is part of their defense and I don't believe that's a manageable way to try a joint trial."

The state objected. They contended that the expense of separate trials was not justified. Assistant District Attorney Boz Zellinger said, "The state's evidence on Amanda Hayes shows her as, not just a conspirator and not just acting in concert, but as a principal in this crime."

Judge Stephens spoke of his concern that each defendant might not be capable of receiving a fair trial and of the possibility that a mistrial would occur if they proceeded with the joint prosecution. "I know we can get this right by trying them one at a time. I have serious question to whether I can do it under this situation if we try them at the same time."

With this ruling, Amanda's trial remained on the docket for May 20 while Grant's was moved to late August. The exact order of the two proceedings would be left to the state's discretion regarding who they would like to try first. At the end of April, they made their decision to try Grant first, and Amanda's trial was postponed to early 2014.

IN Grant's pretrial arraignment before Superior Court Judge Donald Stephens, on the afternoon of Friday, August 16, 2013, his attorneys requested that the court allow testimony from Amanda's sister Karen Berry about the confession made to her by Amanda.

Will Durham, another attorney working on Grant's defense with Jeff Cutler, argued that after the state spoke about custody battles and dismemberment, the defense needed to respond. He wanted the jury to know that Amanda was "the one who did this—that she's the one who hurt Laura."

ADA Zellinger countered that the alleged confession was in bits and pieces, taken out of context. "The statements she's made were so essentially choppy and unclear that I think it's difficult to rule on them when there's so much attached to them."

The judge asked Amanda's attorneys, Johnny Gaskins and Rosemary Godwin, if their client would be willing to testify at Grant's trial. Gaskins told the judge that it was too early for them to decide. About the matter at hand, he said, "We will ultimately conclude that it is not a confession and that the use of the word 'confession' is rather loose."

Upon a request from Grant's defense team, the judge delayed the ruling on the matter, pending his opportunity to hear Karen Berry's testimony and a decision from Amanda on whether or not she would appear on the witness stand.

CHAPTER TWENTY-SEVEN

OPENING arguments for Grant Hayes's trial began as scheduled on August 29, 2013. Dark-haired, sharp-nosed, whip-thin Assistant District Attorney Boz Zellinger rose first, looking wound up tight enough to go into orbit, and turned his attention to an array of expectant faces. "Ladies and gentlemen of the jury, as the sun rose over Kinston, North Carolina, on July 13, of 2011, Laura Ackerson woke up excited. For once things were going her way. [She was] the twenty-seven-year-old mother of two little boys, little Grant and Gentle. She shared custody of them with this man," he said, pointing to the defense table, "Grant Hayes."

"You'll hear that morning Laura got her things and she started to walk out the door and walk past her refrigerator covered with pictures of her little boys. Little did she know that those little boys would only know their mother for only three years. Little did she know as she walked out that door that within twenty-four hours, she would take her last breath. Little did she know that that man," he said, pointing again at the defendant, "the father of her children, would be the one responsible for her murder and disappearance."

After introducing himself and his cocounsel, Becky Holt, Zellinger continued, "Evidence is going to come from this witness stand. It's going to come from the people involved in Laura's life. . . . [Investigators] are going to get up there and tell you the truth about what happened. And it's not a story. It's a reality. . . . Ladies and gentlemen, this is a case that is so calculated, so malignant, and so destructive, that Laura Ackerson disappears off the face of the earth for eleven days after she goes to Grant Hayes's apartment.

"You'll ask yourself as you hear this evidence: Where has Laura gone? On July 13, after she heads over to Grant Hayes's apartment, no one hears from her. Grant told Detective Gwartney that when Laura arrived that night, Amanda kept the boys in another room so they didn't know she was there yet. You'll also hear that Grant and Laura were to discuss her and him signing an agreement for her to keep custody of the boys.

"The question still remains that 'Where is Laura?' You'll hear that Detective Gwartney, upon learning the last place Laura has been is Raleigh . . . enlisted the assistance of homicide detectives and the homicide unit there.

"Wednesday, July 20, everyone still is asking: Where is Laura? . . . You'll learn that detectives also learned, as the investigation speeds up, Grant and Amanda rented a U-Haul trailer that could be dragged behind their car. And that they rented that in Raleigh and then they returned it in Katy, Texas.

"Where is Laura? All roads appear to lead to Texas. . . . Ten days or eleven days have gone by of asking: Where is Laura?

"Perhaps, most importantly . . . on Thursday, July 14, at around 2:40 A.M., some six or eight hours after Laura went over to Grant's apartment, you'll hear the Grant Hayes walks into the Wal-Mart at Brier Creek. . . . You'll hear that he bought a plastic tarp, nine foot by twelve foot. That later he bought some goggles. You'll hear that he bought some firm-grip stripping and refinishing gloves. And perhaps most importantly, you'll hear the Grant Hayes purchased a Skil reciprocating saw with six-inch blades. You'll hear talk about some other blades for that saw. And that's at 2:40 A.M., right after Laura goes missing. And you'll hear more about the eleven days that Laura disappeared. And you'll hear about this six days between the time she went to see her children and the time that Grant Hayes took that boat ride.

"Ladies and gentlemen of the jury, when all the evidence has been presented, when all is said and done in this courtroom, were going to come back here and ask you to find that man guilty for murdering Laura Hayes, for bringing her over to his apartment and then dismembering her body so that she disappears off the face of the earth. Thank you."

BOYISH-LOOKING defense attorney Will Durham stood with a demeanor so relaxed, it didn't seem in keeping with the seriousness of the moment. He contradicted the state's theory from Zellinger's first sentence. "This case is about a man covering up his wife's actions," he said. "On July 13, Amanda Hayes killed Laura Ackerson during the fight. It wasn't something that was planned, it was something that happened."

Durham told the jury about Laura Ackerson's little silver recorder that she used to tape all her phone calls with her kids, the exchanges when she picked up or dropped off the kids and every interaction she had with Grant Hayes. He explained that she would download them all on her computer, "But you won't hear any of those recordings or see anything in those e-mails that's violent—no arguments that have a tenor of violence.

"You'll also see from those documents, as well as from Laura's diary, which was seized in this case, there are a lot of hostilities between Amanda Hayes and Laura Ackerson. You'll see that Laura writes in her diary that Amanda sees her as psycho-crazy. And that they're yelling at each other at exchanges. And Laura feels pretty angry that her ex-boyfriend's new wife is yelling at her in front of the children about things related to being late or whatever kind of chastisement is going on. And the evidence will show that Amanda Hayes was extremely resentful of Laura Ackerson. This was her husband's ex-wife that was calling multiple times a day to talk to the kids. Was still constantly e-mailing with her husband, was still constantly involved in their lives. And there was hostility there."

On July 13, Durham said, Laura Ackerson "goes to Grant's house as she's done many times before. And she gets there and they are talking about the custody case and talking about how much money they spend on it. And somehow a joke about how much money has been spent becomes an agreement. And you'll see that agreement," he said, referring to the piece of paper found in the Hayes's apartment. "They agreed to end the custody dispute . . . This what Grant had wanted, he wanted custody of his kids. And he was ecstatic. But standing three feet away was Amanda Hayes, and her husband had just agreed to give his ex-girlfriend twenty-five thousand dollars and they didn't know exactly where they were to get it from yet. And she was angry about it. Grant went to go to get the kids ready for the special visit, something happened and we don't know exactly what that was. But we do know what Amanda Hayes . . . tells her sister five or six days later about what happened." Durham claimed that Amanda said Laura tried to take Lily away from her. "Then Amanda did something serious and Amanda tells her sister that 'I hurt Laura. I hurt her bad.'

"Now what happens next are the terrible decisions of people who are terrified. Grant and Amanda started making terrible decisions because they were afraid to call the police. They were afraid that no one was going to believe what had happened wasn't intentional. . . . They worried about going to prison. They make terrible decisions and Amanda took charge of the situation. Sent Grant out that night. He went and got some money. He said he went to Wal-Mart, hours after Laura's death. He buys a saw and,

the next morning, Amanda calls her daughter Sha and says
come get these children. Come get the boys out of the
house. And Sha does it and leaves Amanda and Grant with
Laura Ackerson's body and the saw in the house.

"And you'll hear that Amanda calls her sister, two days
after Laura's death, and says, 'You know we always talked
about maybe coming down there and you know, we're
coming.' And she says, 'Okay, that's kind of weird, but
okay, come on.'

"And this was a place that Grant has never been before;
this is Texas, rural Texas. Grant Hayes had never met any
of these people before, these were Amanda's kin. And they
drove down there and Amanda went to her sister and told
her what happened, told her what she had done and said,
'Help me.' And her sister helped her. And her sister gave
her keys to unlock the boat, watched the kids, and then
Grant and Amanda unloaded that U-Haul and they dump
Laura Ackerson's body in the creek.

"The evidence will show that the death of Laura happened in a spontaneous, unpredictable way. Grant Hayes
helped clean up, he helped dispose of her body and that's
a serious thing and that's a terrible thing, but it's not murder. The evidence will show that Grant Hayes is not guilty
of murder."

CHAPTER TWENTY-EIGHT

THE first witness of the trial was Laura Ackerson's friend and business partner, Chevon Mathes. She told the jury how they'd met, and the essence of the business they'd operated together. A broad smile went across her face when she was asked about Laura's children. "Two lovely little boys . . . Grant was just the leader. He's the oldest and little Gentle just followed him around. They were high energy, very sweet and well-mannered children."

Prosecutor Boz Zellinger had Chevon tell the jurors about the custody exchanges and the nature of the dispute that arose over midweek visits the month before Laura's death. Then he questioned her about Laura's skills as a parent. Chevon said, "She was a very loving mother. She took a lot of time out for the kids. She would stop whatever she was doing to make sure they were okay."

After a discussion of Laura's habit of recording all interactions with Grant Hayes and keeping copious notes about those encounters, Zellinger asked, "Did Laura ever express any concerns to you that she had for her safety?"

"Yes," Chevon said. "She told me that she feared for her life."

"Was this one occasion or did she express that multiple times?"

"We spoke about it numerous times" in the months before her murder, Chevon said.

"What did Laura say?"

"She told me she didn't know what Grant was capable of and if anything happened to her, Grant did it. Basically, she just told me she feared for her life."

When the prosecution shifted gears, Chevon responded, "Her main priority was to get her children back before anything else—even our business, even when she was working at the store, she would drop whatever she had to do for her kids. There was a time when she had meetings and I had to take the meetings when Grant called, and that was when Amanda was about to give birth and he wanted her to have the kids for a little period of time and we'd have things set up but I just had to take care of them because she dropped it to be with her kids."

Chevon described the many contacts she had with Laura on Tuesday and Wednesday, July 12 and 13, the success of company sales Laura made and the abrupt end of communication. She testified, "I was waiting for her to give me a call back that evening because we were going to get together and go over everything." She added that when she called Laura on Thursday, the call went straight to voice mail.

"Was that unusual?" Zellinger asked.

"Very," said Chevon. "She always had that phone on her or had that phone near her, in case those kids ever needed to call her. . . . I was concerned. She never had that phone off. She always had that phone on. It was just very odd that it was going straight to her voice mail." Chevon described how she went over to Laura's apartment complex and saw that her car wasn't there. "Friday, I sent her an e-mail and said, 'I'm concerned. I'm worried. Give me a call.'" She told the jurors about going to the police station in Kinston and filing a missing persons report, then talking to the Wilson and Raleigh police departments as well.

The state used the witness to introduce the recovered notebooks from Laura's apartment. Chevon looked through them and testified that she recognized Laura's handwriting. Despite the serious nature of her appearance in the courtroom, Chevon could not help smiling and laughing as she read over Laura's humorous comments about the potential clients who'd turned down their company's proposal.

Zellinger asked, "Did Laura ever talk to you about giving up custody of her children?"

"No."

"Did Laura ever express to you whether or not she wanted to have custody of her children?"

"Yes," said Chevon. "She wanted her kids back."

On cross-examination, Jeff Cutler pushed Chevon to explain why Grant had custody, but she didn't know. Then he asked, "Did she tell you that she consented to him having custody?"

"No."

"Did she tell you that she allowed Grant to take little Grant to New York back in February of 2010?"

"Yes."

"Did she tell you she signed a consent order in the summer of 2010, consenting to the arrangement that they had for the next year?"

"No," replied Chevon. "I didn't know about any consent. I did know that she allowed Grant to go with his father to New York. . . . She did not tell me there was anything through the courts but that he just took him to New York with them." She further explained that her understanding was that the arrangement for the boys to be with Grant during the week and with Laura on the weekends was court-arranged and wasn't by Laura's choice.

"Did she ever offer to introduce you to Grant?" Cutler asked.

"No, she told me she didn't want him to know about me."

"Do you think it's possible that she just didn't want you to get to know Grant?"

"No."

At the probing of the defense, Chevon admitted that she had no idea of the kind of parent Grant was or how much he loved his kids. On re-direct, Zellinger asked her what Laura told her about what happened in court.

Chevon said, "She told me that he painted a picture that she was a prostitute and a drug user and that's how he got custody of their children."

"Why would Laura never go to Grant's apartment?"

"She was scared," Chevon said.

ANOTHER one of Laura's friends, Heidi Schumacher, assumed the witness box wearing a tight updo. Her face was pale and she had a haunted look in her eyes that intensified the longer she answered questions. She told the jury that Laura was her best friend and that they'd first met in late 2004 or early 2005.

After Heidi discussed Laura's belief that she'd been married to Grant and outlined the legal wrangling over the custody of the children, Zellinger asked, "Were you involved in any hearings involving that ex parte?"

"I was involved in the entire custody battle. . . . I was a character witness to Laura." Heidi told the jury that when the court suggested that Grant have the children during the week and Laura have them on the weekends, Laura went along with it because she had not seen her children in months at that point and believed that "any time was better than none." Heidi explained that she was the one who'd told Laura "to go get a tape recorder immediately. I also told her to keep a log of any contact she had with Grant and with the boys." Heidi noted that Laura even kept a log of their food, because of accusations and recriminations from Grant and Amanda that what she fed the boys made them sick.

"She kept a log of when she fed them, what times, when she had diaper changes. She kept a log of every activity she did with the children and every contact she made with Grant. . . . Laura loved her children more than anything and it showed in every action that she took."

Heidi wrapped up her direct testimony by telling the jurors about Laura's prescient statement that if anything ever happened to her, Heidi should know that "Grant did it."

On cross-examination, Heidi insisted, "She told me she would never go to his apartment."

When Cutler pressed her on that belief, pointing to Laura's obvious visit on July 13, Heidi said, "The only reason I can think of was because he was going to give her custody of the kids. That's the only reason I can think of that she would have gone."

With those words, the court adjourned.

THE following morning, Friday, August 30, 2013, when court resumed but before the jury was brought in, the judge said, "I've been advised at the bench that the witness on the stand, Heidi Schumacher, is a witness who has information in reference to what we refer to as 404(b) evidence, dealing with other acts that might constitute crimes for which the defendant is not charged. In previous motions, I have deferred ruling on the admissibility of any such evidence, and since the witness is here and the jury is out, it would seem appropriate to listen to what that evidence would entail so I can be in a position to make some ruling on it in the event that the state decides, at this time or at some time later in the trial, to offer the evidence."

Heidi resumed her seat in the witness box, wearing the same black cardigan she'd worn the day before but replacing the previous day's drab gray dress with a bright blue one. First, she related to the judge the incident of her phone conversation with Laura in 2008, when Grant was ranting in the background and she'd arrived to find Laura injured. Heidi then moved on to the time Grant threatened both her and Laura in a parking lot.

Defense Attorney Cutler got Heidi to admit that Laura never "specifically said that Grant hit her," although Laura had said that Grant caused her injuries.

"When Laura told you Grant went to the US Virgin Islands, did she tell you he went with another woman?"

"No."

Heidi also said she'd seen the pictures of Grant and Amanda's wedding in Las Vegas and that little Grant had been in the photos. She testified that it was her understanding that Laura did not know they were married until she received the photos from Grant.

Cutler tried to discredit that statement by claiming that Laura had sent an e-mail to Grant talking about his marriage to Amanda before it happened. He claimed in one of them Laura wrote, "I'm glad you found your perfect match, Grant." The defense however, did not produce that e-mail or any other proof to corroborate that statement.

Cutler did, however, have Heidi read the January 2011 e-mail chain between Grant and Laura (in which Grant made a number of negative comments about Laura) into the record. In the e-mails, Laura didn't argue about the validity of Grant's remarks, but did say that she was laughing at what he said.

The judge reached a decision, saying that anything regarding arguments and physical confrontations was rel-

evant. "I'm inclined to hear testimony from Heidi Schumacher on anything she actually saw, but not what happened
out of her sight, based on what the victim said to her three
years prior to her death." In short, Heidi's testimony about
the threats and the physical injury were admissible, as long
as Heidi didn't mention Laura's comments.

The jury took their seats in the courtroom and the direct
examination continued with a recitation of the events that
occurred on the day Heidi saw Laura with a black eye and
a bloody nose. She then related Laura's surprise when she
realized that she was not legally married to Grant.

When the prosecutor asked Heidi about introducing
Laura to Oksana Samarsky, she said that she had done so
because "Laura was always good at meeting people and
marketing and Oksana was a fantastic artist and Laura was
also an artist. I introduced them because I thought they
would hit it off and I thought they could help each other."

The state then questioned her about Laura going to
Grant's apartment. Heidi insisted that Laura would not go.
"She would not be alone with him." Heidi said Laura was
afraid of how a situation could be twisted when there were
no other witnesses.

She continued on with testimony about Laura's physical
fears, telling the jury about the threat Grant had made to
both of them in the parking lot, and how it had led to her
getting a concealed-carry permit, and—since Laura was
uncomfortable with guns—why Heidi gave her a knife for
her protection.

On re-cross, the defense tried to shred her testimony,
but Heidi stood her ground. The defense accused her of

never having previously said anything about Grant's threat to kill both of them, but she vehemently denied that allegation.

Finally, when asked about what she told the police when Laura went missing, Heidi testified that when she spoke to them, she'd shared her belief that Grant had either had Laura murdered or had murdered her himself.

THE next witness on the stand that day was Kinston Detective James Gwartney. Gwartney, a man in the proximate vicinity of forty with brush-cut light brown hair, sharp cheekbones, deep-set eyes and a downturned mouth, wore a light gray suit, a blue oxford button-down shirt and a yellow tie. After Chevon Mathes had filed the report about Laura with the Kinston police, his supervisor had given him the missing persons file to investigate.

Through direct and cross-examination, Gwartney detailed the steps he took during the two brief days the case had been in his hands before he turned it over to the Raleigh homicide unit.

SBI Special Agent Lolita Chapman, a black woman with short, neat hair and a prominent chin, followed him on the stand. An investigator with the State Bureau of Investigation, assigned to Greene and Lenoir Counties, Chapman became involved in the case on July 19, when she received a request from the Kinston police for assistance with interviews because of a manpower shortage. On cross-examination, Cutler directed her to read passages from Laura's journal that reflected poorly on Amanda.

Sergeant Dana Suggs of the Raleigh Police Department testified about the discovery of Laura Ackerson's Ford Focus in the parking lot of her former residence at Camden Crest apartments.

Oksana Samarsky next took the stand. She had long, light brown hair, parted in the middle, with long bangs; deep, dark eyes; and smooth skin. Oksana described how Heidi Schumacher had introduced her to Laura in February 2011. She remembered that first encounter well. Laura's two little boys had crawled all over their mother, who displayed a bubbly personality. "We became very quick friends," Oksana said. "Laura believed in me and thought I could make money on my art. She was going to help me with marketing and was going to try to use her connections to get me into a gallery."

Oksana chatted with Laura on July 12, and they were going to try to get together on the evening of the thirteenth. Laura left Oksana a voice mail message that night but they didn't connect. "I was in study group and I saw my phone ring. I wish I'd picked it up. If I'd known what would happen . . ." Oksana said, choking up with emotion as she fought tears and her voice cracked. "I would not let it ring and then just kind of ignored it because she left me a voice mail. And I listened to the voice mail and it said she couldn't make it, she's doing something else. And that's fine, it happened before, it didn't work out. But two weeks later, it was very important that I should have picked up the phone." She paused to capture her composure, pulling out a tissue and blotting her eyes. "I got a call two weeks later from a detective who asked to meet me to get that message off my phone. I ended up meeting him and he had a tape recorder and I played the message and he recorded it," she said through sniffles.

"Have you listened to that message?"

"Yes, several times."

The state entered the taped message and a transcript of it into the evidence and then played the tape of Laura. By the time it ended, Oksana's sobs ripped through the courtroom.

The prosecution continued. "After that message, did you ever talk to Laura again?"

"No," Oksana choked out through her tears.

The judge gave her a moment to compose herself. She blew her nose and looked up at defense attorney Will Durham.

Durham asked her about a Facebook chat she'd had with Laura on July 12. "You and Laura talked about how the custody case was going and Laura said, 'It's going. I joined a group online of ladies in a similar situation—people who have had to deal with assholes. LOL. And my situation is so, so, so, so good comparatively.' She said that to you on that Internet chat, didn't she?"

"Yes," Oksana admitted.

On re-direct, the state had Oksana read a chat string from earlier that summer, when Laura expressed confidence that she would soon be regaining custody of the boys and congratulated her friend for selling some of her art online. The defense then asked if Laura ever showed her any cell phone cases with art on them.

"Yes. Ones Grant did. She spoke very highly of his

work." With that, Oksana, with a tear-stained face, was finally released from the stand.

ANOTHER young woman stepped into the box in her place. Sha Elmer, now Sha Guddat since her marriage the year before, was twenty-four years old and had short, thick, light brown hair and a pretty, sweet-looking face with a warm smile that lit up her eyes. She told the jury that her mother, Amanda Hayes, was married to Grant Hayes.

On direct examination, she sketched out her family history for the jury. Then, she told them about picking up the boys and taking them to Monkey Joe's on the morning of July 14, 2011. She admitted her frustration about having to drive across town and back to loan her mother the vacuum cleaner that belonged to her boyfriend. She talked about the cancelation of the weekend's moving plans and her surprise at her mother's sudden trip to Texas.

On cross-examination, Sha went over her mother's comments about the trip to visit her sister halfway across the country. She said that, although she did not know it until after the fact, her mother wanted to move an antique piece from the 1800s that she inherited from her second husband to Fort Bend County, Texas, for safekeeping.

When asked about her relationship with Grant, Sha said that it was pretty good. She told the jury that on April 30, 2011, she'd posted a message on his Facebook page that read, "Happy Birthday, Daddy." She added, "That's what I called him because that's what the boys called him."

Questioned about what she told police about Grant, Sha

said, "Grant thought he was a good dad and not in danger of losing custody. He just wanted it to be all over—we all did." She said she'd assured detectives that she'd never seen Grant lose his temper or raise his voice and that he'd never been violent in front of her.

On re-direct, the state asked, "During the summer of 2011, how would you describe the financial situation of your mother and Grant Hayes?"

"Swirling down the drain."

"Would you say they were losing money?"

"Anything my mother had at that point had been sold." She continued in that vein, describing the many items her mother had lost: a Rolex, an engagement ring, a wedding ring, a diamond tennis bracelet and other jewelry from Nicky Smith, as well as an unset green-yellow diamond.

The state handed her exhibit 45, a manual for a handheld reciprocating saw. Sha testified that she found it in a stack of papers when she was packing up the family's belongings after the arrest of her mother and Grant.

When the defense asked questions again, Sha told the jury that sometimes when Laura called, Grant would put the phone on speaker or just set it down and let her rant. Grant, she said, wouldn't yell back in front of the baby.

CHAPTER TWENTY-NINE

O N the third day of the trial, September 3, 2013, Tracy Tremmlet, certified crime scene investigator with the City/County Bureau of Identification, explained her part of the investigation—photographing, videotaping and collecting evidence at the scene where Laura's Ford Focus was found.

She was followed by Grant's longtime friend Lauren Harris, the general manager at Monkey Joe's. Lauren had long blonde hair, pouty lips and dark eyes. She wore oversized earrings and chewed gum on the stand. She testified that she and Grant met at Cinelli's, a restaurant in North Raleigh. They'd seen each other all the time for a while and then lost touch for a few years. They renewed their friendship after that and saw each other several times a week. She said she met Laura when Laura was dating Grant, several months before she became pregnant with little Grant.

Lauren added that, occasionally, Laura would be with Grant and the boys at Monkey Joe's. The admittance charge was seven dollars, but she always let Grant's kids in for free.

LAURA'S half brother Jason Ackerson told the jury about the good relationship he had with Laura and the negative one with Grant. His sister had been told not to see him, but he said that they'd continued to maintain contact in secret—just as she had done with her friend Heidi Schumacher.

THE next person to testify for the state was Matt Guddat, Sha's husband, who had been her fiancé at the time of Laura's murder. He related the vacuum cleaner loan, the trailer hitch story and Sha's trips to the police station for questioning.

DETECTIVE Mark Quagliarello, with the homicide unit of the Raleigh Police Department, a balding man with tight lips and deep-set eyes, told jurors about his role in searches and interviews for the investigation. He was the one who'd initially brought Sha in for questioning about Laura, Amanda and Grant.

On cross-examination, the defense asked Quagliarello about his interview with Sha. "Do you recall her telling that Laura had told Grant that if he didn't come down to North Carolina, his kids were going to be abused?"

"In my supplement, I do note that."

After making the detective repeat that remark in a different way, Durham asked, "And [Sha] said that Grant would put the phone on speaker phone sometimes when Laura was calling, and Laura would be screaming and threatening Grant."

"I don't recall that."

"Did she tell you that Grant didn't respond angrily? He would always just say, 'Laura, I can't do this right now. I've got to go'?"

"I don't recall that specifically."

When defense attorney Jeff Durham asked if Sha told the detective that she remembered times in the past when Laura was yelling at her mother, Quagliarello said, "Yes."

"She told you that she never saw Grant Hayes being abusive to her mother?"

"That's correct."

"And that she never heard him even raise his voice at her?"

"I don't remember that specifically."

On re-direct, the state established that Quagliarello did not know the source of any of Sha's information. Then, Assistant District Attorney Becky Holt asked, "Mr. Durham also asked you about times in the past where she remembered Laura yelling at her mother. Did she also tell you that her mother, being Amanda Hayes, was always cordial with Ms. Ackerson?"

"Yes."

THE next witness was Detective Amanda Salmon, head of the homicide unit for the Raleigh police in the summer of 2011. Her round face and small nose were framed by brown hair pulled back tight in a bun. She told of her involvement in canvassing the apartment complex where Laura's vehicle was found, helping in the search of the bedroom and bathroom area of Grant and Amanda's apartment, interviewing some of Laura's friends and other investigative tasks.

The defense wanted to know if the Hayeses' sofa could have been moved with the table and chairs in place as they were. She said it was possible. Then they tried to obtain testimony from her allowing that the bleach stain by the front door could have been there because the children had made a mess at the dining room table. Salmon did not give them what they wanted.

THE seventh person on the witness stand that day was Raleigh Police Detective Keith Heckman, with the Technical Assistance Response Unit (TARU). He testified that there had been no activity on Laura's cell phone after 4:59 P.M. on July 13, 2011. He also tracked the record of pings from Grant's phone's location on Google Maps to a remote area in Texas backed by a creek.

On cross-examination, the defense went over the times of the text messages between Lauren Harris and Grant Hayes and the messages and calls between Grant and Laura on July 13, 2011. The point of this exercise was nebulous at best.

CHAPTER THIRTY

THE day's final witness on September 3, 2013, was another investigator from Raleigh, Detective Sergeant Robert Latour. Latour had a blond buzz cut, round face and downturned eyes, and wore a light khaki suit that made him look quite pale. He testified that on the first day of his involvement in the investigation, he'd interviewed a distraught Chevon Mathes and secured videos from the security cameras at Sheetz that tracked the movements of Grant and the boys on the preceding Friday as well as those from Laura's apartment complex that showed what she'd been wearing on July 13, 2011. He'd worked all day and had still been at it at three in the morning, arranging to secure Laura's spare car key from Chevon in Kinston.

Latour told the jury about his involvement that week in other interviews, in searches of Laura's and the Hayes's apartments, in researching U-Haul rentals and trash pickups and his trip to Texas with Detective Dexter Gill that Friday.

Shortly thereafter, the trial concluded for the day and Detective Latour stepped back into the witness box in a light gray pinstripe suit to continue his testimony on September 4, 2013. He introduced photographs from the Sheetz location, where Grant went to supposedly hand over the boys to Laura on Friday for the weekend of July 15, 2011.

Additionally, he offered the evidence of a receipt from U-Haul for the rental of the trailer and the purchase of some moving supplies, a mount and ball for the trailer hitch and a lock. He showed the jury a video of Grant Hayes making that transaction.

Then his testimony moved to Texas, where Latour presented photographs of Karen Berry's street, house, the johnboat on Oyster Creek, and the path leading to it. Latour explained that his main responsibilities at that scene were interviews and the retrieval of videos and other relevant materials not at the house while Detective Gill assisted the Fort Bend County Sheriff's Office in the processing of evidence.

On July 26, 2011, Latour said, he drove to the medical examiner's office in Galveston to observe the autopsy performed by Assistant Medical Examiner Dr. Nobby Mambo on the upper and lower torso found the day before in Oyster Creek, then briefed Dr. Deborah Radisch, the medical examiner in North Carolina, on his observations. Latour also attended the second autopsy after the discovery of the skull before returning to North Carolina.

On cross, defense attorney Jeff Cutler drew the jury's attention to the fact that it was Amanda Hayes—not Grant—who drove her nephew Shelton Berry's pickup to the end of Skinner Lane and offloaded the boxes of muriatic acid. He also questioned Latour about the drive from North Carolina to Texas, eliciting testimony that there were many swamps and bodies of water along the way where a body could have been dumped.

On re-direct, Latour established that there had been no calls to 911 from any of the Hayeses' phones on the day Laura went missing, diminishing the believability that a confrontation on July 13, 2011, had accidentally turned deadly.

Shelton Berry, Amanda's nephew, replaced the detective on the stand. Shelton had a sharp nose, long neck, and short brown hair that was slightly spiky on top. He was tanned and muscular from his long hours of work outside in the Texas sun. He told the jury that he did groundskeeping and maintenance work and operated a side business, Critter Catchers.

His testimony was littered with "yes, ma'am"s as he answered prosecutors' questions. He said he'd been asleep when Amanda arrived with her family. It had been more than a year since he'd seen his aunt Amanda, and he'd never met Grant or the children before. Although he knew about Lily's birth, he'd never heard about the two boys.

He related the conversations he'd had with Grant about alligators, fishing, sharks and operating the johnboat, but said that Grant seemed to be on the phone most of the time he was at their house. He also appeared to be nervous throughout the visit. Shelton said that he had removed the trotline for catching catfish and a knife from the boat after Amanda and Grant left but before the detectives arrived. He did not, however, use the boat or move it from where Grant and Amanda left it.

On cross-examination, Shelton admitted that both Grant and Amanda talked about alligator hunting, and on re-direct said that although Amanda asked him to take Grant hunting with them, she never indicated any desire to go along.

Shelton's brother, Dalton, testified next. He had the same nose as Shelton, but was heavier and paler than his brother, with dark brown hair, a round face with dark circles under his eyes, and a sideways slant to his mouth. He told the jury that he hadn't been at home when Amanda and her family arrived. When he got there, around five thirty in the morning, they were all asleep.

He said that Grant and Amanda were both upset and worried that they might be in trouble because they were not supposed to take the boys over state lines but said they'd had no choice because the boys' mother hadn't picked them up on Friday.

Dalton also testified that Grant talked to him, too, about alligator hunting and shark fishing.

He said that when Grant and Amanda were packing up to leave, he helped Grant clean the coolers. He said that the trailer remained hitched to their vehicle the whole time they were at his house and it was returned to the U-Haul in Katy on their return trip to North Carolina.

CHAPTER THIRTY-ONE

THE next witness was Fort Bend Sheriff's Office Crime Scene Investigator Kim Oreskovich. She wore a brown uniform and tie and wire-rim glasses with brown stems and pulled her long curly light brown hair back in a ponytail.

She presented a series of graphic photographs of the body parts' recovery. Out of respect for the victim and her family and friends, these were not displayed on the large screen but on a smaller one that was pointed directly at the jury. Oreskovich stood next to it and described the pictures to the jury as she recounted the story of recovering the first body parts from Oyster Creek. At the end of that grisly recital, court was adjourned for the day.

Oreskovich returned to the stand to resume her testimony on the fifth day of the trial, Thursday, September 5, 2013, wearing her hair pulled back from her face but hanging loose and free below her shoulders. In this session, she introduced a massive amount of evidence that she had gathered at the crime scene in Texas, including the DNA swabs and the two coolers that likely once carried the remains of Laura Ackerson. The larger cooler looked grimy because of the layer of fingerprint powder spread on the exterior in a vain attempt to locate fingerprints.

She was followed on the witness stand by Detective Brad Wichard from the robbery/homicide unit of the Fort Bend County Sheriff's Office. He had a big, bushy mustache with lots of grayish hair receding at his temples and put on reading glasses whenever he needed to look at writing on the exhibits.

Wichard presented diagrams of the property and a layout of where the evidence had been recovered. He described his role in the search of the Berry home and the surrounding area, and the materials he discovered there including the Motel 6 receipt in the name of Amanda Smith of New York City, a shotgun from the spare room, a jar and a green towel found in the barn, a suitcase belonging to Amanda pulled out of a trash pile, and the video of Amanda driving Shelton's truck and dumping the muriatic acid boxes at the end of the cul-de-sac on Skinner Lane.

He also submitted samples of dirt taken from the hog pen, some from the dark spot and others from other locations around the pen that he had collected and turned in for analysis. On cross-examination, he told the jury that he had noticed the dark spot in the animal containment area on July 26.

Next in the box was Houston Police Department dive team member Brian Davis, looking very pale and quite nervous during his testimony. He explained to the jury the obstacles he faced during the dive in Oyster Creek: poor visibility, rampant lily pads, overhanging weeds and the hot Texas sun. He entered photographs of the water search into evidence.

Dr. Ricky Carlyle, a Kinston dentist that Laura Ackerson visited, provided patient notes including all missing, canceled and attended appointments. He also provided a full mouth series, a panoramic x-ray that went from ear to ear showing all the teeth, jaw and sinuses along with a computer graph of the existing work in the victim's mouth. His testimony and exhibits backed the state's contention as to the identity of the skull found in Oyster Creek.

Raymond Boyd, an employee at the Home Depot in Katy, Texas, next took the jury step-by-step through Grant Hayes's visit to the store on the day the accused purchased gloves, a trash can and the muriatic acid. He detailed his conversations with Grant and the reasons he'd discouraged him from purchasing the acid for odor removal. He then identified a photo of the packaging recovered on the Berry property as being for the long-cuff neoprene gloves that Grant had bought that day.

When Raymond Boyd finished his testimony, Brian Davis returned to the stand, where he identified photographs of the head wrapped in a sheet laying on a body bag, and the head itself. On cross, the defense asked questions that seemed to bolster the state's case, asking about the gruesome condition of that body part. Davis reiterated the slipping and sliding of the skin on the skull.

Voir dire testimony outside of the presence of the jury

was required of the next witness, Dr. Paul Stimson. An elderly man with bags under his eyes and sagging jowls, he'd served as the forensic odontologist for Harris County, Texas, from 1968 until his recent retirement in February 2013.

Stimson testified that all of the teeth were in the mouth when he x-rayed the skull. When he returned at the request of the medical examiner, Dr. Stephen Pustilnik brought him just one tooth, the maxillary left central incisor, for examination. Using a 100X magnifying glass, he observed what appeared to be acid etching on the front surface. He told the judge that the other teeth that were missing had detached from the jaw somewhere between Texas and North Carolina.

The judge was concerned about the tooth being removed and asked, "Is it normal to remove teeth in making this kind of analysis?"

"It is not unusual," Stimson said. He stated that "it's not unusual for teeth to slip out in the body bag while the body is in the morgue waiting for the family and funeral directors to pick them up."

"I see."

"Especially anterior teeth. Back teeth, because they are multi-rooted, usually stay in place."

"I see."

Answering a question from the defense, Stimson explained that teeth were put back in with soft wax—not glue—to ensure a tooth is placed in the right socket and can be moved if it's placed in error. He said that in the past, "I've seen acid-etched teeth clinically, not forensically."

Laura Jean Ackerson smiling at a happy time shortly before her death.

In her Kinston apartment in Nantucket Lofts, Laura had a separate bedroom for her two boys. Little Grant slept in the car bed on the right, and Gentle in the white bed on the left. Between them, on the little table, Laura placed a photo of herself and her ex, Grant Hayes III, because she wanted the children to know that both Mommy and Daddy loved them.

Amanda and Grant Hayes with Gentle and their newborn daughter, Lily.

J Ackerson, ten
agree not to pursue custody
our children Grant : Gentle the
urrendering Parental Rights.
nsent to leaving them in the s
their fathers for now. further
Drop all pending Litigation ag
dear in the Lenior canty fami

lling counsel Jonn Sargent of
nt less the monetary compensati
and that I will be able to see m
want to at the discretion of their

7ª 8/13/11   Laura Ackers

The contract in which Laura Ackerson signed over custody of little Grant and Gentle to Grant Hayes III. Friends and law enforcement insisted that she would not have done so of her own free will.

The big, suspicious bleach stain that police found on the carpet next to the entrance in Grant and Amanda Hayes's apartment.

The Woodfield Glen apartment complex where the Hayeses lived. In the foreground is the Dumpster area where they tossed the shower curtain, rugs, a vacuum cleaner and more in the aftermath of Laura's death.

The pile of debris originating at the Woodfield Glen apartments' Dumpster that law enforcement needed to examine at the East Wake Transfer Station before it was transported to the landfill.

Right: Two of the coolers that Grant and Amanda used to transport Laura's dismembered remains halfway across the country—North Carolina to Texas.

Below: The back porch of the Berry home, where law enforcement found another of the coolers that had been used as a temporary coffin for Laura's remains.

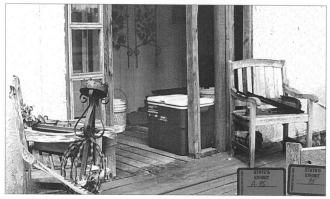

Houston Police Department divers Brian Davis and Mark Thorsen, in Oyster Creek.

The path leading to Oyster Creek, where Grant and Amanda Hayes dumped Laura's dismembered body. The johnboat they used is secured on the left.

Views of Oyster Creek showing the obstacles presented by the extraordinarily dense lily pads that obstructed the search for Laura's remains.

Top: Law enforcement believed that the notes written by Grant Hayes on the back of this envelope were bullet points for a press conference he was planning.

Middle: Amanda Hayes caught by a stealth camera unloading the boxes of muriatic acid from Shelton Berry's Critter Catchers pickup, parked at the end of Skinner Lane.

Bottom: Amanda Hayes at an ATM in Texas, getting cash for her family's trip back to North Carolina.

Booking photos for Grant Hayes and Amanda Hayes, after their arrests for the murder of Laura Jean Ackerson.

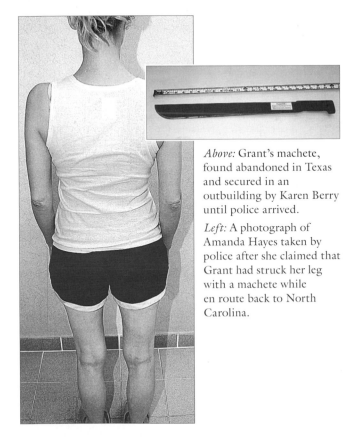

Above: Grant's machete, found abandoned in Texas and secured in an outbuilding by Karen Berry until police arrived.

Left: A photograph of Amanda Hayes taken by police after she claimed that Grant had struck her leg with a machete while en route back to North Carolina.

Chevon Mathes, Laura's business partner and friend who filed the missing persons report to the Kinston police, testifies in the courtroom. *Courtesy of the* Raleigh News & Observer

Laura Jean Ackerson's final resting place, in Tuttle Cemetery in Ionia, Michigan. *Courtesy of Tracy Rademacher*

The judge asked if there was any way the acid etching could have occurred naturally, and Stimson replied, "Yes. If individuals have lemon-sucking habits or individuals who eat a lot of sweet candy or individuals who have bulimia and regurgitate, you get acid etching of the inside of the teeth and so it's a natural phenomenon that can occur."

He also explained the use of acid etching in some dental procedures, like veneers, where "the tooth, which is kind of roughened and the inside of the porcelain is roughened. This gives the glue something to bond with." Likewise, "you acid etch it to do a filling, helping the glue hold them in place."

"How long would the acid etching last?"

"It's permanently there. Once you take the enamel away, it's gone."

The defense continued the cross, asking, "Is it possible that the etching could be anything else but acid?"

"This is not toothbrush abrasion—no," Stimson answered.

The defense then reviewed the chain of custody for the tooth in question. When they finished that line of questioning, the judge announced that Dr. Stimson could testify to, and Grant's attorneys could elicit information about, other ways that the etching could occur.

The defense objected, saying, "The teeth never came to North Carolina from Texas for examination by a North Carolina doctor."

The judge said, "A North Carolina doctor is not a requirement. Objection overruled."

CHAPTER THIRTY-TWO

DR. Paul Stimson resumed the stand on Friday, September 6, 2013, the sixth day of the trial—this time to testify before the jury. The prosecution took him through his extensive experience in his field from dental school to his professorship to his appointment as a forensic odontologist for the medical examiner's office. Since 1968, there had rarely been a year in which he hadn't appeared before the bench as an expert witness in courtrooms all over the world.

He explained to the jury that, although acid etching could happen naturally, it would take years of lemon sucking to strip through enamel or demineralize teeth, because enamel is the hardest structure in the human body. He detailed his examination of a tooth from the skull of Laura Ackerson and then read the addendum to his identification report into the record.

"Forensic examination of acid etching on the left central incisor (number nine) in case RA-2011-280. In a previous conversation, you had advised me that muriatic acid had been used in some of the dentition in this case. On August 9, 2011, I had occasion to be in the area and traveled to the morgue and examined the upper left central incisor in your presence, tooth number nine. For viewing magnification was one hundred times using a magnifying glass provided by you. There was visible acid etching in the facial surface of this tooth. When you felt the facial surface of this tooth with your fingernail, there was a depression caused by the acid action with a small ridge on one edge.

"The dental tubules could be visualized with the aid of the magnifying glass in this area. I agree with your opinion that there was acid etching of the facial surface of the maxillary central incisors in this case."

Through this witness, the state submitted photographs of the remains with some of the teeth missing from sockets but showing the tooth Dr. Stimson had examined in place. Stimson told the jury, "I can't specify the acid—only that etching is present." Knowing the actual substance would be "dependent on the length of exposure time combined with the strength of the acid."

On cross-examination, the defense asked if anyone else had been called in to examine the tooth. Stimson said he didn't know whether or not that had happened.

THE next witness, Detective David Moore of the Raleigh Police Department, was a veteran of twenty-six years with

very short hair and a round face plagued by a perpetual
look of worry. He explained to the jury that on August 19,
2011, he'd used a Cellebrite unit with special software
to transfer data from Grant's and Amanda's phones and
put it into a readable report. He read a number of text
messages—some with dates, some not—to the jury. He
started with the very last text message Laura Ackerson ever
sent, on July 13 at 4:12 P.M. "Okay," he read from Laura's
cell, "I'm leaving Wilson now. I'll call when I get past the
traffic. Where will you be in an hour or so?"

Other texts included messages from Laura about a "pee-
pee accident" that had delayed her departure with the kids
to meet Grant at Sheetz, requests for respect for her phone
time with the boys, accusations of Grant lying about her
and others, as well as apologies and requests for photographs.

He also read texts from Grant to Laura that had an edge
of hostility, including one message where he seemed to be
calling Laura a "brat," and another where he ordered: "Get
them dressed now!" In another he got in a dig: "I'm used
to being around them a lot more than you are, Laura. My
whole life is them. Day in and out. The park, the mall,
Monkey Joe's, meals, messes and bath, that's the kind of
parent I am. 'Thank you.'"

On cross-examination, the defense established that
what Detective Moore read was from an edited version
of his original report. Grant's attorney also asked if the
word "brat" was name-calling or an acronym for the
Bananas-Rice-Applesauce-Toast diet. Moore did not
know.

RALEIGH/WAKE City-County Bureau of Identification Agent Mike Galloway was the next to testify. He explained that he responded to any crime in Wake County when requested by any law enforcement agency. He took photos and looked for fingerprints as well as blood and other body fluids.

He detailed his role in the search of Grant's Dodge Durango and spoke about the difficulty of obtaining fingerprints from the cloth center console. He talked about the search of the Hayeses' self-storage unit and apartment, where he witnessed the bleached-out section of carpet by their front door. He explained his examination of the sofa that had been sold on Craigslist, and the wild-goose chase after a blood droplet trail at a nearby apartment complex. Finally, he related his smelly encounter with Dumpster trash as he documented the contents with photographs and processed the items found at the lab. When he finished his work, he repackaged all the potential evidence and turned it over to lead CCBI Agent Shannon Quick.

THE final witness of the day was Dr. Nobby Mambo, the assistant medical examiner from Texas who had performed the autopsy on the remains of Laura Ackerson. Dr. Mambo was a native of Africa with short hair and deep-set eyes, who spoke in softly accented English with a slight stutter. He detailed his education and experience starting with his attendance at medical school in Zimbabwe and covering his further studies in the United States and work in Canada and New Jersey before he settled in the Houston area in 2007.

He presented his autopsy report to the jury detailing the cuts on all of the body parts, the location of internal organs and the moderate state of decomposition of the torso and leg. He used actual photographs—not projections on the screen—to show the jury the other injuries made by marine life while the remains were in the waters of Oyster Creek.

He explained to the jury that he'd examined the cartilage around the neck looking for any signs of choking, particularly in the larynx. Unfortunately, he said, the muscles were gone and, because of that, it was impossible to find evidence of internal bleeding in any of the locations that it would normally be found. His conclusion was that Laura Ackerson died from an act of homicide by undetermined means.

On cross, defense attorney Jeff Cutler questioned the inclined cut on the clavicle bone, and Dr. Mambo told him that there was no way to determine if that injury had been made by an up or down motion. When he asked about the blood pooling inside the back of the skull, Mambo admitted that it could have been caused by premortem or postmortem trauma or by positioning of the body that caused the fluid to seep back there through lividity.

CHAPTER THIRTY-THREE

THE seventh day of trial began on Monday, September 9, 2013, with Officer Kevin Crocker from the Raleigh Police Department Fugitive Task Force. He detailed his surveillance of the elder Hayeses' home, including the signs of increased nervousness by Grant Hayes III.

Crocker was followed by Timothy Suggs, a forensic chemist with the North Carolina State Board of Investigations, who had tested soil samples from the hog pen in Texas. He determined that some of the samples he received were strongly acidic and tested positive for the presence of chloride—a key component of muriatic acid. While he explained the scientific evidence, Grant was busy writing, not seeming to be paying much attention to the witness at all.

Detective Thomas Ouellette was up next and told the court that he had been part of the search team at the senior Hayeses' home on the evening of July 25, 2011. On cross, defense attorney Jeff Cutler asked about the handwritten document found in a spiral notebook that awarded custody of the three children to Grant's parents. Ouellette said that he photographed that note in place but didn't seize it. The detective who did was Zeke Morse, the next person on the stand.

Detective Morse had also confiscated the family computer and two blue coolers, and he told the jury that he was the one who had collected as evidence the copy of the psychological review for child custody found in the Durango. He'd also reviewed Facebook accounts, and he read aloud many of the messages to and from Grant into the trial record.

The jurors got a break from the long run of official witnesses with the arrival of Mark Herbert, a sanitation truck driver whose responsibilities included picking up, emptying and returning the Dumpsters from Amanda and Grant's apartment complex and delivering them to the East Wake Transfer Station. He described how he emptied the contents next to an eight-foot-wide open pit, where the trash was pushed directly into a tractor trailer parked below and delivered to its final resting place at the South Wake Landfill. The defense had no questions for this witness.

Then it was back to law enforcement, as Sergeant Brian Hall, who'd obtained and served the arrest warrants on Grant and Amanda Hayes, submitted a large number of exhibits.

Raleigh/Wake City-County Bureau of Identification Senior Agent Shannon Quick was the final witness for the day. She'd become involved in the investigation with the discovery of Laura's car. She processed that and also was a participant in two different searches of Grant and Amanda's apartment. She presented a myriad of evidence, including the bedding from the bedroom closet and the chunks of bleached-out carpet she had cut from the floor. She wrapped up her testimony the following morning.

Agent Jennifer Remy, a hair-and-fiber analyst from the North Carolina State Crime Laboratory, took her place on the witness stand on September 10, 2013. She had identified all hairs submitted into evidence as either animal or human. Then she determined whether or not they had a portion of root or a skin tag that would be suitable for nuclear DNA analysis.

Two additional technical witnesses testified next. First, SBI body-fluid analyst Agent McKenzie Dehaan discussed the samples she'd tested for the presumption of blood and the positives she'd sent for further analysis. Then Sharon Hinton, a forensic DNA analyst for the North Carolina State Crime Lab, talked about the results of her testing. Hinton told the jurors that the genetic evidence on the blue latex gloves found in the trash was predominantly from Laura Ackerson. Although she found DNA from other contributors present, the samples were too small to determine whose it was.

Computer forensic analyst Courtney Last of the Raleigh Police Department then took the stand to testify about the contents of a number of computers, including Karen Berry's computer, which Grant had used to access his e-mail while he was in Texas. She read several e-mail exchanges over the last year of Laura's life, including those with friends, as well as messages between Laura and both Amanda and Grant. Last said that Grant stored all the e-mails from Laura in one of two folders, one labeled "Ljhaze," the other "letters from a ho."

When it was the defense's turn to ask questions, they requested Last read other e-mails into the record that they felt either reflected badly on Laura Ackerson or positively on Grant. On re-direct, the state had even more e-mails read into the record.

Barbara Patty, Laura's church friend and mentor, took the stand next. The white-haired older woman told the jury that Laura had attended Grace Fellowship Church and had participated in house church, a small group of fifteen to twenty-five people who met for Bible study, praise and worship, prayer and fellowship. Beginning in the late summer of 2010, Laura also came to her home on Monday nights, when the two women had dinner and a one-on-one Bible study session.

Barbara told the jury that in July of 2011, Laura was thankful to finally have the psychological report and was planning on attending Lenoir Community College to continue her education with a goal of teaching high school science. This surprised some others who had never known that Laura's interests went in that direction. Laura was very focused on the upcoming hearing in August in which Barbara had agreed to testify on her behalf.

Attorney John Sargeant, Laura's child custody lawyer, was the final witness on the eighth day of Grant's trial. He went through his history with Laura and the court proceedings from the time he became involved on June 17,

2010. He refuted the defense allegation that Laura and Amanda were the two at odds. To the contrary, Sargeant told the jurors that Laura was grateful that Amanda was there watching over her boys when they were with Grant. He finished his testimony the following morning by saying that there were no requests by either party for child support—both Grant and Laura were focused only on the custody issue itself.

CHAPTER THIRTY-FOUR

THE first new witness on September 11, the ninth day of Grant Hayes's trial, was Dr. Ginger Calloway, the psychologist tasked with conducting the evaluation of the parties in the custody case. With her curly hair, prominent nose and wire-rim glasses, she looked ready to be typecast as an academic. The state presented her with state's exhibit 406, the copy of her evaluation report that had been found wedged beside a seat in Grant's vehicle.

She pointed to the place in the document where she'd written that Grant alleged Laura Ackerson was chatting online with other guys while he was out of town working. Next to that line was a handwritten notation, presumably made by Grant, that read: "Not alleged. I have proof."

She directed attention to another spot where the report mentioned Grant, Amanda and Sha Elmer's first meeting with Dr. Kristen Winns. Someone had circled Sha's name and written "never" beside it.

At the instructions of the prosecutor, Dr. Calloway went through the steps of the process involved in doing an evaluation for the court in a custody case. In between reading passages from her report to the court, she followed the trail of questions, explaining her process and what she had learned. In addition to Laura and Grant, she said, "I spoke to Heidi [Schumacher], Amanda [Hayes], and Gentle's surgeon."

She said that the surgeon, Dr. Timothy Bukowski, felt that Laura was insecure and unsure with him. She added, "Laura is handicapped by her extreme anxiety and underdevelopment. . . . She also obviously has no family supports evidenced by the fact that no family members came to her assistance when she and Grant separated and terminated their union. She may have been intimidated by Grant and systematically isolated from others by some of his actions. . . . Although Grant portrayed her as a flight risk in the ex parte motion for temporary custody, she had many opportunities to flee and did not."

"Dr. Bukowski noted that Grant seems to need to exalt himself by repeatedly mentioning the famous musicians for which he played," Calloway said.

On cross-examination, defense attorney Jeff Cutler asked about Laura chatting online with other men while Grant was out of town working. Calloway said, "She and her attorney admit to poor judgment when she engaged in online sex talk with men she did not know—consistent with her immaturity and ineptness. There is no evidence that I am aware of that she actually met any of these men. What is most important for the purposes of this evaluation is that she did not expose the children to these men in any way."

She also told the jury that Laura admitted to going on-line and posting pictures of herself and telling Grant about it. "I do not believe it involved the children in any way."

When Cutler asked about Laura's substance abuse, Calloway said, "Both Grant and Laura reported a period of alcohol and drug use."

Then Cutler asked about her interview with Heidi Schumacher and the bias Laura's friend displayed. Calloway said, "Heidi is unequivocal in her dislike for Grant."

The prosecutor, on re-direct, asked about her recommendation for drug testing. Calloway answered, "My concern about drug use centered on Mr. Hayes."

When asked about Laura's need for a coach, the doctor said Laura needed one to "help her with job choice and supervisors that don't repeat the patterns of abuse, control and domination she'd grown accustomed to."

The state wanted to know about the depth of her investigation into the households of both parents in assessing their ability to care for the children. "I don't look at anyone's bank records," she said, "but I do look in refrigerators to make sure that there is adequate food for the children."

In contradiction to the impression the defense tried to make, Calloway said that in interviews she conducted, "No one spoke to me about Amanda and Grant moving to Kinston."

_____

FBI forensic document examiner Lindsey Dyn had examined the note in which Laura gave up custody of her boys in exchange for twenty-five thousand dollars. She determined that the top part was in Grant's handwriting and the bottom part was in Laura's handwriting. However, she could not determine who had written Laura's signature. The defense tried to press her on the latter point, but she insisted that she could reach no conclusion about that signature.

FORENSIC anthropologist Dr. Ann Ross, from North Carolina State, first explained to the jury that people in her profession are called in to examine remains when they are badly decomposed or skeletonized. In this case, she was asked to determine what tool was used to inflict injuries on and dismember the body.

She received sections of bone and the skull for her analysis. On one end, the cuts she observed were smooth—consistent with those made by a Stryker saw, the tool used at autopsy to cut the bone portions for examination. However, there were striations in the cuts on the other end. She analyzed the cuts to determine the number of saw teeth per inch and to look for false starts and effort level.

Using pig leg bones as a proxy, she eliminated a long list of saws as the possible implement used. She concluded that the saw marks on Laura's remains were consistent with and matched those made by a Skil reciprocating saw using a Skil wood/fast saw blade operated at speed five.

Dr. Ross also reported on a knife stab wound to the throat that was deeper, but not as long, as the cuts made to separate the limbs and torso. She determined that it could not be an antemortem wound (one inflicted sufficiently prior to death to allow for some healing); however, she could not state whether it was a perimortem injury (one occurring within a window around the time of death) or a postmortem stab, inflicted after Laura had already died.

On cross-examination, Ross said that there was no visible trauma on the skull itself, prompting the defense to ask, "Did you see anything that would suggest that acid was applied to the bones?"

"No, I did not."

"Or to the teeth?"

"No, but I do believe there were some teeth missing, however."

The defense tried to put the knife wound in the context of the severing of the body parts, but Ross insisted that the knife wound to the throat was not consistent with a dismemberment injury because it came from a thrust but had required less force to penetrate the surface of the spongier cervical vertebrae than was needed for a more dense leg bone.

THE final person on the stand for the day was Pablo Trinidad, a federal prisoner serving twenty-one years for conspiracy to traffic cocaine and possession of a firearm. In August of 2011, he was incarcerated in a processing unit in the Wake County Detention Center awaiting his transfer to the penitentiary. He told the jury that the areas of cells in that facility were labeled by floor number and a color. Pablo and Grant Hayes were housed together on the fifth floor in "five yellow pod" for about a week and a half. The two men had several conversations together during that time.

One morning at breakfast time, about ten men were in the dayroom watching the news. A story about Grant came up and one of the men pointed him out to Pablo. A few others made verbal comments about doing Grant harm, causing Grant to leave the room and go back to his cell. Pablo reminded the others that if they did anything, everyone would be put on lockdown.

Later that day, Grant approached Pablo and said he appreciated Pablo for standing up for him. Pablo shrugged it off, saying it was in his own best interests. Grant asked him where he was from and Pablo said, "Eastern North Carolina, near Greenville."

"'I went down to Greenville a lot to play music and have friends at ECU [Eastern Carolina University]. My mother lives near there—twenty miles away—in Kinston,'" Pablo said Grant told him. Grant went on to ask if he could relay a message through Pablo's girlfriend to Patsy Hayes, asking his mother to set up a Pay-Tel phone account for him and to put some money in the commissary.

In another conversation, Pablo reported, "Grant said he wanted to speak to an attorney because it was impossible for him to do the crime because during years of playing a musical instrument, he developed some kind of handicap and could not use force, and it would not have been wise for him to do it either, because her vehicle was parked near his residence. He wanted to explain that to someone who would hear him out so that he could be released ASAP.

"At the time, he didn't seem to get the seriousness of what he was being charged with. After that, he went to an attorney visit and when he came back, he was very down in spirits and I asked, 'How did it go?' Grant said, 'Well, they're telling me I'm going to have to be here for a while' and his defense attorney told him when you have two co-defendants in a case, a lot of times codefendants will turn on one another. It was a possibility that his wife would do that and he was upset about that."

When the state asked what Grant had said to him about the case, Pablo answered, "He told me that Laura was the mother of his children. He said that she was an unfit mother and they'd been in a custody battle for years. She was soliciting herself on the Internet, doing drugs, continuously asking for money. He was tired of going back and forth with that. He placed a call to Laura and lured her to his apartment. He and his wife subdued her and strangled her and after that dismembered the body and took a road trip to a family member's home. . . . His exact words about what he did with the body were: 'I just got rid of it.' "

The prosecution was pleased. For the first time in trial they had presented evidence of a scenario of events the night Laura was murdered. "What did he say to you before talking about the case?"

"Grant said that Amanda was a good woman and he wished she was the mother of his kids instead of the victim. Amanda was a better person and a good wife."

When asked more details about Grant's physical limitations, Pablo said Grant told him that "it was a handicap with his hand—he could no longer grab anything with force."

Pablo Trinidad faced cross-examination by the defense attorney the following morning. Jeff Cutler resurrected Pablo's record, which included an escape from custody in 1996 and recapture in 1997. He reviewed the charges of conspiracy to distribute five kilograms of cocaine or more that had resulted in his current sentence. He also brought out that Pablo faced a mandatory minimum of fifteen years to life and could have gotten as much as one hundred years to life for the charges.

Then Cutler moved to the specifics of Pablo's testimony, contradicting the time he was in the same pod with Grant, saying it was only five days, and Pablo agreed that was possible. "And you're telling me that in five days you developed such a strong bond that he was telling you his deepest, darkest secrets? Is that right?"

"Yes, it's correct."

"Because you are both from about the same part of the state?"

"That's correct."

"And these are secrets that he didn't tell anyone else in that pod?"

"I don't know if he told anybody else. I know he told me."

"So you're testifying that you were sitting in the dayroom and Grant Hayes walked in and his case is playing on the TV, isn't that right?"

"No, when we were let out for breakfast that morning, after breakfast, that's when we were watching TV and one of the other inmates noticed that he was in the front of the crowd watching television."

Cutler asked, "At some point, someone explained to you, the way it works with the feds, the way to make your situation better is if you can give evidence to the government on other people, isn't that right?"

"Yes."

"And you made an agreement with the feds that you would give up names of people in exchange for getting a better deal, isn't that right?"

"That's correct."

"Grant Hayes . . . was your meal ticket, wasn't he? One of them, at least?"

"If you want to put it in those words—that's your words, not mine," Pablo said.

Cutler continued, "You testified yesterday that he also told you he lured Laura—that was the word wasn't it—lured Laura to the house?"

"That's correct."

"That was a headline," Cutler noted. "That's where you stole that word from, wasn't it?"

"I don't—no."

"And the press also reported, didn't it, after the autopsy came out that strangulation was a possible cause of death, [you] heard that in the news, didn't you?"

"No, I didn't, sir."

"You didn't get that from the news?"

"No. Not at all."

"Is that a part you just made up?"

"No. I done gave my testimony way before I ever heard anything of that nature in the news."

"And you said you were interviewed by the police— that was a year after you were here in Wake County jail, wasn't it?"

"Probably so."

"Press also reported there was a custody dispute, didn't they?"

"Um, when I was in Albemarle Jail in Elizabeth City, they don't cover North Carolina news, so once I left Wake County, I never heard anything about Grant Hayes case on the news."

Jeff Cutler insisted that Pablo Trinidad had been facing a twenty-one-year sentence before he spoke about Grant Hayes, and Pablo contradicted him saying that it was only 360 months. Cutler then alleged that was proof that he'd already been given an advantage for just saying he would appear today and testify for the prosecution. "If you've already been paid for making those statements, you've already benefited from those things you told the feds, isn't that right? So this is your only real chance to get it reduced again, isn't it?"

"Hoping—I'm hoping that I'll get some relief, but once again I was never promised—I haven't spoken to anybody saying to me I am going to get some relief from this testimony I'm giving today."

On re-direct, prosecutor Becky Holt asked a series of questions about what Pablo had seen on the news. Pablo responded negatively on each point she raised. Then she said, "Was there anything—anything in the news about the victim being an unfit mother?"

Pablo said no.

"Was there anything in the news about the victim?"

"No, ma'am."

After a few questions about specific information about Laura Ackerson, Holt asked, "Was all that information provided to you by the defendant?"

"Yes, ma'am."

To his great relief, Pablo Trinidad was finally released from the witness box.

CHAPTER THIRTY-FIVE

DR. Deborah Radisch, chief medical examiner for North Carolina, had been with the department nearly continuously since 1983 and had served as chief since July 2010. Her record of effective performance on the witness stand was legendary.

Dr. Radisch had chin-length white-blonde hair and wore glasses, and she told the jury that she first became involved in the case when Detective Robert Latour of the Raleigh Police Department called her from Galveston, Texas, to inquire about preserving material to make tool-mark comparisons. She explained her examination of the remains prior to sending them to Dr. Ann Ross for analysis on the dismemberment cuts.

When asked about the stab wound, Radisch told the jury that if the puncture in C4, the fourth cervical vertebrae, came from the back, it could have struck important arteries or veins. From the front, it would probably cause a leak in the airway or a cut on the esophagus. For most of the possible angles for this wound, the damage would not be immediately fatal, although if the weapon hit the carotid artery, it would have been a very quick death.

The prosecution asked about her conclusions in the death of Laura Ackerson. Dr. Radisch said that there was a "possibility that injuries represent an asphyxial cause of death or means of death. . . . There was not enough information with the parts we received to determine the exact cause of death." She could not determine if Laura was stabbed to death or strangled to death because of the decomposition to the head. However, she said, it was clear that Laura died by "undetermined homicidal violence."

On cross-examination, the defense alleged that, according to Dr. Nobby Mambo's testimony, the doctor had crushed the thyroid cartilage during examination. Dr. Radisch admitted she had no knowledge of that since it was not in his report, but said, "There's no evidence of healing, so it's an acute injury, but there's no evidence if it happened before she died or just after she died at the time of death, you just can't tell. It's kind of a fresh injury."

The defense pressed her about the broken and glued tooth in the skull. She said with a shrug, "When you work with them, they kind of fall out and you put them back in."

DETECTIVE Jerry Faulk, with the homicide unit of the Raleigh Police Department and lead investigator in the case, enumerated and presented into evidence the exhibits he collected from Grant and Amanda's home. Among them were receipts for many different purchases around the time of Laura's death, including Grant's shopping trip to Wal-Mart.

It had to be a challenge for the jury to absorb all these details, but nothing compared to getting their minds around the idea of someone going into a store and picking out a power tool and blades knowing he was going to use to cut up another human being's body.

Over strong objections from the defense, Faulk read into the public record the lyrics to "Man Killer," one of Grant's compositions. "Give into me, I want it all, I want your scream, I want your crawl. I'll make you bleed, fall to the floor. Don't try to plead, that turns me on. I'll take the keys to your car and some more. . . . I'm not the one to make you scream. I'm just the one to make you bleed. Don't raise your arms, you can't stop me. I'll put my hands on your throat and squeeze."

THE jurors then heard from one of the last people to see Laura Ackerson alive, Randy Jenkins, the owner and operator of Bill's Grill, a small restaurant in the farming community of Black Creek, North Carolina. Randy described it as a "quaint little, sort of like Mayberry, type of place."

Randy said he'd found Laura to be "very poised and very excited about her new business venture" and he'd signed a contract with her for menus. He noted that he'd urged her to change her appointment in Raleigh because of the heavy traffic at that time of day but she'd insisted that she had to go there anyway.

The defense had no questions for this witness.

Susan Dufur, the assistant manager at the Brier Creek Wal-Mart in July 2011, stepped into the stand next. The state played the video of Grant shopping in her store just after two A.M. on July 14. She took the jury through the details of her interaction with the defendant regarding his purchase of a reciprocating saw, goggles, plastic trash bags and tarps. "He was very inquisitive and laid-back—not excited or rattled or panicky," she said. "He was calm the whole time he interacted with me."

THE state then played a recording of "Broomstick Rider," another one of Grant Hayes's songs. The defense objected, but the judge overruled.

As the music played in the courtroom, Grant bopped and bobbed his head along as if he were so totally caught up in his creation that he was unaware of his surroundings.

The prosecutors provided the jury with a transcript of the lyrics. "Baby Mama. I got two kids by you. I can't take any more from you. The way we slept was so cold, I'd wake up every morning wondering which of us would go. I'm paying her bills. Find another sugar daddy. You tryin' to take my kids. That's the way you live. I warned you—don't say I didn't warn you. I don't want your drama. I have two kids by you. I can't take anything more from you. Price tag on your head. You must've told your attorney, I have intentions of killing you."

With that, the state rested its case.

CHAPTER THIRTY-SIX

THE same day that the state ended its presentation, the defense called its first witness, Amanda Hayes's sister Karen Berry.

Karen took the stand, appearing beaten down by the direction life had taken in the last couple of years. Her long platinum blonde hair was pushed back from her face with a headband.

She explained to the jury that she was much older than Amanda and had always been more like a mother to her than a sister. When asked about the last time she'd seen her sister prior to July 2011, Karen said, "I saw her two years earlier, in June 2009, but I don't think I saw her in between. We stayed in contact by telephone but not regularly."

Karen didn't remember exactly when Amanda called, but she knew it was after their mother had died in June 2011. "Amanda said she wanted to see me, she missed me and her husband sold his computer equipment so she could come to see me because she's [been] missing me really bad."

Karen told the jury that Amanda and her family arrived early Monday morning, July 18, 2011. The next day, she said, "Amanda wanted to speak to me alone. She said, 'I hurt Laura and I hurt her bad.' She needed to talk to me." Karen said, after that, she had a conversation with Grant and Amanda about the creek across the street.

"What about the creek across the street?" the defense attorney asked.

"I don't know. They knew about the boat because there had been a discussion about taking the boys fishing before they came."

"Did you at some point put two and two together that Laura was with them?"

"I can't say I put two and two together but I had suspicions that something was wrong."

"Did you come to the conclusion at some point that Laura was dead?"

"I think so. I did come to realize that Laura was dead."

After going over the arrival and departure times, the defense asked, "Did there come a time when Grant and Amanda used the boat?"

"Yes sir," Karen said. "They had asked to use the boat or they asked when they first got there or maybe even before because they asked—they were planning to take the boys fishing in it. . . . I told them they could use the boat but it wasn't safe for the little ones."

When asked about the arrival of the detectives the next Sunday, Karen said, "I told the detectives that I didn't want to go to court and testify against my sister but I was afraid I was going to have to one day. . . . I had chest pains when I was talking to them because of the difficulty of saying what I had to say and the stress of the situation. . . . I told the police that Amanda came to me because she always came to me—to my house."

On cross-examination the prosecution focused on what Amanda had told her sister about hurting Laura. "At one point, you told detectives that you weren't sure if she told you she hurt Laura real bad or that Laura was dead. This morning, are you sure she said Laura was hurt bad or did she say Laura was dead?"

"I'm just . . ."

"Back when you told detectives you didn't know if she told you she hurt Laura real bad if she told you she was dead, correct?"

"If I said it back then, it's correct. 'Cause I don't remember right now what exactly."

The pain and distaste battling for control of Karen's face were washed away by relief with the realization that court was adjourned for the day. The questions, however, continued the next morning, September 13, 2013.

While they were at her house, Karen said, Grant spent almost all of his time outside while Amanda was in the house with the babies.

Regarding Amanda's newborn daughter, the prosecution clarified, "And Lily was a little bit over . . . a month old?"

Karen's mouth twisted, her face contorted, and she choked out a response laden with emotion, "Yes, sir." She sniffed, sobbed and grabbed a tissue. With deliberation, she inhaled deeply and exhaled a jagged breath through pursed lips. She wiped away tears and said, "I'm okay."

"We're not in any hurry, Ms. Berry. Just take your time," the judge told her.

Karen held a tissue to her eyes with one hand, clutched her elbow with the other and pulled both arms protectively into her chest. After a few sniffles, she said, "Go ahead."

Assistant District Attorney Boz Zellinger asked, "Grant wasn't with Lily much at all, was he?"

"No, sir. . . . He only wanted her to take pictures or something."

She responded to Zellinger's questions by saying that she hadn't noticed the coolers until an hour before they left her house. She saw Grant wash out the U-Haul and told herself that it must have rained in North Carolina and it was all muddy in the back. She didn't want to think, she said, she'd just wanted them to leave. Karen's lower lip and chin started to quiver again and she grabbed another tissue to wipe her nose.

She said that Wednesday morning, she and Amanda sat down with a cup of coffee "and we were fixin' to talk about my mother, 'cause she just passed away. We just got started—really didn't get started good" when Grant interrupted and told Amanda she needed to get ready to go right away. Later they did talk briefly, and Karen asked if she was covering for Grant, and Amanda nodded.

On re-direct, the defense put Karen on the spot about Amanda's comment saying she hurt Laura. They pushed her so hard that the prosecution objected and the judge reminded the defense attorneys that Karen Berry was *their* witness.

Defense attorney Jeff Cutler pulled out transcripts of Karen's interviews with law enforcement and entered them into evidence. "Did you tell detectives that Amanda wanted to tell you about something serious?"

"Yes, sir."

"Did you tell detectives in that first interview that she hurt Laura?"

"Yes, sir."

"She told you she hurt Laura and hurt her bad?"

"Yes, sir."

"Do you remember Detective Gill asking you specifically, 'Karen, what did she say?' He asked you that question?"

"Yes, sir."

"You remember saying, 'She said she hurt her.'"

"I remember because I looked over the statements, yes, sir."

"Did you say you asked her, 'How did you hurt Laura?' Do you remember that?"

"Did he ask me if she told me how she hurt Laura? Yes, he asked me that."

"And you said it was bad?"

Karen paused and turned her head, thinking, "Yes, I probably said that, yes."

"Amanda never told you exactly how she hurt Laura?"

"No, sir."

After hammering away at that point for a few more questions, Cutler asked, "Do you remember telling Detective Latour that Grant came over, Grant said he loved her, he'd taken vows and he was going to take care of Amanda?"

"I don't remember saying it."

The attorney handed her a page of the transcript. She reviewed it, but although she still did not remember saying it, she believed she must have because it was in the document.

"Do you remember if Amanda ever said anything to you about Grant hurting Laura?"

"No, sir," Karen replied. "She never told me anything about Grant hurting Laura except the time she shook her head and told me she was covering for him. That's the only time."

"You wanted to believe your sister didn't you?"

"I can't say that I wanted, because I don't know what I wanted. I just know I looked her straight in her face as I've always done to get her to tell me the truth. And at that moment, I believed without a doubt in my mind that she was covering for him. And she looked me straight in the face and shook her head yes."

The defense returned to the statement Karen had made about not wanting to testify against her sister in court and asked her if she'd said that. Karen broke down again and choked through the tears coursing down her cheeks, "Yes, sir. Yes, sir, I did."

JEFF Cutler called Detective Faulk back to the witness stand. They used him to introduce a number of newspaper articles designed to undermine the credibility of Pablo

Trinidad's testimony. The defense attorney then had Faulk read a number of pleasant e-mail exchanges between Grant and Laura.

On cross, Assistant District Attorney Becky Holt established that Pablo Trinidad had given his information to the federal prosecutors before many of the articles just read into the record had been posted online. Then she elicited from Detective Faulk the information that they had never found Laura's phone, her recorder, the two bags she had with her when she left the apartment that morning, or the black blouse or brown pants she was wearing that day.

On re-direct, the defense confirmed that Grant had texted Lauren Harris about a visit with Laura and the boys to Monkey Joe's on July 13, 2011. Detective Faulk was excused from the stand and the defense rested their case.

CHAPTER THIRTY-SEVEN

WILL Durham delivered the first part of the defense's closing arguments in a mocking, flippant tone of voice, as if the prosecution's case was one big joke. "I told you on the first day that this case is about a man trying to cover up his wife's actions. And the state has not proven anything different now. Your Honor will tell you that proof beyond a reasonable doubt is proof that fully satisfies you—entirely convinces you of the defendant's guilt."

He reminded the jurors that they promised not to convict unless guilt was fully proven and now they needed to decide between first or second degree murder and not guilty. He, of course, urged the latter.

He explained that first degree murder required malice, premeditation, deliberation and planning. "The evidence in this case—all the evidence you've heard—doesn't make any sense with a planned-out killing. If it was, it would be the most incomprehensible plan in the world. The saw was purchased after. The cleaning supplies were purchased after. The U-Haul trailer was rented after. They didn't even have a hitch on the car."

Durham went on, "And you heard about this note—and you saw it, it was one of the last things you saw—where Laura Ackerson gave up custody for twenty-five thousand dollars. We know it's Laura's writing on that. The FBI examiner examined her handwriting and said, 'She wrote that.' You've seen the signature. The FBI examiner couldn't come to a conclusion on that because she couldn't get copies of Laura Ackerson's signature.

"If you're going to kill someone to get custody, you don't need an agreement that says you get custody. Doesn't make any sense with a plan. And that would be the dumbest plan in history to have someone come to your house so that you could kill them in your home, with your children present?"

Without evidence of planning, Durham claimed, a conviction for first degree murder was clearly not in the running. As for second degree murder, "You have to decide who killed her, why they killed her, what happened. And you may not have good answers to that question because the state has not proven beyond a reasonable doubt about anything that happened in that house.

"Now, the state has put on a case . . . to show you that this was a malicious killing, that they had such a horrible relationship—I think in their opening, they were kind of, you might remember them talking about hate—hate that leads to this stuff. But the best evidence in this case shows that they didn't have a hate-filled relationship. They had arguments. They didn't get along that great. They were an ex who fought about custody and kids and insurance. Hate-filled?"

Durham mocked the prosecution's contention that Laura was afraid of Grant. He patted the rail of the witness box as he spoke of how, despite Laura's diary being right there, "They didn't have that witness read one word out of it because there's nothing in it—nothing in it that showed it was a hateful, spiteful relationship.

"We had the witness read something out of it, remember that, about July fifth, the custody exchange, going to Grant's house. And there were some statements in there about how Amanda called [Laura] psycho crazy, but there was nothing in her diary that [would] suggest a hate-filled relationship.

"Now they had problems, I'm not trying to tell you they got along all the time and never argued—they did argue a lot and some of it was petty and some of it was mean, nasty. But then the next day, they'd be sending pictures, saying thanks for the pictures . . . and trying to raise the kids."

Furthermore, Dunham said, "The state relies on evidence of Heidi Schumacher and Chevon Mathes to present this picture of this supposedly, this hate-filled, fear-filled relationship. That testimony is not reliable because Laura sold her friends a bill of goods. And I don't mean that in a nasty way—everyone wants their friends to be on their side. And she told them some things and explained the relationship in a way that wasn't accurate.

"She may have told the she was afraid to go to Grant's apartment. But it's not true. She went there—over and over. Remember Sha testifying about watching a video of Gentle's birthday? There's Laura at Grant's apartment. Laura's own words say that she went there over and over again."

Durham also dismissed Heidi's testimony about Grant's abusive and threatening behavior. "And then you heard about this wedding certificate where they supposedly went to the justice of the peace and said, 'I do,'" Durham said, holding a hand in the air. "And somehow Grant didn't fill out the paperwork, never signed it and the wedding wasn't real? That just doesn't make sense. Doesn't make sense. If that happened, those records are easy to get, the state would have gone and got 'em. They would have gotten the record and shown it to you," he said, waving an imaginary piece of paper in the air. "'Here's where Laura signed it and Grant didn't.' They never happened and that's not even how it works. You go get a marriage certificate, you fill it out and then you go to the justice of the peace. If everything's in order, that's when they swear you in.

"What had happened is that . . . Laura told her friends that they were married. It just wasn't true. . . . And they also said, Laura would never, ever, ever, ever give up custody of the kids. She would never do that. But she did that once before, she already signed an agreement decree giving Grant custody five days a week and her two days a week.

"And that agreement later signed in Grant's house doesn't say she gives up her parental rights, she doesn't want to see her kids again. She said that Grant could have primary custody. She would do that. She did do that."

Durham moved to the recording of "Broomstick Rider" and said it was a parody. "I mean, there's jokes in there about sending goons to his parents' house cause Laura was living with his parents at the time. What? 'I'm going to send a hit man to my parents' house'? It was a joke. And it's not a funny joke now, in light of what's happened," Durham admitted, but added, "It wasn't him writing a song saying, 'This is what I'm going to do.' He was blowing off some steam.

"All the reliable evidence in this case points straight to Amanda Hayes. They want to tell you Grant Hayes wanted to kill Laura Ackerson because he wanted custody of his kids. But she already signed an agreement giving him custody of those kids. At the house, that day, she already signed an agreement: you get custody of the kids, twenty-five thousand dollars." He claimed that any motive Grant might have had no longer existed once Laura signed that document.

"And there was this Facebook chat about Grant telling somebody, 'Maybe I'm just gonna give Laura the kids to make this go away.'" Durham tried to twist to something Grant wrote after Laura was already dead into an event that occurred before she died. "Instead it ended with Grant having custody and them having to pay twenty-five thousand dollars to Laura—twenty-five thousand dollars they didn't have . . . and now Laura's going to be a part of their lives forever." Durham theorized that custody of the children was Grant's only motive. With that motive gone, the only one with a motive was Amanda, who didn't want Laura involved with the kids and did not want to go into further debt to pay her. He claimed Amanda did it and that is why they took Laura's remains to Texas. He pointed to the state not calling Karen Berry and presenting Pablo Trinidad instead. "And, he, in exchange for helping the state out . . . instead of being in prison forever and ever and ever and ever, he's going to be in prison for twenty-one years. . . . And he was in the same pod with Grant Hayes for five days. Five days. If Grant Hayes was telling people that he had done something like this in five days, don't you think there'd been more than one person who came to court and said that?"

Durham shifted then to Amanda's confession, calling it sufficient to raise reasonable doubt. "They went to Amanda's family—Amanda's kin—people Grant didn't even know in Texas. Rural Texas. He wouldn't have done that if it was his plan. It wasn't his mistake—it was Amanda's mistake, so they went to *her* family.

"Grant Hayes helped dispose of Laura Ackerson's body. It was his wife [who'd killed Laura] and he wanted to protect her. And his motives were not all pure, he was concerned about protecting himself. That's a terrible thing and it's a serious crime," Durham admitted, but "that isn't what this case is about. This case isn't about disposing of a body, as terrible as that is. Disposing of a body is a terrible thing but it is not murder. The state has not proven—has not proven beyond a reasonable doubt that Grant's guilty of murder. And that's why we would ask you to check that third box, the not-guilty box."

_____

WHEN Will Durham finished, co-counsel Jeff Cutler rose to give the concluding remarks for the defense.

"I think one of the key challenges you have," he told the jury, "is to take the emotion—the raw emotion—possibly the disgust, whatever you despise. There's no reason not to be disgusted with what Grant Hayes participated in. There's plenty of reason to be upset about what the state has proven in this case about how they worked together to cover up Laura's death. . . . But the challenge you are going to have is to take those emotions, those feelings, and put them in the proper place as you said you would do in jury selection. Put those aside and be objective about the facts and the evidence."

Cutler reiterated Durham's scorn for Pablo Trinidad. "If you believe Pablo Trinidad, then you have to believe she was choked, she was strangled in some way. That's what he says Grant told him happened—she was strangled. And again, whatever happened, your common sense will tell you, if they strangled her, why is there bleach spots on the carpet? . . . You don't need bleach if you strangled somebody."

Cutler said of Karen Berry that "she knew and she truly believed—that her sister had done something to Laura." He remarked that "she testified about [how] on the morning when they were leaving, taking Amanda aside saying, 'Now, look, I'm not going to bring this up again, I'm not gonna ask again, just tell me, are you covering for

Grant?' . . . And I would suggest to you that that nod was Amanda paying her sister what her sister wanted. . . . But that is not what happened. And the evidence from Karen Berry is that Amanda never said to her that Grant hurt Laura—that Grant—that *we* hurt Laura. It was: 'I hurt Laura.'"

Cutler then belittled the state's contention that Grant and Amanda had acted in concert. "If one kills her, then they both can be guilty of murder if they have a common purpose," he said. "But, again, there is no evidence of that. They may ask you to make inferences, conjectures and that this was a terrible custody battle and that that makes sense. But . . . we put on some e-mails in our evidence. And if you remember, those e-mails are around in May, about the time of . . . the custody evaluation. And the state says, 'Now Grant is mad—he didn't get what he wanted and that's his motive to kill.'

"But if you look at what they did, days after this custody evaluation . . . they were actually working together to get as most time with these kids with both parents. . . . That custody evaluation wasn't an impetus for anything."

Cutler said, "Ladies and gentlemen, I could probably stay here another hour but I'm not. I'm going to wrap it up. This is a sad case. This is a nasty case—very nasty things occurred. But I trust you will do your job. You will not let your emotions decide this case. You will not let your disgust over what happened in this case lead you to a verdict. You will look and you will hold the state to its burden of proof.

"'Have they proven to me how Laura Ackerson died?

Have they proven to me who killed her? . . . Am I truly convinced of what happened to Laura Ackerson in that apartment and how she died?' And I would suggest to you, they have failed to prove beyond a reasonable doubt these things. And I trust that you will return a verdict of not guilty."

CHAPTER THIRTY-EIGHT

ASSISTANT District Attorney Becky Holt began the closing arguments for the state. "Let's get this right from the get-go. I'm not going to stand up here and ask you to convict Grant Hayes of first degree murder because you feel sorry for Laura Ackerson," she said. "The State of North Carolina asks [you] to find him guilty because that is the verdict that is called for by the law and the evidence in this case.

"Laura Ackerson, in July 2011, had every reason to be optimistic about where she was going, where her life was heading, and specifically about what was going to happen with the custody of those two children."

Holt brought up Dr. Ginger Calloway's report. "The judge will tell you how you can consider Dr. Calloway's report. He'll tell you, as it impacts on your decision making of the state of mind of Laura Ackerson or the defendant, or any motives that you can consider it for that purpose. Not for the truth of what necessarily was reported in that report, but what affect it had on Laura Ackerson, on her state of mind, on the defendant, on his state of mind.

"Now that report, it is in evidence. You recall where it was recovered from. It was in the Dodge Durango by the passenger seat, right there in the console. You recall that it had coffee stains on it. It had markings. 'Never.' 'BS.' Why is that important?" Holt asked rhetorically. Because "although Dr. Calloway's report recommends fifty-fifty—a two-three-two plan—it's really bad for the defendant. While Laura, according to Dr. Calloway and her report she provided, she needed to work on her being more assertive, she needed to work on her anxiety." Regarding Grant Hayes, however, Calloway "recommended [he] needed to go see a psychiatrist . . . because of his 'illogical, disturbed thinking that he exhibits. It is disturbing,' she wrote in her report, 'that his intense rage towards Laura may serve as an anchor for his disturbed thinking. It is obvious that they do not want Laura included in the children's lives. The defendant believes he should have total control through legal and physical of the children with supervised visits only for Laura.'

"So what do you have? On one hand, you have Laura Ackerson, who over this year period has really worked to get herself into a good spot. She's gotten a job, she's moved out, has gotten a place to live, has set all these things in motion.

"The defendant over that period of time, over that year, I would suggest to you, found himself in a very different spot. He found himself in a situation where things were *not* going well, where things were *not* looking good for him to get custody of these boys."

Leaving Dr. Calloway, Holt moved on to March of 2011. "It was about that time that the defendant makes a report to DSS [Division of Social Services] regarding child abuse, which was not substantiated . . . but it was around that time that Laura expresses to her attorney [John Sargeant], 'What if something happens to me? I'm concerned.'

"[Grant Hayes] was losing control of the situation," Holt said. "And as we move closer and closer to that August fifteenth hearing, where Laura, on one hand, is lining up the witnesses," Grant knew "his options are limited." The ADA mentioned that things were getting strained. "In June—you heard testimony and you saw digital evidence about a midweek exchange that took place at Monkey Joe's . . . Laura said: 'I'm not going to do that again—it was too hard.' You heard Chevon say, 'She called me and she was very upset.' Grant wouldn't let her say good-bye. It was a scene. It was at the Monkey Joe's.

"And then, on June the twentieth, there's a request by Laura to the defendant: 'Can we do the midweek thing again?' And the answer was: 'No.' . . . You don't hear anything more about the midweek visits until July the twelfth—the evening of July the twelfth. And that's instigated by the defendant. And what he says is: 'Do you want to give the midweek visits a try—you wanna give it another try?' . . . The defense would have you believe that would show they were getting along. That might make sense, if it were not for the events that followed."

Holt said again, "This is a case in which the defendant was in a place where he was losing control." She pointed out that Grant "had great aspirations that he would be this songwriter that would go to Nashville or travel the world with his children and move forward. He wanted Laura to just go away. . . . But what the defendant didn't count on was that Laura was not going to give up on those children. And he knew that and it became more and more clear."

She referenced the defense's argument that the case was just about dismemberment and disposal, and that the jury "shouldn't consider that in your deliberations on whether or not he is guilty of first degree murder. The judge is going to tell you, you can consider that: the defendant's actions before, during, and after the killing. The judge is going to tell you, you can consider all of that. And what do those actions tell you?

"The defense will tell you that the fact that the defendant went to Wal-Mart a few hours after this killing and bought a saw, bought goggles, and bought plastic tarping, that you shouldn't consider that. Well, you should consider that. They say it was a bad plan—a stupid plan—well, the law doesn't say it has to be a good plan. The law doesn't say that it has to be thought out in every respect. The defense says that [the Hayeses] didn't think about how they were going to get her out of the apartment—it was a dumb plan.

"Well, the plan was to kill her. Whether or not they'd thought out exactly how, doesn't mean there wasn't a plan to kill Laura Ackerson. Listen carefully to the judge's instructions when he talks to you about those things.

"The defense argued to you that it didn't make any sense to go to Texas—that that wouldn't have been the defendant's idea. Would it have been his idea to take [her] to Kinston where his family lived, where he was getting ready to move to?

"It's all about Grant Hayes. It's all about it not coming back to him. It's him, through his lawyers, who's arguing that it's Amanda Hayes acting alone—-his wife acting alone—who killed Laura Ackerson—the mother of *his* children—the woman to whom he'd been engaged in a custody battle for over a year—one he was getting ready to lose."

Becky Holt moved on to what Grant told Pablo Trinidad, and how the defense's skepticism was unwarranted. "He talks to members of the Greenville Police Department in January of 2012. That's before Dr. Radisch's reports come out, I mean it hadn't even been published. And he told them about the choking. And Detective Faulk said what [Pablo] told [him] was consistent with what he told Greenville.

"What else does the defendant tell Pablo Trinidad? You remember when he first started testifying, he said, the defendant said, 'I couldn't have done it because her car was parked near the apartment and I had trouble with my hands from playing instruments for a long time.' Then as he continued to talk, you learned that, what the defendant said was what his defense was going to be. 'I'm going to say I didn't do it because who would be stupid enough to leave her car right there near my apartment? I'm going to say I couldn't choke her because of my hands, because of playing instruments, had gotten weak—I didn't have the strength in my hands.' The defendant was planning his defense even then, two days after he'd been arrested. And that's what he told Pablo Trinidad.

"You decide the credibility of Pablo Trinidad. Weigh it with the other evidence in the case but consider those things when you decide. Consider his testimony with great care and caution, but when you do that, if you still believe his testimony in whole or in part, consider that with everything else when deciding this case."

Holt moved on to Karen Berry. "The defense—well, just let me say this: You had the opportunity to observe her. This was a difficult situation as you can imagine. You had the opportunity to see her testify and try to tell you who said what. I would submit to you the defendant's main defense here was Karen Berry. And what did she say? She said that, ultimately—and you remember how you remember it—that she and Amanda had a conversation in which Amanda said, 'I hurt Laura and I hurt her bad.' Mr. Zellinger asked her, 'Don't you recall when the detectives were out you told them that you couldn't remember whether she said, "I hurt her" or "Laura's dead"? And wouldn't your memory be better then?' 'Yes, it would be.' 'Well, what did she say?' 'I don't know, I don't know which of those it was.'"

Holt spoke of the defense grasping at straws with that one bit of testimony and turned it back to Grant. "The defendant in this case was desperate—he was desperate to get rid of Laura—and to do it any way he could. He wanted to erase Laura from his life. He wanted to have a family without Laura in it," she said, holding up a photograph of him, Amanda and the kids. "He didn't want to have to deal with Laura Ackerson anymore. And when she came to his apartment, at his request, on July the thirteenth, he was going to make sure that Laura Ackerson never [again] saw the light of day. That was his plan the night before when he sent her an e-mail and whether he lured her over there initially with the promise of seeing her children, he lured her over there by saying, 'Let's end this custody thing.' But he never intended to let Laura get custody of those children.

"For Grant Hayes, it was more about winning and being in charge. It was more about denying Laura to be a mother to those children. It was more about making sure that he wouldn't have to deal with her ever again. And as the case started going bad for him, he knew the only way to do that was to kill her. Grant Hayes, either acting by himself or together with Amanda Hayes, killed Laura Ackerson," Holt stated.

"Premeditation with deliberation on July the thirteenth, 2011. He then dismembered her body and drove her across the country and threw her in a river so that he could destroy what remained of Laura. He robbed her of her life. He robbed her of her dignity. And he tried to cover it up in every way he could.

"Don't let Grant Hayes get away with this crime. Don't let Grant Hayes not answer for what he did. Whether or not Grant Hayes began making that plan or formed that intent a week before, a year before; whether he formed that intent to kill Laura Ackerson when he wrote a song about killing her; whether he formed that intent and that plan when he sent her an e-mail the night before to tell her to come over—to come over and see the boys; whether he formed that intent when he had her in the apartment and got her to sign that note; whether he formed that intent when he stabbed her in the neck; whether he formed that intent when he wrapped his hands around her throat, cut off the blood flow to her head, cut off her air, for the four to six minutes it would have taken: Grant Hayes planned to kill Laura Ackerson. The judge will tell you that deliberation, the cool state of mind, the premeditation, over a period of time, however short before that takes place—listen carefully to Mr. Zellinger as he tells you about those things and to Judge Stephens's instructions."

Holt concluded by saying, "Tell Grant Hayes, by your verdict . . . that you know that that's what he intended— that that is what he planned on July thirteenth, 2011. Tell Grant Hayes, by your verdict, that you're not going to let him obliterate Laura Ackerson in this way."

ASSISTANT District Attorney Boz Zellinger took Becky Holt's place in front of the jury to add the final arguments for the prosecution's case. "Laura Ackerson loved her kids to death—she loved her kids to her own death. That is the only reason why she went over to that apartment that night. You all know after hearing the evidence in this case that Laura Ackerson was not going over to that apartment for any reason other than to get custody of her kids. Grant Hayes knew that. He tried to control her that night. Now, he's trying to control you with his defense."

Zellinger stated that this was "a terrible case—the awful truth that these courtroom walls have heard has been staggering. . . . What happened to Laura is something that shouldn't happen to a human being—I mean, it's something that shouldn't happen to an animal. To be sliced apart and [have] acid poured on you and then left to rot in a Texas creek.

"It's hard to get past the depravity of the situation. And the question—the reason that it's relevant, the reason that everything that happens after the murder is so important, is because it tells you why and who committed this murder. Someone who takes someone's severed head and pours acid on it—would that be the person who committed this murder or would it be someone else in this apartment? Would a person who wrote a song about killing someone—would that be a person who committed this murder or was it someone else in that apartment?"

Zellinger said, "Simply put: this is a guy who wrote a song about killing someone and then dismembered her body and then poured acid on it and left the body in a creek in Texas—the whole time lying about it to investigators and to people on Facebook and to his friends. If the defendant is lying on Facebook to his friends what does that say about this defense?"

Zellinger explained why "acting in concert" was an important element to this crime despite the defense's mocking of it. Then he contested the other side's claim that the custody dispute in this case was unpleasant but no worse than any other similar situations. "They were at each other's throats. The defense wants you to believe that the defendant and Laura weren't really fighting like this, that they really weren't hating each other as much as they appeared to. And the best evidence of this malice—of this hate—between these two folks, that the defendant hated Laura Ackerson so much, is what happened after she was dead." It was the malice, Zellinger said. "There is so much malice in this case. From that song alone you get a tremendous amount of malice. . . . Grant Hayes hated Laura Ackerson.

"There is so much hate in this case that not only did he kill her . . . this man bought a saw and cut her torso in half."

Zellinger held up the reciprocating saw purchased by law enforcement for demonstration purposes. "You've seen the blades. This is a heavy object. This isn't something that just happened. Yeah, he just disposed of the body and it ended up in Texas. This saw cut someone in half. And then he cut her head off. . . . With malice, there's not much of a question. He had so much malice that he sawed the mother of his children's legs off.

"The next is the proximate cause of death—the cause without which the victim's death would not have occurred. Again, this is not much of an issue. Even the defendant's counsel in closing seemed to concede that it comes down to two people who killed Laura. It could be Grant. It could be Amanda.

"Then the third element is this intent to kill. The judge is going to tell you that the state has to prove beyond a reasonable doubt that the defendant intended to kill the victim. And the judge is going to tell you that 'intent is a mental attitude seldom provable by direct evidence. It ordinarily must be proved by circumstances from which it can be inferred.' . . . Circumstantial evidence is 'proof of a chain or group of facts or circumstances that points to the guilt or innocence of the defendant,'" Zellinger said, reading from the jury instructions document. "We are asking you to use your common sense: whether a guy who wrote a song about murdering a woman was actually the person who murdered the woman. . . . You noticed that the defendant, in his e-mail box, puts all the correspondence from Laura Ackerson in an inbox labeled 'letters from a ho.' The defendant despised Laura Ackerson. Laura Ackerson prevented him from doing what he wanted to do with his life, which is moving with those kids and moving all over the country. And that's why he made this concerted effort to eliminate Laura from his life and from any other person's life," Zellinger stated.

"The fourth element is the one that the crux of this case comes down to: premeditation and deliberation. The judge is going to tell you that premeditation is that the defendant formed the intent to kill before acting over a period of time, no matter how short. Remember that bleach spot is right by the door. And that's interesting. Why is it right by the door? You know when Laura walks in the door; she's not immediately murdered because her handwriting is on that document. . . . Why did we find that? Everything else in the apartment is gone. The carpet is bleached. The rugs are thrown out. . . . Gone is that shower curtain, those mats, the shower rod, and you heard the defendant went and bought a computer cord the next day, that's Thursday.

That's interesting. Why did the defendant feel the need to go out and buy that laptop computer cord—the charger for that computer? Was it because it was used to choke someone? We don't know.

"But everything is missing from that apartment. You saw the pictures of that apartment. You saw that knife block that interestingly was missing some knives. . . . In a case like this, you're not finding the evidence of the murder; you're finding evidence of the cleanup. So why is that note left there?" he asked, continuing, "You have to gotta have some questions about the note. . . . Here you've got your premeditation and deliberation. Here at some point this night, they are signing this. You don't know if Laura is signing this at knifepoint. You don't know what's going on in that apartment. Really, only three people did know—two are charged with first degree murder and one's dead.

"But why do we find this note? Why is it left in that apartment? The defendant obviously knew the police were coming at some point, because he got rid of everything else in that apartment. But we find it there. And why do we find it? Well, it's designed to look like Laura took twenty-five thousand dollars and took off. . . . We find this note because the defendant wants the investigators to think Laura took off with this money. If that was the thought process going on in the defendant's head, then with this note, he had the intent to kill Laura . . . and he acted in a cool state of mind."

ADA Zellinger explained that condition of a cool state of mind does not require a total lack of emotion and that it can be inferred from the defendant's actions, such as how

Grant's behavior appeared when he went to Wal-Mart at two-thirty in the morning. "Twenty-six minutes he was shopping. And you saw him standing there, arms crossed, looking at all the saws—premeditating and deliberating on how he was going to saw up Laura Ackerson's body. . . . At no point in any of this evidence is Grant anything but completely calm and collected."

Zellinger also challenged the defense's use of the word "disposed." "The defense said he disposed of the body. It sounds like you have a wrapper and you toss in the trash can. The defendant didn't just dispose of the body; he engraved his hate for Laura Ackerson by cutting off her head. He cut off her arms. He cut her torso in half. He cut her legs off. He cut her at the knees. He then took those parts and put them in coolers—and at that point, these [aren't] coolers, they're coffins—those four items you saw in front of you. He then drives those items to Texas—halfway across the country. And then when he's there, it's not good enough to just throw it in that creek, he then also has to pour acid on it.

"That dismemberment, ladies and gentlemen, means more than just disposing of the body. It's in an aggressive emotion—this extreme abhorrence toward the person he killed. He's trying to disregard Laura as a person whatsoever. He couldn't control her in life so now he's going to control her death. He's just driven by this power and control to carve up her body. . . . The defendant argues that how Laura died isn't proven. . . . And Dr. Ross and Dr. Radisch through their medical examinations were able to discern as much as they could about the body. But of course, evidence of whether Laura was strangled or stabbed would be much easier if there were muscle or tissue attached to her neck. Remember, those C4 vertebrae, the ones that go down to C5, those were all found at the bottom of her head in very bad condition. I mean, you got to see the picture of Laura's head when it was recovered by the Houston dive team member Brian Davis, it was in terrible condition. But you'll also remember, it was in a different condition than the rest of her body. And the defendant says, 'Well, there's no evidence about acid, there's no evidence on any of her body.' That's because the acid was poured on her head. There's not going to be evidence of acid on her other body parts when Grant Hayes pours acid on her head and it doesn't do whatever he was intending for it to do. But you do see acid on her teeth—on that tooth—and yes, it's only one tooth, but you see acid etching. That's circumstantial evidence.

"And you know there's acid, the pH in that hog pen is very low, you heard about how acidic it was. You hear about the acid etching on her teeth and you know that Grant Hayes bought acid. That's circumstantial evidence."

Furthermore, Zellinger said, "Not only did he send e-mails to Laura to try to cover up what happened and then he goes and in a very deliberate manner, he stands out in front of that Sheetz for an hour, an hour and twenty minutes. And we tried to speed up that video as much as we could but he stands there, waiting, for the woman who's dead in his bathtub. How more deliberate could Grant Hayes get in the aftermath of this murder?

"Then there's this note that says Grant keeps custody

and Laura just gets twenty-five thousand dollars. And that that note is left in that apartment after everything else is thrown out to shown that Laura Ackerson disappeared. And the question for you is: why is that note written? It is written so that so that it looks like Laura Ackerson disappeared. And Grant Hayes intended for Laura Ackerson to disappear when that note was signed before she was dead. And that gives you that premeditation and that gives you that deliberation and that leads to one inalienable conclusion"—Zellinger turned and pointed a finger at Grant Hayes—"that this man killed Laura Ackerson, the mother of his children. This defendant then cut up her body, that then, he did very deliberate things to cover up that it happened and that coverup continues today. And that can lead you to one conclusion that he is guilty, beyond reasonable doubt, and you should find him so."

AFTER Boz Zellinger's closing, court adjourned for the week. The jury had time to ponder over the weekend, and began their deliberations on Monday morning, September 16, 2013.

It took them less than two hours to announce that they had a verdict.

Grant Hayes was escorted back into the courtroom. When he sat down between his two attorneys, Will Durham gave him a smile and an encouraging pat on the back. Grant rocked nervously as if moving to a beat inside his head.

The judge read the verdict: Grant Ruffin Hayes III, guilty of the first degree murder of Laura Ackerson.

A deputy moved closer to Grant and stood directly behind his chair. Will Durham's smiling face turned somber.

Judge Stephens moved immediately on to the sentencing phase. "A jury decision in an hour and a half probably speaks louder than anything anyone can say about this case from the state's perspective, from the family's perspective."

Will Durham made the customary bid to set aside the verdict. As expected, the judge denied the motion.

Stephens continued, "Grant Ruffin Hayes III, having been found guilty of the murder of Laura Ackerson, it is the judgment of this court that you be sentenced to the North Carolina Department of Corrections for the period of your natural life without benefit of parole."

Grant was handcuffed and, after a few mumbled words to his lawyers, he was led out of the courtroom without displaying any emotional reaction at all to this life-altering event. His attorneys announced their intention to appeal. The judge denied bail. Phase one of the search for justice for Laura Ackerson was at an end.

CHAPTER THIRTY-NINE

A Wake County grand jury returned an additional indictment against Amanda Hayes the month after Grant Hayes's trial came to an end. In case the jury at her January 2014 trial did not convict her of first degree or second degree murder, the state's backup plan would be to also charge her with being an accessory after the fact.

A request to allow the defense's investigator to search the Dodge Durango was granted by the court. In doing so, a knife was found that had not previously been collected by police. On December 16, 2013, Amanda's attorney Johnny Gaskins filed another request for the testing of that implement. In his motion, the attorney wrote: "The knife that was found in the Dodge Durango by the Raleigh Police Department appears to be yet further evidence that the defendant's husband was prepared to kill the defendant and their children while they were in the Dodge Durango."

Superior Court Judge Paul Ridgeway approved the motion for testing as well as for an analysis of a biohazard suit and pair of rubber gloves also recently found in the SUV. The State Bureau of Investigation found no blood on the weapon, but Gaskins was not satisfied. He planned to have it examined by a North Carolina State anthropologist to see if it had been used in Laura's Ackerson's murder.

IN early January 2014, the defense announced its intention to call Grant Hayes to the stand during trial. Gaskins hoped that if he did so, Grant would be forced to invoke his fifth-amendment rights, since he had a pending appeal. When the lawyer approached Grant in prison, he insisted he would not claim the fifth because to do so would indicate that he had killed Laura and he claimed he had not.

Grant may have thought he could discourage the state from calling him by previewing his testimony in an interview to Amanda Lamb of WRAL TV in mid-January. He told her that he had not testified on his own behalf because his attorney did not want him to do so. He felt that Jeff Cutler had misled him and had not had his best interests at heart.

Grant also gave a version of the events of July 13, 2011, that placed the blame on Amanda but differed in significant ways from the story his attorneys told the jurors. He claimed that Laura came over to the house to discuss an out-of-court settlement. He said that her opening bid to end the suit was fifty thousand dollars but that amount was negotiated down to twenty-five thousand dollars. It was after that was done that Laura asked to hold Lily.

Grant claimed that, at that time, he went to wake up Gentle to leave with his mother while Amanda was supposed to be scanning the final contract for Laura. "Words were exchanged and Laura jumped Amanda as she walked away from the table with the contract. I was not in the room."

Grant said that after he heard a loud noise, he ran back into the room and saw little Grant standing up looking over the sofa at his mother on the floor. "Amanda was in the nursery screaming, 'Call the police. I want her arrested. Why did you leave her alone with me? Why did you leave the room?'"

Grant said that he slapped Laura's face to try to bring her around and believes she died at the moment he attempted to raise her to a sitting position. During all of this, he said, little Grant was standing two feet away taking it all in.

He said his wife told him that Laura had threatened to take Lily from her and that Laura had grabbed Amanda's hair and pulled her backward. Amanda, he said, claimed that in a reflex action, she slammed her elbow into Laura's throat. When Laura released her, Amanda ran into the nursery, slamming and locking the door.

Grant alleged that all he was concerned with then was his three-year-old son. "Initially, I was more concerned about little Grant seeing his mother die and I didn't want him involved in a police investigation. And all I could see was Child Protective Services coming in and taking all three of our children while there was an investigation. . . . Here I am, a black man in an apartment with a dead white lady who's been suing me. . . . And being a black man for thirty-four years, I have a certain amount of paranoia and distrust for the police." Nonetheless, he said, he told Amanda to leave and take the children, then planned to call 911. Instead, he started drinking and lost his nerve.

Grant said that if he had the chance to do it again, he would have called police so that they would have a record of Amanda's story directly from her and not from his sister-in-law Karen Berry, whom he accused of lying to the court.

He said that he believed Karen had taken a deal to not be prosecuted in exchange for her testimony. "She was as much of an accessory as I was."

Grant also claimed that the state framed him by covering up the truth, hiding exculpatory evidence and eliciting false testimony. "To establish the element of premeditation in first degree murder, they used lies—pure lies, unsubstantiated lies."

He wrapped up his interview with a defense of Amanda Hayes, claiming her actions were the defensive reflexes of a mother defending her child and, thus, Amanda was not guilty of murder. "Laura got herself killed. I don't blame Amanda. Amanda had a duty to herself and me to protect our child. . . . Justice would not be served if she were convicted of murder."

CHAPTER FORTY

THE trial of Amanda Perry Hayes for the murder of Laura Jean Ackerson began with jury selection on Tuesday, January 21, 2014, in the Wake County Courthouse in Raleigh, North Carolina. Much of the prosecution's case was a repetition of the material they'd presented in the trial of Grant Ruffin Hayes III. The defense's case, on the other hand, was remarkably distinct from the previous proceedings. The story they would tell was a direct contradiction of both the one presented in Grant's trial and the one in his television interview.

Opening arguments were delivered on the afternoon of Monday, January 27, 2014. Assistant District Attorney Boz Zellinger spoke first. "'I hurt her. I hurt her bad. She's dead.' Those are the words of Amanda Hayes to her own sister. Those were the words of Amanda Hayes six days after Laura Ackerson came over to the apartment that she shared with Grant Hayes. Those are the words of Amanda Hayes hours before she and Grant Hayes deposited her body in a Texas creek. Those were the words of Amanda Hayes six days before Laura Ackerson's severed torso would be found. 'I hurt her. I hurt her bad. She's dead.' . . . You are going to learn that on July 13, 2011, Laura Ackerson woke up excited. She's a twenty-seven-year-old mother of two little boys, Gentle and Grant IV. She shared custody of those two little boys with Amanda Hayes's husband, Grant Hayes. You'll hear that Grant Hayes left Laura for Amanda Hayes, an actress that Grant met in the US Virgin Islands."

Zellinger described the contentious custody dispute and the excitement Laura had shown about the outcome of the custody hearing and her optimism about the success of her new business.

Zellinger continued, "This is a case that's not just about a crime—it's an inhumane crime. This is a case about killing a human being, and the barbarism and brutality that Grant Hayes and Amanda Hayes exerted on her body such that she disappeared off the face of the earth for eleven days."

He noted that Amanda took her stepsons and newborn to a Chick-fil-A at a quarter to ten the evening Laura died, and "at two A.M. that night, Grant Hayes walks into the Wal-Mart at Brier Creek and you'll see the amount of time that Grant Hayes is out of that apartment. Presumably, Amanda and those children and Laura are left there. And you'll hear that Grant walked into that Wal-Mart and purchased a nine-foot-by-twelve-foot plastic tarp. You'll hear that he bought some goggles and a couple pairs of gloves, Hefty Contractor extra large garbage bags. And, perhaps most importantly, you'll hear that Grant Hayes purchased a Skil reciprocating saw with six-inch blades and he also bought some additional blades . . . And it's going to be clear to you what the purpose was of those purchases. And you're going to estimate and listen to how much time Amanda is home with the kids and presumably Laura's body. You'll hear that she had a cell phone there."

Zellinger went on to describe how Amanda had her daughter come take the boys out of the house for most of Thursday, and how that Friday, when the custody exchange was supposed to happen as usual, "you'll hear and you'll see Grant Hayes go to this Sheetz gas station for hours. And you'll see him outside on the phone. Pay close attention to who he's calling at that time. And again, you'll hear that Amanda Hayes is at home, alone, with her baby and Laura Ackerson's body. After Grant stays at that custody exchange and, shockingly, Laura doesn't show up, he leaves and comes back."

The next day, Zellinger noted that "Grant and Amanda Hayes are out in town buying more items: three bags of ice, multiple coolers—pay close attention to where the coolers end up." He told the jurors that Grant and Amanda asked Sha's boyfriend to install a trailer hitch on the Dodge Durango and about the last-minute arrangements for the trip to Texas. Then, he turned to Grant picking up the U-Haul rental truck. "And you're going to get to see his demeanor in that U-Haul facility . . . more time when Amanda Hayes is at her home with her children, by her cell phone, and presumably Laura's body."

Zellinger told the jury that Laura was reported missing on Monday, July 18, by her business partner Chevon Mathes, who spoke to Detective James Gwartney of the Kinston police. "Detective Gwartney hears about all these custody issues and decides to contact Grant Hayes. Play close attention to what Grant Hayes tells Detective Gwartney. You're going to hear this testimony and you're going to hear that Grant Hayes said that Laura came over to his apartment at 6:40 that day and you'll be able to compare that to the telephone records and what time you think she arrived there." The next day, July 19, "Detective Gwartney comes to Raleigh, since he's learned that this was the last place that Laura was seen, and briefs members of the Raleigh Police Department."

Zellinger notes, "Meanwhile in Texas, you'll learn that Amanda Hayes that morning sits down with her sister and utters those words: 'I hurt her. I hurt her bad. She's dead.' . . . [Then] later that day, Amanda takes some money from an ATM and she and Grant end up purchasing a thirty-two-gallon trash can, four boxes of muriatic acid and a couple pairs of gloves." He told the jury about the creek across the street from Karen Berry's house in Texas, the johnboat her family kept beside it and how Grant and Amanda used it to supposedly go on a nighttime fishing expedition.

"Around that time that they went out on that boat, you'll hear that the Raleigh Police Department finds Laura's car. And they find that car in an apartment complex in a parking space that's not four hundred yards from where Amanda and Grant Hayes lived. . . . And you'll learn that when the detectives find Laura's car in so close proximity to Amanda Hayes's apartment that they execute a search warrant for Grant and Amanda's apartment. And you'll hear when they go there, right by the front door, there's a big bleach spot and you'll hear more about that bleach spot. And you'll hear there's another bleach spot right by the bathroom. . . . That bathroom was very, very clean—cleaner than any other room in that house."

The prosecutor talked of the overlapping cross-country trips of Grant and Amanda and Detectives Dexter Gill and Bob Latour "like ships passing in the night" in opposite directions. "And they sit down with Karen Berry, and you'll hear about Karen's demeanor as she prayed before talking to them. And you'll hear that Karen tells them about something, the things that occurred. About how Karen walked around the property with Grant and Amanda as Grant and Amanda asked if there is a septic tank or a hole or a river—looking for some deep place. And you'll hear also hear that Karen told them, 'I can't stand the thought of standing in court and facing my sister after this but I've got to do what's right. Please take care of her when you pick her up, please.' . . .

"And at that point, the question in detectives' heads—'Where is Laura?'—is leading them across the street from Karen Berry's house. . . . And there, for all of Laura's family and friends, for Chevon, for the Raleigh Police Department, for all the folks at the Kinston police department their worst fears are realized. For there, in the middle of that creek, lies Laura Ackerson's severed torso. Her head has been cut off, her arms have been cut off, her torso has been split in half. You'll hear of the efforts that these investigators take to pull those body parts out of the water."

Zellinger enumerated some of the witnesses ahead, then said, "And you'll get to see Laura's diary . . . where she says Amanda calls her psycho-crazy. Amanda looks at her with disdain. That Amanda says, 'I'm now responsible for your kids because you're psycho-crazy.' Plus you're going to see in that diary many things about Grant Hayes and the bitter, contentious custody dispute that Amanda and Grant were having with Laura Ackerson. You'll hear Laura writes, 'I'm afraid to approach this subject with Grant and Amanda, they act as if I don't exist.' And the whole time, you'll be wondering, who would want to do this and make Laura disappear for eleven days? You'll hear Laura wrote, 'I've done nothing to them but to Amanda, I am psycho-crazy. It's disturbing to deal with them about my children.'

"Ladies and gentlemen of the jury, you're going to hear how this custody dispute grew more and more contentious. You're going to hear how angry and resentful Grant and Amanda were that Laura Ackerson was calling them every day and trying to get in touch with her children. . . . And you're going to learn that on July 13, 2011, there were three adults in that apartment. One is dead, one has been tried for murder and one is here before you. You're going to learn that Amanda Hayes is an actress. That she trained as an actress. That she performed as an actress. And that she attempted to make a living as an actress. Ladies and gentlemen, this isn't a case about movies and it isn't a movie, this isn't a stage. This is a case about a murdered young mother and the two young boys who will never see her again and the role that Amanda Hayes had in her death."

THE defense did not deny that their client had played a role in the murder of Laura Ackerson, but instead worked to make the jury understand that Amanda's involvement had not been of her own free will. Johnny Gaskins was bald on top with a long fringe of gray hair around the sides, somewhat reminiscent of Andy Griffith on *Matlock*. In a slow, plodding southern drawl, he began by saying, "I have to confess to you, after doing this for thirty-five years, I have spoken to many juries now and every time, I feel exactly the same way—very nervous. I have a very important role to play at this moment and I recognize that role. My job at this point is to help you to understand what it is that you are about to hear in this case."

Gaskins said that the story was about "three primary participants. The first of those is Grant Hayes. Grant Hayes is the classic sociopath. On the one hand, he is very talented— he's a talented musician, he is very charming, he is very witty, he is very charismatic, he is very intelligent. But on the other hand, he is also very controlling, he is very manipulative, he is very deceitful, he is very dishonest, and most of all, he is very dangerous. He's already been tried in this case and has been convicted for the first degree murder of Laura Ackerson and for that he is serving life in prison without parole."

The defense attorney pointed to the movie *The Talented Mr. Ripley* and explained that Grant identified with the main character. "That's the sociopath that Grant Hayes believed himself to be.

"There are two victims in this case. One is Laura Ackerson. Laura believed that she was married to Grant. Grant had even deceived her about that. . . . She found out much later, it was not true, it was a trick. In the meantime, they had the two boys, little Grant and Gentle."

Gaskins pointed out that as the custody date hearing neared, "Dr. Calloway had provided Grant with a copy of her report and her recommendations in it and he wasn't happy with that at all. Now, as the time for that hearing approached, Grant and Laura were becoming more and more hostile to each other. The arguments were becoming more frequent. Amanda was playing the role of the peacekeeper. She tried to convince both of them that 'the two of you need to get along, if not for yourselves than for the sake of your children. You need to try to put your differences aside and work this out in a way that best benefits little Grant and Gentle.'

"Now, the second victim in this case is Amanda. You'll find that throughout the evidence that you will hear that there are enormous parallels in how Grant treated Laura and how he treated Amanda. How he manipulated both of them, how he controlled both of them, how he lied to both of them, how he deceived both of them, he treated them the same. Grant saw women as people who needed to be controlled by him. They needed to be submissive to him.

"Now, Amanda was living in St. John in the Virgin

Islands. . . . At the time that Grant met her in St. John, she had $188,000 at her immediate disposal. She had $77,000 worth of jewelry. Grant had nothing. What he saw was the opportunity to maneuver himself into Amanda's life so that he could get her money. . . . They got married in April of 2010. . . . By the end of 2010, seven, eight months later, Grant had all the money. He had sold the jewelry. He was off traveling around the country, at least doing musical gigs or pretending to do musical gigs—we don't know which. And Amanda was the one who was left at home with the two boys. And then by July 2011, she had a baby of her own.

"Grant had managed to isolate her. He had her in the home and he was out gallivanting around the country spending her money. By July of 2011, she was broke. . . . And she and Grant were about to be evicted from the apartment that they shared in Raleigh. The plan at that time was that they'd move in with his parents, who lived in Kinston. There was nowhere else to go.

"So what happened on July 13, 2011?" Gaskins asked. "Arrangements had been made for Laura to come to Raleigh to take the boys to Monkey Joe's . . . but she was running late. . . . At Grant's request, she came to the apartment where Grant and Amanda lived together. What Grant wanted to do was discuss a financial resolution of the custody dispute. But she didn't want little Grant and Gentle to hear him talking about the children in terms of money. So he asked Amanda to take the boys into the bedroom while he talked to Laura at the kitchen table. Laura and Grant sat at the kitchen table and worked out an agreement. . . . It provided that Grant would pay her twenty-five thousand dollars and she would drop the custody suit but could have visitation whenever she wanted with little Grant and Gentle."

Then Gaskins offered up a completely new version of what happened that night. "Amanda was still in the bedroom—she was back in the bedroom with Lily, her now one-month-old little daughter and the two little boys. She came out of the bedroom, walked over to the table and saw the two of them—Grant and Laura—writing out this settlement agreement. Laura asked her if she could hold Lily and Amanda simply turned around and walked away. . . . Laura came up behind her and tripped over the rug and when she did, she bumped into Amanda's back and Amanda called out for Grant. Grant grabbed Laura from the back, in an effort to pull her away, and when he did, Grant—the two of them, Grant and Laura—tripped and fell to the floor.

"Amanda continued on into the bedroom. A few minutes later, Grant . . . told her he was going to have to call EMS to come attend to Laura and he would help her into the bathroom while Amanda took Lily and the boys out of the house—take [them] for a ride, have dinner, or whatever, while EMS took care of Laura," Gaskins said, so she left with the children. When they returned, "Amanda asked Grant, 'Where is Laura?' And what he tells her is: 'As it turns out, everything was fine. She's okay. She's left. She's gone back to Kinston.'

"Amanda went to bed believing that everything was fine. There was nothing to indicate that anything bad had happened. She believed that Laura was back home. She goes to bed and Grant leaves—leaves the apartment at some time around midnight. . . . We have tracked Grant's movement during that three-day period. . . . We can tell you with a great deal of precision where we think he killed Laura. We can also tell you . . . where we think he dismembered her body. Amanda had absolutely nothing to do with it," Gaskins insisted. "She did not know that Laura had been killed. She did not know that Laura had not returned home just as Grant had told her. He concealed everything that he did . . . from her for the next three days."

Grant was the one who wanted to go to Texas, Gaskins said. "He comes up with the idea that: 'Let's go see your sister in Texas. Your mother died. You were pregnant at the time that she died. And you never got a chance to go back and see her while all of this was going on. This would be a good time to go see her. We're moving this weekend, so we can rent a U-Haul trailer and on the trip, what we can do, is take a piece of furniture that we have in storage and give it to Karen,' her sister in Texas."

Amanda, still oblivious, agrees, Gaskins says. "Unknown to Amanda, Grant has been out doing some very, very bad things. He has killed Laura. He has dismembered her body. He's bought coolers. He's bought chain saws. He's bought ice. . . . Unknown to Amanda, Laura's body is concealed in the back of that U-Haul trailer, hid behind furniture that totally concealed what's behind it. They get to Texas. . . . Monday night, July the eighteenth, Amanda sees Grant pacing around the front yard. He's acting very upset and very nervous. And she goes out in the front yard and asks him what's going on. And he tells her that when Laura fell in that apartment and she hit her head and she died, it was an accident. It wasn't intended to happen that way. 'She died and it was an accident and you have got to help me convince your sister to help me dispose of her body. And if you don't do it, none of us are getting out of here alive. And if I can't do it, then I can get it done with one telephone call.' And he pulls out a machete—and I'm sure all of you know what a machete is. It's a knife about this big," Gaskins said, spreading his arms wide. "And he whacks [Amanda] across the leg with it and he says, . . . 'You've got to tell your sister that you're the one who knocked Laura down accidentally and caused her death. Karen will never help me—a black man from North Carolina.'

"The next morning, Amanda tells it to Karen just the way that Grant has told her to tell it—that she knocked Laura down and she hurt her badly and that her body is in the back of the U-Haul, but Karen—Karen's older than Amanda and had raised her. Karen sat Amanda down and said, '. . . Are you covering for Grant?' And she nodded her head affirmatively that she was, in fact, covering for Grant.

"Amanda did help Grant dispose of Laura's body in Texas. But she only did it because of fear of what would happen to her and to the children if she didn't help. Now, Amanda is charged with two different offenses here. She's charged with first degree murder, which, as you know, is the premeditated, deliberate murder of another person. The evidence will show that she had absolutely nothing to do with killing Laura—not a single thing. . . . The second offense that Amanda is charged with is being an accessory after the fact to a homicide that Grant committed by killing Laura. The state alleges in that indictment that Grant, not Amanda, killed Laura. And what Amanda did was to somehow assist Grant with the disposal of the body when she was in Texas. The two offenses are diametrically opposed to each other. On the one hand they say she committed first degree murder. On the other hand, they say that Grant committed the murder but she voluntarily helped dispose of the body in Texas."

The defense attorney argued that once the jury heard the evidence, they would "conclude that Grant the sociopath . . . the master manipulator, the professional liar, a man who has been convicted of first degree murder . . ." was who had committed the crime. "We believe the evidence that you hear from this witness stand will convince you that Amanda did not participate in any way in Laura's death. The question that you will be called upon to decide is whether she voluntarily participated in concealing what Grant had done."

CHAPTER FORTY-ONE

TESTIMONY in the trial began that same afternoon with the state calling Chevon Mathes, Laura Ackerson's business partner and friend, to the witness stand. Just as in the earlier trial, Chevon broke down in tears when she read aloud the e-mails she had sent before she knew Laura was dead. The defense followed up by focusing on any negative comments Laura had made about Grant's lies and her fear of him.

The next witness was Detective James Gwartney from the Kinston police, who had begun the investigation into the disappearance of the young mother before turning it over to the Raleigh police investigators. Gwartney's cross-examination began on the second day of the trial, but consisted largely of questions that Gwartney couldn't answer about Grant Hayes, drug dealers and covering digital trails.

Special Agent Lolita Chapman of the State Bureau of Investigation followed the Kinston investigator to the stand. Like Gwartney, she had only been involved in the case for the first couple of days. She told the jury about her role in searching and interviews.

Prompted by the prosecutor, Chapman read selected passages mentioning Amanda Hayes from Laura's phone call log and her journal, demonstrating that, contrary to the defense's opening statement, there was friction and hostility between the two women. There were multiple instances of Amanda calling Laura psycho-crazy. In response, the defense attempted to show that particular epithet was something that Amanda got directly from Grant.

Raleigh Police Sergeant Dana Suggs explained his role in locating and securing Laura's Ford Focus near Grant and Amanda Hayes's apartment. On cross-examination, defense attorney Johnny Gaskins asked, "If that vehicle had been two or three miles away, that would have indicated that someone had to assist with moving that vehicle, wouldn't it?"

"That's possible, yes," Suggs said.

Randy Jenkins, the owner/manager of Bill's Grill, told the jury about his encounter with Laura on the last day of her life. The defense asked if Laura mentioned that she was supposed to be in Raleigh at three.

"No," Randy said. "She said she was going to Raleigh after our meeting."

"I gather she was alone?" Gaskins asked.

"Yes."

Laura's artist friend, Oksana Samarsky, gave her testimony about Laura just the same as she had in the first trial. She told the jurors that the first time they met, Laura had her boys with her.

"How was Laura with her children?" prosecutor Boz Zellinger asked.

Oksana's face brightened. "She made me smile. She really made me want to have kids someday. . . . She was very bubbly and full of life when she was around them and they were, too. They just loved her to death."

On cross-examination, Gaskins asked if Laura ever mentioned Amanda, and Oksana said that she had not. "Did Laura speak to you about Grant Hayes?"

"Not much," Oksana said. "I didn't even know his last name. She mentioned she had custody issues with him but I really don't know that much."

DETECTIVE Amanda Salmon again delivered the story of her part in the investigation of the homicide. She testified about finding an Apple Store receipt in Grant and Amanda's apartment. Gaskins asked her if Grant paid cash for that purchase. She said he did. Then the defense attorney pressed her on the payments on other receipts but she said that she had not seen any of the others.

Lauren Harris, Grant's friend and one-time manager of Monkey Joe's, stepped forward next. She offered the same information as in Grant's trial.

Heidi Schumacher, Laura's best friend, had briefer testimony, since the state did not ask her about Grant's physical violence toward Laura or the threats made to both of them. But on cross, the defense broached the subject from the first question.

"Were you involved in an incident when Grant attacked Laura?" Gaskins asked Heidi.

"Yes, that was when they were living on Mitchell Mill Road right before little Grant was born."

When the defense pressed her for details, she gave them, but Heidi seemed hesitant to volunteer any information that would draw attention away from Amanda's culpability. Gaskins then provided her with a copy of the parenting report that Laura had prepared for Dr. Ginger Calloway. Once he confirmed that Heidi had proofread the document for her friend, he had her read aloud many of the responses from Laura's sixty-page parental history.

"Grant had very harsh views on the value of women and sex," Laura wrote. "He used sex as a tool to punish and mold my behavior instead of as a way to show affection. If he continues to behave like this, I think it will continue to cause chaos in any relationship. Also, the belief system Grant holds with regard to women will ultimately be passed along to Grant IV and Gentle. I think this will give them lower self-esteem and chaos in their adult relationships. . . . Grant III told me that he was molested as a child. That he has had sex with over two hundred women. He also told me he had sex with his aunt. He showed no disturbance over this. This disturbs me. I don't want our children to think that this is acceptable."

Talking about Amanda, Laura wrote: "I think he married her for several reasons that I don't believe she is aware of yet. Grant III has convinced Amanda that I am crazy and he urgently needs her help saving the children from me. I hear these things had prompted her to marry him very quickly and to stand behind him when he boldly lies to the court. . . . Now because they are married, Grant III has the ability to take Amanda to court for alimony when they divorce."

Laura went on to contend that Grant spoke to her about getting control of Amanda's money and made it clear "I would lose our court case and he would win because in the court system, the one with the most money wins."

Heidi also read aloud Laura's statement about Grant's belief in the imminent demise of the American government and his comment that "the children won't stand a chance with a poor, crazy, weak, white trash woman like me."

Gaskins wrapped up Heidi's reading of the document after more than an hour with Laura's summary of the situation. "Grant III has told his parents he wishes I was dead. . . . Grant III want me out of the picture so that I cannot interfere in the lives of our children. He wants to raise them to be . . . his '401K plan' or 'retirement plan' and his 'empire.' He wants me out of his life so that I cannot interfere with his new wife."

On re-direct, ADA Boz Zellinger had Heidi read a few lines about Amanda Hayes that the defense had not highlighted. "This would also explain her uncalled-for hostile attitude towards me. Please note that I wrote her a thank-you note for everything she'd done for my family and when she bought me a plane ticket to come get Grant IV in March 2010. I have maintained that attitude with her at all times."

AMANDA'S daughter Sha Guddat (nee Elmer) once said, "I would have rather buried my mother than go to her murder trial." But there she was, stepping up as a witness. She began telling the story of her life with Amanda and how her mother met Grant. Sha explained that, although she worked for Grant booking gigs through Rare Breed Entertainment, she was never paid by him. She got any spending money she needed from her mother.

On cross, Sha told the jury about the sad state of economic affairs in her mother's household that had placed them on the verge of eviction. Blaming the financial problems on her stepfather, she said that Grant was "very talented when he could focus, but he couldn't focus on anything for more than five minutes. He couldn't finish anything he'd started. He'd have ten projects going at once and never finish any of them."

She read a short passage from "Broomstick Rider," the song Grant had written about Laura, and which Sha had turned over to the police. In retrospect, she recognized that lines like "I have intentions on killing you" and "My bullets will get you soon" were incredible indications of Grant's premeditation.

"You made references to how you tried to contact your mother after she left to visit her sister in Texas?" defense attorney Gaskins asked.

"Yes."

"Grant was constantly trying to prevent you from having conversations, in fact, with your mother, wasn't he?"

"Yes."

"He didn't want you talking to her on the telephone, did he?"

"No."

On re-direct, Boz Zellinger zeroed in on that latter point. "You talked with your mother during that time period, didn't you?"

"Yes."

"And did you hear the phone taken out of her hand and turned off immediately?"

"No."

"And you talked to her several times during that week, didn't you?"

"I did briefly."

Then, Zellinger got clarification from Sha that when the police searched the apartment, they were working a missing persons case. On the other hand, when she later found the reciprocating saw manual, the body parts had been found in Texas.

THE next witness was Raleigh Police Detective Keith Heckman of the technical unit. He repeated his previous testimony about the location and activity on cell phones of Laura Ackerson on the last day of her life and on those of Amanda and Grant while in Richmond, Texas.

On cross, Gaskins asked him to call a phone number from the old 2011 records to see who answered. The prosecutors objected. The judge asked, "Call it now? In 2014?"

When Gaskins said, "Yes," the judge sustained the objection.

Gaskins launched again into his contention that the phone records proved that Grant was a drug dealer. But Heckman countered a lot of the statements the attorney attempted to establish as facts and gave him no satisfaction.

The state called Sha's husband, Matt Guddat, to the witness stand. He spoke of his first meetings with Amanda, on Mother's Day 2011, and with Grant, on Sha's birthday on June 7, 2011. He answered questions about Sha's irritation with Amanda pushing her around and said that he'd only been in Grant and Amanda's apartment on one occasion, when they all went out to dinner together for Sha's birthday. He said he used the hall bathroom at that time and it had a black shower curtain and toilet seat cover.

On cross-examination, Matt said that Grant had not been with them on Mother's Day because he'd been in Hawaii. On Sha's birthday, Grant had dropped Amanda off at the restaurant but had not stayed for dinner.

PATSY Dwyer, facility manager for the Raleigh U-Haul, a voice not heard in Grant's trial, now stepped up to testify. She told the jurors that Grant said he was going on a fishing trip with his family and wanted plastic to secure the coolers of fish bait and keep them from overturning in the van.

Patsy said that she was used to people coming in very stressed, but Grant was different: "He was glassy-eyed as if sleep-deprived" or "punch-drunk," she recalled. Grant, she said, talked about Jimi Hendrix and "Purple Haze" and told her he'd been up all night playing music with his friends.

When Grant asked to call his wife to make sure he wasn't forgetting anything they needed, Patsy handed him her phone. When he finished, he asked her for a plastic drop cloth.

Gaskins tried to get Patsy to admit that Grant had also purchased moving blankets in her store. However, she insisted that she couldn't remember. He showed her a photograph of the transported piece of furniture, and although she admitted that the blankets it was wrapped in looked like the ones sold by U-Haul, she wasn't certain that they were hers.

THE next witness, Susan Dufur of Wal-Mart, gave a repeat performance of her testimony in the earlier trial, complete with a replaying of the store security video.

RALEIGH Police Detective Dexter Gill, looking like a worried, anxious Jeb Bush, stepped into the box next. He was the one who'd received the call that the Kinston missing person case had ties to Raleigh.

He told the jurors of his trip to Texas with Detective Robert Latour and the interview with Karen Berry. Then he introduced a number of pieces of evidence, including the coolers, the Motel 6 receipt in the name of Amanda

Smith, the khaki green suitcase and the towels from the shed.

Then Gill talked about bringing back the large piece of furniture, Karen's computer, and the body parts found on the first day of the search. Gaskins elicited nothing revealing on cross-examination.

DETECTIVE David Moore of the financial crimes unit told the jurors that he had prepared the cell phone–analysis report using Grant's actual phone rather than cell provider records. He read text messages from Grant to Laura and to Lauren Harris, as well as one from Laura to Grant.

On cross, defense attorney Gaskins took Moore to the phone calls between Grant and Amanda, trying to get him to say that they were proof that the two were in different locations when they occurred. When Moore would not cooperate, Gaskins asked, "Can't you know where the two phones are from triangulation?"

"I don't know, sir. I don't do that."

THE final witness in the fourth day of the trial was Raleigh Police Detective Zeke Morse, sporting a multicolored bow tie. He had participated in the search of the elder Hayeses' home and the canvas around Grant and Amanda's apartment, and had followed up on dozens of small details in the investigation. One of the pieces of information he'd sought was whether or not there was a GPS built into the

Durango. There was, but he found out that it wouldn't have begun collecting data unless an air bag had been deployed.

Gaskins focused on the canvas when he asked his questions. "Did you have anyone that lives near that apartment of Amanda and Grant . . . reporting they heard a Skil saw running on the night of July 13, 2011?"

"Of the people I spoke to, no."

"Did anyone report anything unusual at that apartment on the night of July 13, 2011?"

"Again, of the people I spoke to, no."

TESTIMONY ended for the day, allowing time for the state to present a request to the judge. The problem at hand was the johnboat taken into evidence. Prosecutor Boz Zellinger said that it won't fit in the elevator so they could not bring it into the courtroom. They wanted the jurors to go downstairs to view the close quarters the boat offered when packed with four coolers and two people.

The defense objected, claiming that the same result could be achieved by showing photographs to the panel. After some back and forth and a moment for contemplation, Judge Stephens asked Gaskins, "What is your objection?"

"Whatever," the defense attorney responded. "If they want to look at the boat, we'll look at the boat."

CHAPTER FORTY-TWO

THE fifth day of the trial opened on Monday, February 3, 2014, with Kim Oreskovich of the Fort Bend County Sheriff's Office on the witness stand. She explained to the jurors what she had done for the investigation in and on the banks of Oyster Creek, including the collection of body parts. She introduced photographs and other evidence, including the four pair of women's panties found in the khaki suitcase and a hair found in one of the coolers, though one that was never tied to Grant, Amanda or Laura.

Defense attorney Johnny Gaskins retrieved the machete from the evidence trove, handed it to her and asked her to hold it up. When she lifted it in the air, he asked, "That's not something you'd allow anyone to strike you with, is it?"

Oreskovich flashed him an incredulous look and said, "No."

Gaskins then went into a rambling series of questions

about blood testing that didn't seem to go anywhere. When he finished, Assistant District Attorney Boz Zellinger clarified some possible points of confusion that Gaskins had stirred up with his queries.

The state next called Detective Brad Wichard with the homicide and robbery division at Fort Bend County. He presented photographs of the johnboat and its contents, namely an old red coffee canister and a small pile of ropes and chains.

The jury then took a field trip downstairs to parking level B1. They walked around the boat and looked at it, out of sight of the media cameras. In less than ten minutes, they returned to the courtroom.

Wichard told the jury about how he aided the investigation in July, shipping Laura's remains to North Carolina, and reported on the finding of a portion of a leg on August 11, 2011, during the cleaning of the water gates under a bridge.

Gaskins said, "There isn't room on that boat for four large coolers and two adults, is there?"

"Yes."

"You think there is?"

"Yes."

"Well, as I'm looking at the boat, I see two seats . . . correct?"

"Right."

"Between the two seats, how much space do we have?"

"I'd give an estimate of three feet."

"In front of the first seat, how much room do you have?"

"A little less, probably two and a half . . . from front to back. I'd have to measure to give you an exact number."

"What are the dimensions of a one-hundred-and-twenty-quart cooler, do you know?"

"I would give you an estimate of approximately one and a half by three feet."

"Well . . . we have two one-hundred-and-twenty-quart coolers and two seventy-five-quart coolers, right?"

Wichard quibbled over his knowledge of this fact, only admitting that he had been told that Amanda and Grant transported two of the coolers back to North Carolina. "I was not made aware of, nor do I have knowledge of, the size of those two coolers."

"Okay. My point was . . . was there room for those?"

"Well, if there's room for two, there's room for four, 'cause you can stack one cooler on top of the other cooler."

Gaskins peppered him with queries trying to get the witness to tell the jurors that the boat would not be stable or that it would be too crowded. Wichard brought an end to that line of questioning when he said, "I can say this from my own experience. I've gone fishing on a boat that size with three grown men and one large cooler, with a motor on it and gas and with a battery for the motor for a long while. And I'll say, yes, it can be done if you're not on rough water. That's what I'm basing my opinion on."

FORENSIC chemist Timothy Suggs, who had tested soil samples from the hog pen, was the next witness for the prosecution. He determined that two of the samples were strongly acidic and demonstrated the presence of chloride—qualities consistent with muriatic acid.

Houston Police Department dive team member Brian Davis repeated his testimony from the trial of the first defendant. He described the methodology used to search for and find additional body parts on the second day of the exploration of Oyster Creek.

Another witness, Raymond Boyer of the Home Depot in Katy, Texas, recounted Grant's trip to his store to purchase muriatic acid and Raymond's attempts to dissuade him. The only difference from his earlier testimony occurred during the cross-examination, when Gaskins established that Grant had purchased only one pair of gloves.

Forensic Odontologist Dr. Paul Stimson again told jurors about the examination of the skull and the dental records that provided a positive identification of the victim as Laura Ackerson.

Galveston County forensic pathologist Dr. Nobby Mambo again delivered testimony of what he had done that contradicted what Dr. Deborah Radisch found when she received the remains of Laura Ackerson. Gaskins led the doctor to admit that the trauma on Laura's skull could have been the result of a fall. Zellinger, on re-direct, made it clear that the injury to the skull was not fatal and Laura's death was a homicide by undetermined means.

A quick succession of reruns from Grant's trial took the stand without offering any different or new information. Raleigh Police Officer Kevin Crocker and Detective Thomas Ouellette recounted their participation in the investigation;

Mark Herbert, the truck driver for Waste Services testified about the trash pickup; and Raleigh Detective Brian Hall introduced the video of Amanda's July 13, 2011, trip to Chick-fil-A. The state also used that last witness to emphasize the fact that the packaging for two pairs of kitchen gloves and two respirator masks had been found in the search, as well as two masks and two pairs of blue gloves.

Gaskins followed up with a series of questions about financial transactions, videos and evidence that elicited nothing more from Hall than "I am not familiar with that," "I was not involved in that process," "I do not have an independent recollection of that" or "I did not testify to that."

Zellinger rehabilitated his witness's credibility and professionalism with a few questions. He gave Hall the opportunity to explain to the jurors that Detective Faulk, as the lead detective, was the person who received all the evidence; that bleach destroys biological fluids; and that although the canvas found no one who had heard a reciprocating saw, it also did not find anyone who saw a body carried out of the building.

AMANDA'S sister Karen Berry walked up to the front of the courtroom, slid a back support into the chair in the witness stand, and settled down to tell her story again. The prosecutor brought her quickly to the words Amanda had spoken to her: "She told me Laura was dead and she had done it."

The defense tried to paint a more positive portrait of

their client, to the point of trying to put words in her mouth on several occasions. When Gaskins asked her why Amanda was always the one driving the Berry's vehicles, Karen said, "I wouldn't let Grant drive my car if he'd asked. Amanda was like a daughter to me. She didn't need to ask."

After a series of questions that raised objections from the state that were sustained by the judge, Gaskins asked, "Were you concerned that Amanda was in danger on the trip back to Raleigh?"

"Yes, I was."

"Explain that, if you will."

The judge interrupted, "You can ask her another question."

With a nod, Gaskins tried again. "Were you concerned about Amanda's welfare because you were concerned that Grant was the one who killed Laura?"

A voice raised in objection rang out, loud and clear, from the other side of the courtroom. The judge agreed with the state. "Sustained as to the form of that question . . ."

Gaskins plunged ahead. "Were you concerned . . ."

Judge Stephens cut him off again. "You can ask her why she was concerned."

"Okay."

"Don't tell her why she's concerned."

"Okay," Gaskins said and turned back to the witness. "Why were you concerned?"

In response, Karen explained her fear that Amanda and the children would be found dead somewhere between her house and North Carolina.

On re-direct, Boz Zellinger brought the jury's attention

back to one important moment: the time when Amanda told Karen that Laura was dead, and she was responsible. He also elicited a new nugget. Karen said that while they were sitting together on the swing, Amanda told her, "I will do anything to protect my family. Lily needs her dad."

Gaskins was not ready to give up on this witness yet. "Is Amanda someone who is easily controlled by men?"

"Objection," Zellinger bellowed.

The judge sustained and Gaskins asked a different question. "Do you recall telling the detectives that Amanda's husband Nicky Smith had been a controlling man?"

"Yes, sir."

"And do you recall telling the detectives that Amanda was someone who was easily controlled by men?"

The state objected but the judge overruled. "You can answer."

"I don't know that I said it that exact way. I think that she . . ." Karen paused to reorganize her thoughts. "I think, at times, that she was controlled by men."

The state followed Karen's testimony with that of her daughter, Amanda's niece, Kandice Rowland. She told the sea of expectant faces about her abbreviated visit with Amanda on the evening of July 19. She explained that the money she gave to her aunt that night was repayment of a loan Amanda had provided to Kandice to help pay off her student debt after graduating from college.

With disappointment etched in her face, Kandice told the jurors that Amanda was supposed to call before she left Karen's, but she hadn't. "I called her around lunchtime but didn't get an answer."

Kandice was permitted to step down without any follow-up questions from the defense.

DR. Deborah Radisch, chief medical examiner for the State of North Carolina, as always a most formidable witness, pointed out a number of inconsistencies in the testimony from her counterpart in Texas, including the fact that the cut size was actually at the C5 vertebrae—not at C6, as Dr. Nobby Mambo testified.

Radisch told the jurors about the three false starts on the leg during the dismemberment, and the intentional and violent puncture wound in the fourth cervical vertebrae, which could have been fatal. She explained the crushed cartilage in the throat was the result of another "intentional and violent" act—possibly caused by blunt force trauma or by strangulation or by stepping on a person's neck. She then repeated her ruling that Laura Ackerson had died of an undetermined homicide.

On cross, Johnny Gaskins tried to get her to establish the chronological order of the injuries but Dr. Radisch resisted, saying it was not possible. Then the defense attorney asked, "Do you have any idea of how difficult it would be to dismember a body with a reciprocating skill saw?"

The medical examiner gave him a look of amusement that spoke of her many years of sparring with defendants' lawyers. "I don't have any personal knowledge of that," she said, then continued in a more somber tone, "but I know that some of the difficult factors are actually getting to the bone through the tissue, [because] a lot of saws don't cut through tissue very well. Once you get to the bone, that's where the saw is better—on the bone, not the soft tissue. And of course, it's going to depend on which bone and where on the bone—that sort of thing."

"Would it be fair to say that using a reciprocating skill saw to dismember an individual's body would require a great deal of damage to the flesh and to the bone?"

"I think if you're only using the saw and you're trying to go through the flesh, that would leave more damage than if you first cut through the flesh and soft tissues to get to the bone."

"Say that again, please."

Radisch grinned. "Okay, just say you're using the saw and it's the only thing you have—you started from the skin and going to the bone," she said. "The tissue will catch up in that saw and it will kind of muck it up and make it more difficult. But if you understand that is going to happen, then you go get a knife and cut through that tissue and kind of create a path so that the reciprocating saw doesn't have to go through all that soft tissue, and get right to the bone."

"So if you used a knife, you wouldn't have as much debris flying about."

"Yes, that is what I think."

"If the reciprocating skill saw was used and a knife wasn't used . . . then would you . . . expect to have a great deal of bone and debris flying about, wouldn't you?"

"Well, I don't know about 'flying about.' I don't know."

"But it's causing a lot of damage to the flesh, isn't it?"

"Yes, but whether that's going to be flying about or

whether it's just going to get tangled up in this hole you're trying to create, I don't know."

"Would it be fair to say when that reciprocal saw hits on a blood vessel, there's going to be a lot of blood spray?"

"There would be blood spray, yes."

On re-direct, the state brought the focus back to the central points of the medical examiner's testimony.

Gaskins had a few more questions. "There are many ways to strangle—you can do it with your hands?"

"Yes."

"With a rope?"

"Yes."

"With a cord from an Apple computer?"

"Could be."

AGENT Mike Galloway, with the City/County Bureau of Identification, reprised his testimony from Grant Hayes's trial, telling about his role shooting photographs, obtaining swabs and fingerprints, and testing for blood. The defense had him confirm that he found no blood evidence connected to this case.

Raleigh Police Sergeant Robert Latour, a homicide detective at the time of the investigation of Laura Ackerson's murder, related his actions and findings in North Carolina and Texas. Then Latour mentioned a bit of information that never arose in Grant's trial. He said that when he contacted Wal-Mart to get information about the reciprocating saw, he learned that someone else had already requested that material: private investigator Randy Miller, who'd been hired by Amanda Hayes. That line of inquiry was shut down when the judge sustained the defense's objection.

Latour was followed in the witness stand by the environmental crimes investigator from Texas, John T. Schneider. He explained the placement and workings of the surveillance cameras set up in Fort Bend County to catch illegal dumpers. He told the jury about the one at the end of Skinner Lane and how he came to connect the photos shot there with the homicide case in Raleigh.

Senior Agent Shannon Quick with the City/County Bureau of Identification repeated her testimony from the previous trial, only adding her examination of a pair of black women's pants and a black-and-white shirt splotched with dirt and mildew that had been recovered from the Dumpster trash. Nothing of evidentiary value was found there.

Defense attorney Gaskins took the witness back to the hall bathroom in Grant and Amanda's apartment. She confirmed that the room was not totally empty. There were four bottles of shampoo and conditioner on the edge of the tub, a jar on the toilet seat lid, a roll of paper on the holder and a picture on the wall above the toilet. She admitted that she found no blood—not even in the sink or tub P traps.

The prosecution negated that questioning when Quick told the jurors that there was no test for bleach and that is why it is used in the laboratory to clean up bodily fluids from their equipment. Bleach, she said, destroys hemoglobin and DNA. In response, Gaskins brought up the testing done behind the molding in the bathroom, prompting the state to get on the record that a plastic tarp could have prevented any blood from reaching that spot. Gaskins, referring to the reciprocating Skil saw, asked, "Would you expect to find blood spatter?"

"I have never used a saw," Quick said. "I have no idea."

FBI document examiner Lindsey Dyn went through her process of determining that the two handwritings present on the twenty-five-thousand-dollar handwritten agreement were those of Grant Hayes and Laura Ackerson.

Computer forensic examiner Courtney Last talked about her review of computers owned by Laura, Karen Berry and Grant Hayes's parents, and the cell phones belonging to Grant and Amanda Hayes. During her testimony, the state played the audio of the confrontational October 29, 2010, encounter between Amanda and Laura that Laura uploaded onto her computer. It culminated with Amanda saying, "I would just as soon we would never speak again."

CHAPTER FORTY-THREE

MICROSCOPIC evidence was in the forefront at the start of the ninth day of Amanda Hayes's trial on February 7, 2014. First, forensic biologist McKenzie De-Haan testified that a swab from the linen closet in the hall bathroom, the blue latex gloves found in the trash and the coffee can from the johnboat all tested positive for blood in the lab.

Next, Jennifer Remy, a forensic examiner who had examined the trace evidence, detailed the process she employed to determine which hairs collected would be suitable for DNA analysis. Sharon Hinton, who received that evidence for further testing, found the genetic markers of Laura Ackerson intermingled with that of a male on one of the blue gloves, while others had Laura's DNA on the outside surface only. On some gloves, she found the presence of two or three separate contributors; however, none of the unknown DNA was in sufficient quantity to compare to known samples. In the case of one of those gloves—but not the others—she was able to eliminate Amanda Hayes.

Remy also described her attempt to get a DNA sample from a pair of blue jeans but ran into a typical complication. Very often, the dye used in making denim garments inhibits the amplification of the genetic material to the extent that extraction is impossible.

LAURA'S child custody attorney, John Sargeant, took the stand next. Since the estate had waived attorney-client privilege, Judge Stephens ordered him to answer the questions posed—a formality required by law. The lawyer recounted his interactions with Laura Ackerson from their first meeting in June 2010 until their final one approximately one year later.

He testified that whenever Laura was looking at an employment opportunity, dating someone or making any change in her life, she always called him first and asked if it would affect her ability to get custody of her children. When prosecutor Becky Holt asked about the possibility of Laura accepting cash in exchange for relinquishing custody, Sargeant said that they never discussed anything but Laura gaining full custody of both boys.

When defense counsel queried him about Laura's concerns for her personal safety, Sargeant said, "Yes, she did. I remember specifically on March the second, us talking about Mr. Hayes getting desperate about the evaluation, and she was concerned that Mr. Hayes may hurt her or do something to her. In fact, I know that she and Heidi Schumacher, her friend, had a deal that if something happened to either one of them that the other one was going to contact the police."

"Did she also share information with you about threats that Grant had made to other people?"

"I don't know about threats that Grant made to other people. I mean, she had shared other information about Mr. Hayes having some violent tendencies, yes."

"What violent tendencies?"

"I think she had indicated that he was violent to her when they were together. . . . He would say things like, not that he was going to do it, but he knew people who could do things to her."

"Did . . . she ever use words to the effect that 'if I can't get it done, my goons can do it'?"

"Yes, sir. He said he knew some thugs from the old days that could take care of Laura."

WITH psychologist Dr. Ginger Calloway, the state focused on the comments about Amanda that she'd made in her psychological evaluation for the child custody case. She read a few passages aloud to the jury.

"When Amanda was asked about how the family makes money, she reported, 'Grant has a little money here and there. I've sold some things and we've spent our savings on the custody evaluation.'

"When asked about working after the baby is born, Amanda said, 'No, I'm also an artist. I see myself with three little kids working on art at their little table.'"

Quoting Amanda again, Dr. Calloway read: "For Grant's protection, we didn't want to announce that we were dating. Sha and I moved to New York and we both encouraged him to move there. He said he didn't want to return to North Carolina. His only connection there was his kids." Although, Amanda wrote, he mostly missed "Grant IV. Not so much Gentle because he didn't have a bond with him."

Calloway wrapped up by reading a piece of commentary from her report: "It is concerning that although Amanda is superficially kind and attentive to the children, she does not recognize Laura's importance and centrality to the children."

The defense began their examination of the witness by questioning her about her education and credentials as if the court had not already recognized her as a forensic psychology expert. Calloway seemed a bit exasperated when she said she had received an MS in psychology from North Carolina State and Gaskins asked, "I believe you said you had a master's degree, too, is that right?" She explained that it was the same thing. When he asked about the additional training she had after she received her PhD, she very nearly rolled her eyes. "If you look at my curriculum vitae," which she knew he had in his possession, "you will see all the courses and workshops I attended."

Gaskins then asked if Calloway was familiar with antisocial behavior, and she responded, "Do you mean antisocial personality disorder?"

He admitted that he did, then pulled out a copy of the *Diagnostic and Statistical Manual of Mental Disorders*, published in 2000, and asked her to read three pages to herself to refresh her memory. After she'd done so, he asked her to read several passages from her evaluation report.

She started with: "Grant Hayes is an attractive thirty-two-year-old African-American man of short stature with a bald, shaved head, long fingernails, and relaxed manner. He is very extroverted, charming, gregarious, witty and likable. He is jovial and verbose, was pleasant in manner and rambled extensively in interviews, frequently in a tangential or off-topic way."

Next, Gaskins pointed her to this passage: "During interviews, Grant rambled in his responses, requiring a refocus and a request to limit his verbosity. He was entertaining with his various stories and accounts of his experiences and seemed to enjoy recounting those various reports. Without limit, he seemed he could have rambled extensively for quite some time.

"Grant was extremely negative, at times, paranoid, with regard to Laura, her character and alleged actions. . . . Of great concern is the finding that he scored positive for the suicide constellation on the Rorschach and reports a history of suicidal thinking. . . . This index is not a predictor for suicide. . . . At a minimum, a positive constellation suggests that Grant has significant pathological, emotional disarray. Grant reports suicidal thinking as early as fourteen years of age, reports three significant periods of suicidal thinking, and reports extensive illegal drug use following the last episode of suicidal thinking. In testing and interviews, he looks like an individual with an underlying mood or thought disorder—one who is self-medicating with the use of chemicals or illicit drugs.

"Despite being extroverted and gregarious, Grant looks very uncomfortable with emotions," Calloway read, noting the use of "intellectualization to neutralize emotions" was a form of defense, but that "to the degree Grant is using it, the overuse of intellect to neutralize emotion can lead to delusional thinking. Reliance on this defense mechanism could also cause him to look more greatly impaired than he is. . . . Findings from testing supported by findings from some interviews indicate he seizes upon information before he has gathered all relevant pieces of a problem situation. This leads him into incorrect situations and faulty judgments. His interpretation of events, others' motives and actions, the world about him, is damaged and inaccurate relative to other adults."

The next series of questions regarded the details of Calloway's interview with Heidi Schumacher, and Heidi's belief that Grant was controlling. After that, Gaskins moved on to Dr. Calloway's recommendation that Grant see a psychiatrist for evaluation of a mood disorder or other explanations for his "illogical, disturbed thinking."

At the lawyer's request, Calloway also read Laura's note in the parenting survey: "'I am of the belief that Grant has a personality disorder. After living with him for a period of almost four years, I have found a few labels that fit him but one that is near perfect: sociopath. The others are narcissist, borderline personality and psychopath. He likens himself to the main characters in these movies: *Six Degrees of Separation* with Will Smith and *The Talented Mr. Ripley*. Grant III has told me that he is the character depicted in these movies.'"

Gaskins pressured Calloway to say that Grant Hayes fit the definition of antisocial personality disorder, and she kept insisting that determination should be left to a psychiatrist. She also pointed out that the defense attorney had provided an older version of the diagnostic manual, and that changes had been made to that section since then.

On re-direct, ADA Boz Zellinger asked, "Did you ever give the Minnesota Multiphasic Personality Inventory, parental history survey or the Rorschach—did you ever perform any of those tests on Amanda Hayes?"

"No."

"Did you have concerns about the safety of anyone in this study?"

"I was concerned about the children and recommended a guardian ad litem for them." When prompted by Zellinger about whether or not she had concerns about Grant and Amanda, Calloway read her note that, "Grant and Amanda are convinced that Laura is sick, poisons the children's minds and has some form of mental illness."

"In your report, didn't you say that these people wanted to travel the world and that this desire made it obvious that 'they did not want Laura in the children's lives'?"

"Yes, that's the sentence," Calloway agreed.

"That's not just Grant but also Amanda?"

"Yes."

"Where you talk about 'erasing Laura' that talks about Grant, Amanda and the paternal grandparents?"

"Yes, that's what it says."

Gaskins came back with one question. "And you concluded in your report with the recommendation that Grant see a psychiatrist over the question of a mood disorder or other explanations for the illogical, disturbed thinking he exhibits?"

"That's correct."

CHAPTER FORTY-FOUR

THE proceedings took a gruesome turn when forensic anthropologist Dr. Ann Ross ended the ninth day and opened up the tenth, on February 10, 2014. She told the jury about using the pig proxy, a new Skil reciprocating saw and an assortment of blades to determine what had been used to sever the bones on Laura Ackerson's body.

On cross-examination, defense attorney Johnny Gaskins first asked if flesh was removed from any of the body parts of the deceased that she had examined. All Ross could tell him with any certainty was that she had not macerated any of them.

"Do you start with a live pig?" Gaskins asked.

Ross laughed and said, "Uh, no."

"Did you use a reciprocating chain saw to cut through the flesh of the pig?"

"We removed his forelimbs and hind limbs and those were the ones we actually used."

"And you sawed through the flesh in order to get to the bone?"

"Correct."

"Did that create debris?" Gaskins asked.

Puzzled, Ross repeated the question before answering. "We did it outdoors," she said. "We did it in a field—in a research field."

"And one of the reasons you do that is because you don't want to mess up your room with whatever debris is created by the sawing of the pig proxy, right?"

"No, not necessarily. The reason we do that is because we are dealing with a large hog and the best way to carry him out is with a large truck and place him in the field and start at the field site. But we have conducted comparisons in our laboratory under our hoods."

Gaskins continued to ask questions regarding the messiness of the process, presumably to bolster the defense theory that Laura's dismemberment had not occurred in the hall bathroom.

"When you cut through the pig vessels, did it create a spray of blood?"

"No."

"Did it create a spray of tissue when you cut through the pig proxy tissue?"

"I don't recall a spray of tissue."

"Did the Skil saw jam up . . . with the flesh as you tried to cut through it?"

"Not to my recollection."

Switching direction, he asked, "Is there any way to tell what occurred first, the dismemberment or the knife wound?"

"No there is not."

Her final words were, "Dismembering a body in general is very difficult."

COURTNEY Last returned to the stand to complete her testimony from the previous Thursday and tell the jurors about her examination of Grant's and Amanda's iPods.

Gaskins began his cross by showing photos from Amanda's iPod at her sister's house on July 18, in which she looks happy and asked if she agreed with his assessment. When she did, he moved to a photo of Amanda in a motel room from July 21, and asked her if Amanda looked happy in that picture, too.

Courtney said, "Yes."

"She also looks haggard in that picture, doesn't she?"

"It's a matter of opinion. I guess."

"She looks haggard."

The judge interrupted, "Is that a question? If so, reword it."

"I withdraw the question, your honor," Gaskins replied.

DETECTIVE Jerry Faulk, the lead investigator in the case, talked about the investigation in general and then focused in on the trip Amanda made to Target on July 14, 2011, at 5:31 P.M. At that time, the defendant purchased a bottle of bleach, a pack of bath tissue, two pairs of gloves, a package of electrical tape, an eraser-scrubber and a lint roller.

At Gaskins's request, the detective read the transcript of an anonymous Crime Stoppers tip to the jury. "I played music and recorded a song with Grant Hayes in late 2007 or 2008 but quit dealing with him because he creeps me out. I only knew him about three weeks and during that time I practiced at his home a lot but felt uncomfortable because of the type of friends he had," the transcript read.

"I do not know if he had anything to do with his wife's disappearance but it is possible. I say so because one night we were drinking and we both went upstairs and while we continued drinking, he told me that he chokes people. He said that he was going to tell me something but I should promise him that I'll not tell anyone. Then he said he killed a man when he was younger and was never caught and no one knows he did it.

"I did not go back to his house from that night because I did not know what to make of what he told me. And I have not seen him since. We recorded a song but he edited me out of it and rerecorded it without my voice," the tipster said.

"Grant Hayes is creepy and had shady friends who were drug dealers, both sellers and users of cocaine. At the time, he lived in a brand-new house valued at somewhere near $600,000 and I often wondered where he got the money from to afford it.

"I will speak to a detective but I want to remain anonymous because he will know it is me if I mention I recorded with him," he said.

When Gaskins followed up, asking if Faulk had found information that Grant associated with "shady characters," the state objected. The judge said, "Shady characters? Sustained."

Gaskins substituted the word "criminals," and the detective said that they found no evidence of that. When Gaskins moved on to ask him about three specific individuals and their criminal records, Faulk said that he had talked to two of those men but did not recall seeing any reports of charges or convictions.

"Were you there when Grant was arrested?" Gaskins asked.

"No, sir."

"Were you aware that he was held in a holding cell at the Raleigh Police Department for approximately six hours?"

"We don't have any holding cells, so, no sir."

Gaskins next produced three receipts for purchases made at gas stations in the Raleigh area July 14 and 15, 2011, which he insisted proved that the body was moved far from the Hayes's apartment probably to Kinston. Detective Faulk countered that all of the gas stations also had convenience stores, meaning there was no way to know if all of those purchases were for gasoline.

After Detective Faulk stepped down, the state rested its case.

CHAPTER FORTY-FIVE

As is usual, the defense requested a dismissal on the grounds that there was insufficient evidence to sustain a first degree murder charge. Judge Stephens rejected that motion.

Defense attorney Johnny Gaskins next asked to recall Detective Jerry Faulk to read the transcript of Grant Hayes's interview while the video (which had unintelligible audio) played on the screen. The judge wanted to know if the defense planned on calling Grant as a witness. When Gaskins said they were not, the state objected and the judge asked how they can admit his words if they don't. He further explained that an interview taken ten days after the alleged offense might indicate a lot about Grant's state of mind at the time of the crime but that it would not be relevant to Amanda's.

Stephens sustained the state's objection. He told the defense team that the tape could be made part of the record but it could not be produced as evidence or referred to unless they came up with a more compelling argument for inclusion.

THE first witness for the defense was Mel Palmer, who'd been a licensed private investigator in North Carolina for more than twenty years. Continuing the disputed assumption that the gas station receipts all reflected the purchase of gasoline only, Palmer described how he'd driven the Durango to Wilson and back to Raleigh and then to Kinston once the defense had permission to search the vehicle. When he reached that town, he drove around to all of the properties listed as belonging to the Hayeses, covering 598 miles in the process.

Palmer also supported the defense theory that Grant used his answering service to make indirect contact with drug dealers. Then Gaskins brought up *The Stepford Wives* and *The Talented Mr. Ripley*, which Gaskins now wanted to play for the jury.

The state objected to wasting time watching movies. The jurors were adjourned for the day for the judge to listen to arguments from both sides. After doing so, Judge Stephens said, "We'll allow Mel Palmer to describe the movies and allow them to be entered into the record. However, the state's objection to playing the movies is sustained."

The next morning, Palmer returned to the stand and presented a written description of both movies. He then went back through the details of his December 2013 recreation of the trail the defense claimed the Dodge Durango had followed on July 14 and 15, 2011.

On cross, the state questioned the validity of the miles-per-gallon figures he'd given but Palmer sidestepped the issue by saying that he did not have the manufacturer's pamphlet. He also admitted that he had no independent knowledge of the real estate in question and only knew what the lawyer told him.

Then, Palmer said that the movie descriptions he'd read aloud were not written by him but by the attorney, or more accurately, he admitted, were both from Wikipedia entries with minor revisions. (For instance, the word "murder" in the Wikipedia version was replaced with "killing"; the phrase "young man" in first sentence had changed to "young sociopath"; and that the phrase "lie and deceive" was added by the defense.)

On re-direct, Gaskins gave Palmer the 2009 Dodge Durango manufacturer's book and Palmer corrected the testimony he'd made on cross regarding highway mileage. Then he confirmed that what he'd seen in the movies was consistent with the description he'd read on the stand.

When prosecutor Boz Zellinger was back in the fray again, he verified that the private investigator hadn't verified the report about the Hayes's rental properties. Then he acknowledged that the tax records for 2011 did not show that the property was owned by Grant's parents or by Grant or Amanda.

All in all, Palmer's testimony did not appear to do much for the defense case. The next witness, however, was the one who had to win the day.

CHAPTER FORTY-SIX

THE moment every courtroom watcher hoped would come arrived on February 11, 2014. The defendant, Amanda Smith Hayes, stepped up to the stand to testify on her own behalf. She wore a pastel pink suit with a white blouse and spoke in a very soft, childlike voice. After asking her to identify herself, the first question from her attorney Johnny Gaskins was: "Did you kill Laura Ackerson?"

"No, sir, I did not."

"Did you help Grant kill Laura Ackerson?"

"I absolutely did not."

"Were you present when Grant killed Laura Ackerson?"

"No, sir, I was not."

"Did you know Laura had died before you got to Texas?"

"No, sir."

Gaskins then took her through her childhood, eliciting a comment about her relationship with her sister Karen

Berry. "She and I have always been very, very close. She and my mother were not so close and so my mom kind of tried to prohibit me from seeing [Karen] a lot during my life growing up, which actually probably made us closer—just the defiance, you know," she said with a soft laugh.

"She definitely treated me just like her kids. You know, she has two daughters that are also in the same age range [who] I am very close to also; whenever I was growing up and she treated me—groundings and spankings—just like the rest of them."

Then Gaskins had her continue through her first three marriages and on to her stab at making it as an actress in Los Angeles. "It was awful. I hated it. I hated the industry. I didn't like the people. It was so fake and phony and it really turned me off acting," she said, also listing ageism and casting-couch issues amongst her problems with the field. "I didn't want to be involved in the industry anymore."

Gaskins then guided Amanda through the beginning of her relationship with Grant Hayes to their arrival in North Carolina and the custody battle over little Grant and Gentle. Amanda said that when they moved down to North Carolina to get custody of the boys, she did not want to go. "I felt obligated because I married him and I took that commitment very seriously."

After the move south, she said, she tried to keep everything between her and Laura polite. "Grant would get upset with me for being too nice to her. He would tell me that, whenever I was nice to her, it would make it seem like he was the problem—that they weren't able to get along. And so, he would really try to keep us from communicating."

Then Amanda launched into her version of the events of July 2011. She said that on July 12, Grant was supposed to be watching the boys while she was making dinner "but little Grant found Gentle in the hall bathroom. He had pooped in the potty chair and tried to empty it by himself and got poopy everywhere. And he had flushed a whole bunch of toilet paper in the toilet and stopped it up. It was overflowing." Grant, she said, put all of the kids' stuff in her bathroom and Amanda told him she was not going to clean up the hall bathroom.

She said on July 13, when Laura tripped and bumped into her while she was holding Lily, Grant got hold of Laura and pulled her back and told her to chill out and she started fighting him. "She kicked that little wall by the love seat and when she did, they both went over the chair and went on the floor. I just went straight into the bedroom with Lily. I didn't even stick around to see what happened. And when I got to the bedroom, little Grant was coming out the door. And he asked me what that noise was and I told him the chair fell over."

Amanda said that five minutes later, Grant came into the bedroom and told her that Laura was hurt and he needed to call for an ambulance, and he asked Amanda to take the boys out of the house so that they didn't see anything. He said that he'd take Laura into the bathroom and that Amanda should hurry up and get dressed to go out. Amanda complied, and she said that when they returned, "Grant was sitting on the sofa and the house smelled [of cigarette] smoke. We don't usually smoke in the house but I could tell he had. I sat next to him and asked him about what happened and he said everything was fine." She added that he told her to be quiet because he didn't want to talk about it in front of the kids.

When she went to Target on the afternoon of July 14, Grant called and asked her if they had any bleach because the bathroom still smelled bad. When she said they didn't, he asked her to pick some up and get a pair of gloves to clean the bathroom.

After she came home, Grant left the house. When she got up to feed Lily on Friday, July 15, Grant asked, "Would you like to go see your sister? Since we're getting ready to move, we've got a little money." Amanda explained that Grant had sold his computer on Thursday.

She said on Friday that Grant got rid of the rug under the dining room table because the boys had made it nasty from spilled drinks and dropped food. That day, Laura did not show up at the exchange in Wilson, so instead of traveling to Texas with just the baby, the boys were now going along. "Three car seats and our vehicle was plumb full." Grant suggested getting a U-Haul and taking the piece of furniture in storage to Karen. "I was afraid it was going to get ruined in storage and I wanted to bring it in the house. And, honestly, I was afraid that he would try to get me to sell it. And it was the last thing of any value I had, so whenever he suggested it I jumped on it."

Grant then went out for the night and she did not see him again until Saturday afternoon, when they all went to the storage unit with the U-Haul trailer. Then, Amanda said, Grant dropped her and the kids off at the apartment and went off again and didn't return until late that night.

"We had actually gone to bed and he had come in and told us, 'Let's go.'"

Amanda said that Grant did most the driving with the children sleeping the whole night through. Amanda took over for a bit. She got sleepy and couldn't wake Grant, so she pulled off to get a hotel. "When I pulled up, he said, 'What are you doing?' And I said, 'I'm going to get a hotel for a little while.' And he said, 'I'm just fine. I can drive.' And I said, 'Grant, I tried to wake you up and you didn't respond at all. We have three kids and it's better for us to just rest for a little while. You can take a shower or whatever.'" She said that Grant gave her cash and she got a room using her New York driver's license.

"On the way to Texas," she said, "Grant told me he had a dream that he was in a forest and that he'd killed Laura and that if I didn't help him get rid of her, I was going to be next. And I told him it's probably from all the crazy TV he watches—he watches a lot of crime shows."

"On the trip from Raleigh to Texas," Gaskins asked, "did you pass over numerous swamps and bridges and secluded places?"

"Yes, sir, many, many, many places. The ocean, bridges, swamps, yes, sir."

"On the trip to Texas, were you aware that Laura's body was in the back of the trailer?"

"No, sir, I was not—not at all."

"How many places do you estimate that you passed where her body could have been disposed of had you known she was there?"

"I don't know but I know for sure in Louisiana there

are lots and lots of swamplands. There are bridges and oceans—there's a lot, a whole lot."

Amanda said that she arrived at her sister's house at five A.M. on Monday, July 18, and they all took a nap. She said that she and Grant went to bed at the same time, but she was later awakened by a noise and saw car lights outside and Grant walking across the yard. She went outside to see what he was doing and found him emerging from the back of the trailer and he had a machete.

"We walked over to my nephew Shelton's truck and we sat down on the tailgate. And Grant lit a cigarette and . . . I told him that he should probably come in and probably try to sleep so he could get up tomorrow . . . and be around people instead of sleeping all day.

"And he told me he was trying to figure some stuff out. And I asked him 'What?' And he, well, I'll never forget it, he was smoking a cigarette and he was like really calm and he looked at me and said, 'What would you say if I told you Laura is dead?' And I was like, you know, 'What?' you know? Basically, he told me the night that Laura had come over to the house that she had died. And whenever I left, he just panicked and freaked out. And I started freaking out and I was asking him why he didn't call the cops, why he didn't call for help like he told me he was going to do. And he told me that he got scared—he was a black man with a dead white woman and no one was going to believe him that it was an accident and that he had taken her to Kinston and then he stopped himself and said that he shouldn't be telling me any of that stuff.

"And then he told me that the Kinston police had called.

I assumed they'd found Laura's body since he told me he took her to Kinston. And anyway, I was freaking out and he had the machete and he whacked me on the leg and told me to shut the eff up and that this was not the time for me to start challenging him. And he told me that I didn't understand because I had said something about the cops finding her. And he said, you know, I didn't understand."

She said that Grant told her she had to help him get rid of the body or none of them would make it back home and asked her to get Shelton to help. When she resisted, she claimed, Grant told her then Karen would have to be involved. "And I said, 'I don't trust my sister like that.' And he told me, 'Well, you better figure out how to make her trust, you know, to trust me.'

"Then he told me that the best thing he could think of was that I needed to tell her that I was the one who pushed Laura so that she would help, 'cause she certainly wasn't going to help him because he was a black guy and it was the first time she had ever met him and I better figure out how to make her help us." She added that Grant threatened her that she would never see Sha again.

"And it wasn't long and Shelton pulled up. And he got out and I started asking Shelton all sorts of questions just about his job and the vicinity. And I asked about his work because I really don't know anything about hogs and stuff like that. I just started asking him a bunch of questions and, anyway, Shelton, he's kind of an airhead, he said he was going to go in and go to bed.

"And so Grant told me we were all going to go in and

go to bed together. And so we went in and Lily's in our bed and Grant snuggled up to me and I remember being really scared and I was unsure of what to do. And so the next morning, whenever I woke up, Grant wasn't in bed with me. And when I got up, Grant and my sister were in the kitchen together. And so I told my sister that I really needed to talk to her. And she said, 'Okay.' And I said, 'It's really important. I need to talk to you right now.' And she said, 'Okay,' and asked if she could get some coffee and I said, 'Yeah.'

"And Grant's just in the kitchen and so she and I both just get a cup of coffee and we go outside and Grant follows us and she and I go to where the swing is at and Grant just goes to the driveway, which is right there . . . you can see him and he can see us. And so, I was just really scared and I just—I didn't know how to tell her. I just blurted it out and I just told her something really bad had happened and I needed her help and if she didn't want to get involved I understood.

"And I told her that Laura had come over to our house and that she and I had gotten into an argument and she had threatened to take Lily away from me and that I had shoved her and she fell. And that she was hurt really bad. I don't really recall saying that she was dead just because I was afraid to say it and, somehow or another—you know Grant's watching us and I could tell he wanted to come over—so I asked her if it was okay and he came over. Oh, and this is another thing. Whenever he and I were out there at night, he told me it was my fault that this had happened.

If I had just let [Laura] hold the baby that none of this would have ever happened. So, I remembered when talking to my sister and I kept telling her it was my fault.

"And I was crying and she kept telling me that I wouldn't be in this position if it wasn't for him and he wouldn't be in it if it wasn't for me—you know, we were in it together, at this point. And anyway . . . I was just trying to figure out how to get her to help us and she did ask if I wanted an attorney and I told her no."

Gaskins asked, "Did you tell your sister Karen what Grant told you to tell her?'

"Yes, sir, I did.'

"Did you push Laura?"

"No sir," Amanda said, shaking her head back and forth. "I never touched her."

"At some point later did Karen sit you down and talk to you about what you said?"

"The next day—a lot of stuff had happened through that day. It was very stressful. It was very, very stressful."

"Well, what happened that day?"

"Well, anyway, during this conversation with my sister and Grant—there, honestly, I don't remember exactly who said what and where—but I know something was said about the well because there's a well in the front yard. And we all got up and talked to the backyard and it was primarily my sister and Grant talking and I was just following. And I know that whenever, we go to the septic system back there and she had said she thought maybe at one point, that one of the kids might want to build a house so she didn't know for sure if it would be a good idea but she said it was out there."

Amanda said that they then borrowed her sister's car and went to the ATM for cash and to Home Depot for the muriatic acid. While there, Grant told her to call Sha to tell her to go to their apartment to meet a guy who wanted to buy the couch.

Amanda said that, after they returned, she picked up Dalton's phone and tried to dial 911 but couldn't figure out how to press Send. "When Dalton got his phone back, he said, 'Oh my god! You almost called 911.' And I just kinda made it sound like an accident. And Grant told me if I tried that again, I would never see Sha again. So from that second on, I was just scared."

She said when they returned to her sister's house, "Grant was outside a whole lot. He was on the phone the whole time. I didn't know who he was talking to. And honestly, I heard so much stuff—Grant's told me so many stories. He told me one time that Laura . . . left with little Grant whenever he was firstborn, and within an hour he had someone pick her up and brought her back and told her she wasn't leaving and taking the baby. She could leave but she wasn't taking the baby." Amanda continued telling stories about Grant killing and assaulting others—the stories that Grant often told others to appear tough and ruthless. "And I know whenever he sold a lot of drugs, he hung out with a lot of bad people. He told me about these mafia guys that owned a restaurant that he used to hang out with a lot. . . . There were a bunch of stories about different people he knew. So not only was I afraid of him but I was really fearful for Sha because I wasn't there to be able to protect her and I was scared. I was scared that he was going to have someone get her," Amanda said as she burst into sobs on the stand.

Amanda said she was trying to act normal when her niece Kandice visited on Tuesday night, "because I didn't want anyone else to be involved. I was so scared that I'd brought this guy to my family. I wanted to get him away from my family. I was scared because of the kids."

While she was talking to Kandice, Grant said he needed Amanda and she joined him outside. Grant told her the acid wasn't working and to see if they could use the boat across the street. He also said he was thirsty. Amanda went back inside, retrieved two bottles of water and got the key to unlock the boat, a long-sleeved shirt and a pair of sweatpants from her sister.

She said when she got out to the johnboat, there was black plastic over what was in it. She helped Grant push the boat into the water and sat down in the rear, facing out. They started paddling backward to turn around and they started taking on water. Amanda told the jury that she'd grabbed a coffee can and started bailing.

At this point, Amanda hung her head and held tissues in front of her eyes as the sound of sobbing and sniffling filled the courtroom.

She described feeling scared of the dark, the unfamiliar terrain and the unknown animals. She also claimed she wasn't facing Grant as he did whatever he did, which "seemed like it took forever. We headed back and I was scared we couldn't find where to go back to shore. As soon as we got to the dock, he told me to give him my clothes. I still had my shorts on underneath."

She said she handed him her borrowed shirt and pants and got his permission to go back to the kids. "As soon as I walked in, my sister had to leave," Amanda said but noted that when Karen came back, Grant tossed all their stuff in a nearby apartment building's Dumpster, "and he asked for my shoes and he threw them away too."

"Did you ever see Laura's body?" Gaskins asked.

"No, I didn't," Amanda said, shaking her head.

"During any time, did you?"

"No. The last time I saw her was when she fell. When I came back out, she was already in the bathroom. I never saw her ever. Whenever we got to the boat, it was all covered up. Honestly, I didn't even know there was a middle seat until we saw the boat the other day," Amanda stated.

"That night, he started cleaning everything up. I was trying to keep the kids calm and my sister was freaked out. I could tell she wanted me to go and I couldn't blame her," Amanda said. She went to get some provisions for the drive home, and Grant told her to toss the acid while she was out. "I was afraid to throw it out at the apartment Dumpster 'cause I didn't know if it was flammable or explosive. So I got the idea to throw it in the bushes."

Talking about Grant, she apparently had forgotten that law enforcement found Grant's machete in Texas because she said, "He was really paranoid driving to Raleigh. He had the machete with him the whole time and he had the other knife that he always took with him to the club. . . . One time on the road, when Lily was crying, he told me, 'If you don't shut her up. I'm going to throw her out of the car.' . . . And when we hit the North Carolina state line, he was crazy. He wouldn't get out anywhere. He wore one of the kids' hats and sunglasses.

"I prayed to God to keep us safe the whole way. He wouldn't let me talk to Sha. When she called, he answered and said it was against his better judgment but he'd let us talk for a minute. Sha was mad because I wasn't telling her what was going on but I wanted to protect her.

"When we got near Kinston, we got a hotel room. Grant asked where the meds were from my C-section and I told him I'd left them at my sister's and he got mad. He said, 'We could have all just gone to sleep.' . . . He was afraid to go to his parents' house because he had an aunt next door and he didn't trust her."

Amanda said that she kept trying to be normal, because "I didn't want to scare the boys. I knew it was closing in and I was scared. Once we got to Grant's parents' house, I wanted Sha to come to me because I wanted her to take Lily. But she wouldn't come because I wouldn't tell her anything—I couldn't.

"Friday, I asked him if he trusted his dad enough to tell him. Grant said, 'No. If you tell anyone, I'll slit your throat.'"

Gaskins asked his client, "Did Grant write you a letter from the Wake County Detention Center after he was arrested?"

"Yes, sir."

Gaskins handed her the letter and the envelope. In the return-address portion, he had written the name "Sharon Clay" but Amanda recognized his handwriting. Gaskins asked her to read it to the jury.

Amanda opened the letter and read. It started with a dense joke and then referenced "her love child" in a way that did not make it clear if he was referring to Sha or Lily. He told her she had some homework and that she needed to write everything down. Then he wrote another disjointed comment: "You and your beau are getting raped right now. Hell what do I know—I'm just saying what it looks like but for all I know GrantHaze.com is taking in millions of ninety-nine cent downloads and y'all will come out of this shit rich as fuck. Yo, stranger things have happened in these here Americas—from a nude beach in Jamaica with Nicky to strip searches in North Carolina with Haze. . . . Remember your friends, bitch, or else I'm coming after your ass sideways, karate style." After mentioning the hive mentality of bees and ants, he wrote: "It's all the same for us big birds—consciousness is all connected—bowling balls in a trampoline, we are the lens of self."

He rambled on with that point and wrote, "You're good people, Mama and the good thing about it is the seeds you planted in the rain will see to the fruit. Always does. So chillax." He continued on urging her to keep writing in her journal and then wrapped up with another comment from out of the blue. "Fucking Obama health care, my ass, just make it rain, niggah. Peace and I'm out. I'm thinking about psycho-cybernetics for Grant. I know you have the book in your collection, do you recommend it?"

When she finished, Gaskins asked a few more questions about finances and the property owned by Grant's family. Then it was time for Amanda to face prosecutor Becky Holt.

CHAPTER FORTY-SEVEN

AMANDA Hayes started out her cross-examination looking confident, her innocent face and sweet voice totally intact. She didn't flinch when Assistant District Attorney Becky Holt asked, "Did you yourself take pieces of Laura Ackerson and start throwing them into the water?"

"Ma'am, I never saw anything."

Amanda answered the state's questions, telling the jury about the boat rocking and her exhortations to Grant to be still or he would capsize the boat. While all the while, Amanda said, she was paddling and bailing simultaneously.

"What were you doing out on that boat that night? What was your plan?" Holt asked.

"I didn't have a plan. I was just doing whatever he told me to do."

"Miss Hayes, isn't it true when you were out on the boat, you were taking Laura Ackerson's remains . . ."

"Ma'am, I never saw anything."

"Wait till I finish the question before you start answering. Isn't it true that you were taking Laura Ackerson's remains, which included her torso and her head and parts of her leg, and throwing them over the side of the boat?"

"Again," Amanda said in a sugary sweet voice, "I never saw anything that was going on behind me."

"You're saying you were in the back of the boat and you didn't see anything going on behind you?"

"I was facing toward the water. That is correct."

"Well, what could you hear? What could you smell?"

"I heard the animals and, honestly, I didn't smell anything."

"Don't you remember saying on a previous occasion, it smelled so bad it was making your stomach roil?"

"No, ma'am, I don't recall that."

"You testified earlier that, that Monday night, Shelton had come home and you started talking with him about his business. You talked to him about wild pigs?"

"Yes, ma'am."

"You talked with him about whether they would eat human remains?"

"Yes, ma'am, I did."

"You talked with him about alligators?"

"Yes, ma'am."

"You talked with him about whether alligators would eat human remains?"

"I don't remember exactly the entire conversation but, yes, to generalize, yes, I was asking him different questions. I had just found out and he was my first source and I was just asking him because if anyone knew, he would, at this point."

"So let me get this straight: you just found out according to your testimony . . . that Laura Ackerson was with you there in Texas . . . and you needed to dispose of her body?"

"Yes, ma'am, that's correct."

"And your response to that is to wait until your nephew got there and ask him if wild pigs ate human remains, if alligators ate human remains? What did he tell you? Did he tell you whether or not wild pigs will eat human remains?"

"Yes, ma'am, he did say that wild pigs would eat anything. Yes, ma'am, he did."

"Did he tell you that alligators would eat human remains?"

"I don't really recall what he said about the alligators and remains, honestly. I know my sister told me before that they did go alligator hunting and I don't really recall. But she said that they had gone over into that area."

"You knew there were alligators in that area before you got in the Dodge Durango and traveled across the country to your sister's house, didn't you?"

"Yes, ma'am," Amanda replied, but insisted "that is not at all why I was going to my sister's."

Becky Holt then switched over to Amanda's conversation with her sister Karen Berry. "And your testimony is that on the morning of the nineteenth, you told your sister . . . that Laura was dead?"

"Yes, ma'am, that's correct."

"At that time, you told her that you had done it."

"Yes, ma'am, that's correct."

"And you asked for her help to help get rid of Laura's remains?"

"Yes, ma'am. Can I explain?"

"Sure," Holt answered.

"I was doing that because Grant told me we needed to tell her that. It was not my idea to tell her, it was his idea for me to tell her and what to tell her because he felt that was the only way she was going to help us. And at that point, that was the only solution that he had."

"And did she help you?"

"Very basically."

"And she helped at that point by showing you the hog pen?"

"She helped by keeping the children safe."

Holt asked Amanda in an incredulous tone of voice about her story regarding the septic system, with Amanda painting herself as someone who was just following Grant and Karen around without a thought in her head.

Then Holt asked, "Okay, tell me how this happens. When you say, 'We want to get rid of a body, how do we do it?' How did you end up at the hog pen?"

"I honestly don't have an answer for that question. I mean, I was just following them. We were just kind of brainstorming. I don't think there was much rational thinking at this point at all, from anybody."

"What I'm trying to understand, Ms. Hayes, and ask you about is, you've indicated that you go to your sister and say, 'I have brought you the body of the mother of these two boys that I brought to your house. I need help disposing of this body,' and you all being a brainstorming session to come up with solutions and ideas?"

"Well, first of all, I did not intentionally take a dead body to my sister's house. It was a position I was put in involuntarily, totally against my will. I would have never, ever, ever in a gazillion years done such a thing—ever."

"You would have never taken a body to your sister's house to dispose of . . ."

"Never."

"And yet, when you were asked to help get rid of a body, your response is to set down and, first of all, ask your nephew for ideas about alligators and wild pigs and then to talk to your sister about throwing her into a septic, going to a hog pen and doing something?"

"Honestly, ma'am, I wasn't really asking, I was told . . ."

"Told what?"

"He told me I had to help him."

"When you were going through the brainstorming session with your sister and Grant Hayes, at some point, you all settled on acid?"

"I think that Grant came up with that idea and we let him go with it. We weren't going to argue, dispute with him or anything anymore."

"And what was the acid idea?"

"Honestly, I don't know one hundred percent."

"What percent do you know?"

"I just know that he said he wanted some—was going to get some acid. What or how he intended to use it, I don't know. He didn't share that information with me."

Holt questioned her about the purchase of the acid and

again, Amanda played the innocent empty-headed blonde who had no idea of what was happening, claiming she wasn't looking the right direction when Grant loaded the acid into the truck.

"When did you realize there was acid in the truck?" Holt asked.

"Whenever he asked me to get rid of it the next day."

Amanda then responded to questions about her activities on Friday morning after they'd left the hotel. She said they went to attorney Ford Coley's office in Kinston and spent a long time there before going to Grant's parents' house.

At that point, court adjourned for the day. But Becky Holt wasn't done with Amanda Hayes yet.

THE next morning, Holt questioned Amanda about the time when little Grant was with them in New York. "At some point, you and Grant decided you weren't going to send little Grant back, is that right?"

"It was Grant's decision."

"Do you recall telling Dr. Calloway that you and Grant didn't want to return Grant IV to Laura?"

Amanda answered that they had had a discussion about it and that she had told Dr. Calloway that Laura was untrustworthy and had "done several things that were not on the up and up, it appeared to me." She then denied that the plane ticket she bought for Laura to fly up to New York was in exchange for dropping the lawsuit.

Holt continued on to the move down to North Carolina,

which Amanda had said on direct was only supposed to be for three months. If so, Holt asked, why did Amanda sign "a lease for a year?"

"Yes, ma'am, 'cause once I got there I realized it was definitely going to take longer than three months." She added that she had intended to sublet or wiggle out of the lease in some other way.

Amanda continued on, painting herself as the peace-keeper who urged her husband to let Laura have the boys. She said she told him that if all Laura wanted was money, then she'd give the boys back as soon as she realized how difficult it was to work, go to school and be a single mom.

Amanda then launched again into her story of what happened on July 13, 2011, adding a few details to her earlier testimony.

Once more, she placed herself in the bedroom with the three children watching the animated movie *Cars* at Grant's instruction. Amanda said she emerged to take Lily to the changing table and saw Grant and Laura sitting at a table looking over a document. She read over Grant's shoulder and became very upset because they had discussed Laura keeping the kids and now he was offering her twenty-five thousand dollars that they didn't have.

"I was upset at both of them. I just turned around and walked off. I didn't want to be around either of them. That's when Laura asked to hold the baby and I just ignored her. I didn't want her to hold the baby. I didn't want to be around either one of them. And it upset her, 'cause she said, 'You have my kids and you won't even let me hold yours?'"

Amanda said then that Laura "approached me, I guess she tripped over the rug. She bumped into me. But Grant saw the whole thing and he came to her and he just grabbed her to pull her back."

Amanda said she just huddled around the baby as Grant and Laura were struggling and Laura yelled, "Get your hands off of me!"

Amanda then reiterated the same tale as before, about Grant sending her and the kids out, but now added that she first went and got a pack of cigarettes for herself and slushies for the boys. She said that little Grant needed to go to the bathroom but she took him over to the far side of the drive and let him "pee-pee in the grass."

Next, she said, she stopped at Wendy's and got a soda for herself. After that, she drove to the mall and drove around the parking lot. She had planned to take them inside to walk a bit but they had all fallen asleep, so she just kept driving. "When I returned home, Laura's car was still there. When I started to get out of the car, little Grant was hungry and I knew Grant hadn't gotten to the grocery store to get something for dinner so I took them to get something to eat."

Amanda interjected that when she saw Laura's car was still there, she assumed that "the ambulance had already come and Grant rode with Laura to the hospital. When I left the Chick-fil-A, Lily was crying really hard, so I drove around to try to calm her down but she kept screaming."

After a stop to console her, Amanda said, she went home and Grant told her Laura was fine. In the next series of questions, Holt talked to Amanda about her family. Amanda mentioned that she was upset with her siblings for disposing of their mother's ashes without speaking to her about it.

She contradicted her nephew's testimony about moving the piece of furniture, and said both of her nephews and her sister were mistaken about the time when it was unloaded from the trailer.

Becky Holt then asked, "You testified that Laura called twice a day, every day, to talk to those boys."

"Yes, ma'am."

"Did she call Thursday?"

"Not to my knowledge."

"Did she call Friday?"

"Again, not to my knowledge."

"Did you have your phone on Thursday?"

"Yes, the phone was always on."

Holt next asked about Randy Miller and Amanda admitted that he was her private investigator. "Were you aware in August [2011] that he went to the Wal-Mart inquiring about the saw purchase?"

"It's possible."

"And that was prior to getting any discovery, prior to the police department even knowing about the saw?"

"It was before I got any discovery, that's correct."

Holt then wanted to know if Amanda had been in communication with Grant at that time and, if so, how they'd communicated. Amanda said, "Several different ways. Whenever I was incarcerated, he contacted me through the pod telephone system, if you will, and he told me that I needed to keep my mouth shut and not trust anybody—that there were a lot of crooked people in the system."

When Holt asked for an explanation, Amanda said, "You actually speak with people through the sink. . . . There's several floors, I believe ten floors. And I believe if you blow water out of your sink, you can communicate on difference floors. . . . One of the girls told me to go to my room and that he was trying to speak to me."

When asked if she shared information with others in the jail, Amanda claimed it was very minimal. "My attorney advised me from the get-go not to speak about my case," she said.

"Do you know an individual named Michaela Haywood?"

"I met her one time when I first came but I did not have a conversation with her in regards to my case—no, I did not."

"Do you recall telling her that when Laura came over to your house on July 13 that she fell and she didn't seem to be moving?"

"No, I don't recall that."

"Do you recall telling her that you and Grant tried to wake her up by putting a wet towel on her face?"

"No, ma'am."

"Do you recall telling Ms. Haywood that you had taken Laura's body out to the boat to dump in the creek in hopes that the alligators would eat it and that the alligators were at the other end?"

"No, ma'am, I didn't tell her that."

"Do you recall telling her that your sister called the police?"

"No, ma'am."

"You believed for a time that your sister called the police, didn't you?"

"I was upset at my sister . . . because I lost my baby and I felt my sister had something to do with me losing my baby."

"Did you believe your sister called the police?"

"I believed my sister had spoke to the police, that's correct."

"And you were upset with her for doing that, weren't you?"

"I was upset—yes, I was."

"You were also upset at Sha for turning over 'Broomstick Rider,' weren't you?"

"I wouldn't say I was upset with her over that. I was upset because I wanted her to try to stay out of it. I was just trying to protect her."

Holt then brought up another inmate, Michelle Clark, and Amanda also denied speaking to her about the events, too. "So it's your testimony today that you never told Michelle Clark that Grant Hayes stabbed Laura to death and cut her up and put her into coolers?"

"No, ma'am, I did not."

"And it's your testimony here today that they—meaning you and Grant—loaded up the coolers and went to Texas?"

"I never told her that—ever."

"And finally, you don't recall telling her that you were there when Grant did the dumping and it was stinking, it made your stomach roll and you were wearing gloves when you did it?"

"Again, I never had a conversation with Michelle Clark about my case in any shape, form or fashion," Amanda insisted.

Holt went through questions about what the two other inmates said Amanda told them, and got denials on each detail. Then Holt asked, "Miss Hayes, you loved little Grant and Gentle, didn't you?"

"Yes, ma'am. I still do."

"And you wanted them as part of your life. You wanted them as a family so you could travel the world."

"I loved to travel. I traveled all my entire life since I was a little kid so, yes, I loved to travel. I married Grant Hayes and so I knew that Grant and Gentle would be part of my life," she said, adding that, "Yes, so I would like them to be able to travel, too. That doesn't mean I was trying to eliminate or take them away from their mother in any shape, form or fashion."

On re-direct, Amanda's lawyer Johnny Gaskins asked about Grant's variety show in New York and then jumped to asking about Grant telling Amanda that Laura did not want to go to the hospital, then delved into the origin of the bleach stain. Amanda said that the kids had knocked over the bucket that Grant used to clean the carpet and caused that discoloration by the door.

Gaskins then covered much of the same territory that he had during direct, over the objections of the prosecution, and wrapped up with a few repetitive questions about the boat.

Holt plunged into that topic herself. "Mr. Gaskins just asked you about the boat and what was happening on the boat. What you testified was, 'I knew what Grant was doing'?"

"That's correct."

"But that's not what you said yesterday. You said you were in your own little world, listening to the animals and looking towards the back of the boat, bailing out or having no idea what was in the boat and having no idea what Grant was doing?"

A hard expression crept across Amanda's face. "I knew what he was doing—that is correct."

"Tell the jury what he was doing right now."

Amanda's voice turned harsh and sounded angry. "I'm sure that they just heard me. I knew what he was doing."

"I didn't," Holt pushed. "What was he doing?"

"He was getting rid of Laura's body," Amanda said, her voice strained as she struggled to control her features.

"Okay. How was he doing that?"

"I am assuming he was putting it in the water."

"Okay. Could you hear the splash as her head went into the water?"

"Again, I heard lots of things. I heard splashing noises. I heard animals. I heard lots of animals."

"What kind of animals did you hear?"

"I don't know what kind of animals they were. I have no idea."

"So, what you recall about the boat trip is that there were splashing noises and there were animals and you were bailing out the boat."

"Yes, that's correct, and I was trying to keep the boat from going into the grassy areas."

"And why was that?"

"Because I didn't know what was in those grassy areas."

"So during the time you were out in the boat, knowing that Grant Hayes is taking Laura Ackerson—the pieces of her body—and throwing them into the water, what you're concerned about is your personal safety and the animals that are in the water?"

Amanda regained control of her demeanor and again spoke in the voice of a little, innocent girl. "I am concerned about my safety. I am afraid he's going to tip the boat over, we're going into the water—I'm afraid of a lot of things. I don't think you can imagine the kind of fear I was under. I honestly don't think you can imagine."

"The fear that you were under was that the boat would tip over and the animals would . . ."

"I had lots and lots of fear."

"Thank you," Holt said with disgust dripping off each word. "I don't have any more questions."

CHAPTER FORTY-EIGHT

THE thirteenth and final day of testimony began on Valentine's Day, February 14, 2014, with the state wanting to introduce new evidence. They had received a fax that morning from Grant Hayes Jr. consisting of three letters that Amanda Hayes had written to Grant Hayes III and mailed to Patsy Hayes for her to read over the telephone to her imprisoned son. Mr. Hayes said that he'd sent them to the district attorney's office to set the record straight after he heard that Amanda claimed to be frightened by his son and in fear for her life. The state wanted to introduce them as evidence using Detective Jerry Faulk on the stand.

Defense attorney Rosemary Godwin presented the objection to admission on two grounds: that it was hearsay evidence and that, since they had given advance notice of presenting a duress defense, the state had had two years to find and secure the correspondence.

After some argument, the judge ruled that the letters were not admissible in the manner that the state wanted to present them, as rebuttal evidence. The only way they would be admissible would be if Patsy Hayes took the stand herself and explained to the jury how she'd received them and what she did after they arrived. At that point, the prosecution started to scramble. Assistant District Attorney Boz Zellinger stepped away from the table as the defense again objected—this time on the grounds of late discovery.

"I am very aware of late discovery with no notice," Judge Stephens said, adding, "I note your objection and understand it, but that would not preclude the evidence if it is offered in some lawful way, as the rules permit."

By this point, Zellinger had made a hurried return to the table. The judge asked, "Does the state intend to offer this evidence in any manner than the one you first described?"

"Yes, the state intends to offer this evidence not through Detective Faulk but via Patsy Hayes."

Judge Stephens told the defense counsel that, after they presented their next witness, he would grant them time for any needed discussion to determine if they had any further relevant testimony to offer on this evidence or if they possessed any other newly discovered material before they rested their case.

Although the state now wasn't going to use Detective Faulk, the defense had plans for him. They called him back to the stand so that he could present the last hour of the videotape of Grant Hayes in the interview room the night of his arrest.

It was an odd thing to watch. Grant was alone but talking as if he were having a conversation with someone sitting across the table in the empty chair, occasionally chuckling as if his invisible friend had made an amusing comment. He rambled on about the music business, engaged in a philosophical discourse that had references to Cro-Magnon man, metaphysics, asteroids, and the government.

At one point, he sang Johnny Cash's song, "The Long Black Veil." He also napped, stretched out on the length of the table. At other times, he closed his eyes and rested his head on his arm—still talking away as if answering questions from someone who wasn't there.

On cross-examination, Zellinger asked Faulk if anything in that last hour was relevant to the investigation, and Faulk replied no.

"Have you ever had a defendant use an insanity defense in one of your cases?" Zellinger asked.

"Yes, sir."

"And can a video like that be used by someone attempting to use an insanity defense?"

"Yes, sir."

Zellinger elicited testimony that the camera was obvious and not hidden, that Patsy Hayes didn't know the address of Grant and Amanda's apartment, and that there were no cell phone tower pings in Kinston at the time the defense claimed Grant had been there dismembering Laura's body, all to establish the lack of complicity on the part of the elder Hayes couple and to undermine the defense theory that Grant had taken the body to one of their properties. Since Amanda had told her daughter and her sister that she'd kept her phone off to preserve the power, he asked the detective if he'd heard Amanda testify that her phone had been on all the way to Texas.

"Yes," Faulk said and looked over the record of the cell report handed to him by the prosecutor to verify his answer.

"Did you hear Amanda testify that she was hit on the leg with a machete?"

"I did."

Zellinger produced several photos of Amanda Hayes taken on July 25 and asked, "Do you see any damage to Mrs. Hayes's legs whatsoever?"

"None."

THE state called its first rebuttal witness, Patricia Barakat, who had been in the Wake County jail awaiting trial on embezzlement charges. Beginning in May 2012, she said that she saw Amanda nearly every day. She said she was a trustee, a position with benefits that nonviolent inmates can earn through good behavior, and Amanda seemed to be the only intelligent person in there. "We connected."

When Becky Holt asked her about what Amanda had said about Laura Ackerson, Patricia replied, "That they hated her, that she was a liar."

"And when you say 'they hated her,' who was she referring to?"

"Her and her husband Grant."

When asked why, Patricia said, "She had told me that Laura didn't care for the kids, that she was only trying to use the boys to extort the money from Grant. She didn't really love the boys."

When asked if she knew of Amanda's feelings for Laura's children, Patricia said, "Oh, she loved them boys—she loved them like they were her own."

"During the course of the conversations you had with Amanda Hayes, did she talk to you about Grant Hayes, her husband?"

"Yeah, she loved Grant very much . . . and she missed him."

"During the course of the time that you spoke with Amanda Hayes, did she provide you with information about Laura's death?"

"Yes," Patricia said. "We were talking about it every now and then—little bits and pieces. . . . Amanda really didn't come out with everything at once. She . . . had to feel me out, I guess. She had to know that she could trust me." Patricia then talked about the environment in lockup and how some people will befriend an inmate for the sole purpose of using her or getting information from her to help themselves, and mentioned that she'd cautioned Amanda about some of those types.

Holt asked about the circumstances under which Amanda had first spoken to Patricia about the night Laura was killed. Patricia said they were in the recreation area, a sunny room where inmates could get away from others.

"What did she tell you?"

"She said that Laura was supposed to bring the boys to

the apartment and they were supposed to meet. And Laura was all late on her behalf of them meetings and so that—oh, this is too much for me." Patricia took a deep breath. "They had both decided they were no longer going to bring the kids to Laura that Laura would have to bring the kids to them," because Laura was always late.

"What did Amanda indicate to you happened when Laura got to the apartment?" Holt prompted. "What did she tell you?"

"She said that she was in the room with Lily in her arms and that Laura had come in and asked her if she could hold Lily. Amanda said no. Amanda—now she told me two different things," Patricia said. "She said that she said no and she yelled for Grant, and Grant and Amanda struggled. They knocked into the wall, the chair fell over, Laura was on the floor."

"And that initial time, did she tell you that Amanda had yelled out that Laura was going to kidnap the baby?"

"Yes. . . . She said Grant knocked her to the floor and Grant was over Laura, and Grant looked at her and said—and Laura was not moving—and Grant looked at her and said, 'She's dead.'"

"And did she indicate she was standing there the entire time?"

"Yes."

"And did she indicate that she knew Laura was dead?"

"Yes. . . . She went to the back bedroom where the boys were. And she was supposed to call Sha to come pick up the boys and she was going to leave with Lily. . . . She got more detailed the second time she told me." Patricia told the story again, this time relating the newly revised "Laura tripped and fell into me" version.

"Did she tell you the second time what happened after that?" Holt asked.

"She said—well, this was when Grant was over the body and looked up and told her that Laura was dead—and I asked her, 'How did that make you feel?' And she said, it didn't make her feel anything—she felt nothing. Then she went back to the boys—that was her concern, to go back to the boys."

Holt asked if Laura gave a reason for the dismemberment, and Patricia said, "They couldn't very well carry Laura's body out—so the only way to get it out would be to cut it up. . . . She said Grant had gone to premed and knew how to cut up a body."

The prosecutor asked, "During this conversation and subsequent conversations, did you have an occasion where she basically told you it was an accident?"

"Yes," Patricia said. "Before she really went into detail with it, she had looked me straight in the face and said, 'It was an accident. It wasn't supposed to happen like this.' And then, a few minutes after that, she'd be like this to me," Patricia said as she pantomimed the movement of Amanda grabbing both of her forearms. "'Do you understand me? It was an accident. It wasn't supposed to happen like this.'"

"And did you question her about that statement?"

"I did. I said, 'If it was an accident, why not call the police, 911?' She didn't have nothing to say with that. . . . She was very—I mean, she loved Grant. She felt she was doing the right thing, I think, standing by him. But then she would get very agitated about it and didn't want to talk about it anymore."

"You remember an occasion when she said that if it was an accident, then they can't convict her of murder?"

Nodding her head, Patricia said, "If it was an accident they can't convict her of murder, yes."

"And what was her demeanor or expression when she said that?"

"She was sort of sarcastic with it—sort of."

"Did she smile?"

"She smiled."

The prosecutor switched over to Amanda's comments about Sha. Patricia said, "She was glad that Sha was sent away because she would probably think this was all pre-meditated, but she wanted Sha away from it all. . . . She said that Sha had given the police 'Broomstick Rider' and she had directed the police back to the house to find some sort of letter."

Patricia then told the jurors that Amanda said the U-Haul was rented to carry Laura's remains and that her sister Karen didn't want to have anything to do with what Amanda and Grant were doing.

"Did she indicate to you that she was angry because her sister called the police?"

"Yes, she said she was very angry with that."

"Do you recall any conversation about if things would have been different if Lily had been a boy rather than a girl?"

"Grant liked the boys so she had said that if Lily had

been a boy, things wouldn't have happened like they happened." Apparently, Amanda believed that if she'd had a son instead of a daughter, Grant would have been willing to relinquish custody of his first two boys to Laura.

Holt had Patricia remind the jurors again of the many times that Amanda proclaimed her love for Grant, and then asked, "Did she ever mention, when this happened, ever being threatened?"

"No."

"Did she ever mention being afraid of Grant Hayes?"

"No. She had mentioned that she was scared in the minutes after Laura was dead and she did say it was scary but never once did she say she was afraid of Grant. No."

"Did she ever mention him hitting her with a machete?"

"Nope." Patricia went on to say that she'd observed Amanda's testimony in the courtroom.

Holt asked, "And in terms of her demeanor and how she came across, how does that compare to the Amanda Hayes you knew for those two and a half months in 2012?"

"It's not the same."

"What's the difference?"

"Amanda, if she was like that—she was very nice, I don't know how to describe it, with the COs [Commanding Officers]. With the people, she was not like, 'Hey, how are you?'" Patricia said in a breathy imitation of Amanda's tiny voice, "She was not like that. It's almost like, if she needed something from you, she was very nice and very pleasant. But if she didn't, she was just normal—as you could be in jail."

"During the time that you were around Amanda, did

you see her get any preferential treatment from the COs?" Holt asked.

"Sure. . . . They would talk to her separately. Like, if we were all locked down, she wouldn't necessarily be locked down. They would visit her at her room and stuff like that. I mean, she had a good rapport with them."

"You said she used a certain tone or a certain approach with the COs that she didn't use with the other prisoners."

"Sure. She was would be all smiles and 'yes' and—this is going to sound horrible—but sound innocent—can I just say that? Very sweet, very—like the other day, when she was up here and you pushed and pushed and she finally answered you, that's the Amanda I knew in jail."

"And the sweet sounding voice is not the way she dealt with you, was it?"

"That was not her normal everyday way, no."

Defense attorney Johnny Gaskins, on cross, accused Patricia of listening to the news media talking about Grant and Amanda's case almost every day before she was arrested, and accused Patricia of trying to get her own sentence reduced by turning Amanda in to the authorities.

"I didn't use anything of this information to my advantage to cut my time at all," Patricia replied. "I didn't gain anything by letting Detective Faulk know any of this. It was never brought up at all. When I got in front of that judge, none of this was ever brought up in front of that judge."

"You knew that if you told the police that Amanda had told you that 'this was an accident, that it was never intended to happen this way,'" Gaskins said, "you couldn't use that to your advantage."

"I didn't use any of this to my advantage."

He continued, "You knew to get any advantage, you had to embellish what you were told, didn't you."

"I didn't embellish anything. I know I did bad by what I did and I had to serve time, but I didn't lie. I took what I did and I did my time for it."

Gaskins nevertheless tried to make it sound as if Patricia had received special treatment by getting credit for time served, even though that was standard procedure.

On re-direct, Becky Holt asked if Patricia ever saw "Amanda show any remorse over Laura Ackerson's death?"

"I never saw Amanda show any kind of remorse, not any kind of that. I've only seen Amanda cry twice when I was there. Once when she got off the phone with [someone] who was—I believe—her mother-in-law, and once when she got into an argument with one of the COs. That was it, she got frustrated."

"And when she got off the phone with her mother-in-law, was she frustrated because they had stopped putting money in her account?"

"I don't know what the purpose of that conversation was but I know that they had stopped putting money in her account. Her niece [also] stopped putting money on her account. She was frustrated with that. You've got to understand, being in jail is very frustrating. So when you're stuck behind them walls and you can't get the help you need, it's very frustrating," Patricia explained, adding, "I would sometimes get her stuff from canteen because she didn't have anything."

"You indicate to Mr. Gaskins that you didn't use any of this information to your advantage."

She nodded and said, "Not once."

"Then why did you think it was important to bring this information out?"

"Because, morally, I thought it was wrong. I just don't see how somebody can do that to somebody. If it was an accident and it was caused by that one person you said you were afraid of, you could have gotten help. She wouldn't have been sitting in there. She would have been with her babies if she had just called 911."

"She also told you that if it was an accident she couldn't be convicted of murder, didn't she?"

"Correct."

"And she smiled."

"Yes, she did."

Gaskins covered the same territory. "Every time you talked to her, she told you it was an accident, didn't she?"

"She did. She was adamant that it was an accident."

"And that no one had ever intended that Laura die."

"No, she didn't say that. She said it was an accident and wasn't supposed to happen like *that*. That's what she said. Whether the intent was there, I don't know. But that's what she said."

"And when you talked to the police, you went to a potential ten-year sentence to time served."

Patricia shook her head. "I didn't use none of that to my advantage, again."

"And you got out of jail?"

"I got it because I had time served. None of this was brought up in my case," she said, wagging her finger back and forth. "When they judge me, none of this."

"So you didn't get the old wink and nod."

"Did not."

Then Becky Holt asked one more question: "Did Amanda tell you that she hated Laura so much that she wanted to throw her from an airplane?"

"She did say that once, yes."

CHAPTER FORTY-NINE

THE final witness of the trial stepped into the stand at 3:37 on the afternoon of Friday, February 14, 2014. Grant Hayes's mother, Patsy Ann Hayes, clearly did not want to be there but realized that she was the only way the jury would hear of the letters Amanda Hayes sent to her to read to her son and she wanted to set the record straight.

The prosecution played the voice message Grant left for his mother telling her they would be moving in with them on the weekend of July 16. "I know your house may not be ready for me but we have to be out of here right now."

Then Patsy Hayes was asked about the properties owned by her and her husband in Kinston. She testified that all the rentals were occupied at the time of Laura's death and the remaining deeds were for vacant lots.

She read into the record a letter from Amanda written

in September 2011 thanking Patsy for sending photos of the children and chatting about her life in jail in very optimistic terms. She ended by writing: "Thank you both so much for caring for our children. Please tell my husband that I love him very much and think of him every day." Amanda had also included a note addressed to "Chicken man and Lil Monkey," the nicknames for little Grant and Gentle, sending them "big hugs and fishy kisses" and exhorting them to be good for their grandparents. She signed it, "Love, Daddy and Mama."

In the January 2012 letter, Patsy read more appreciative comments addressed to her and her husband and then Amanda gave her information on her clothing sizes and measurements and asked for a pants suit in white or off-white and "a baby pink shirt, something I can take the jacket off if I want."

She also sent another piece of paper. On the side margin, she had written: "To Grant, please read it to him." It began, "Hello, my baby. I love you so very much and I hope you're doing good. Please take good care of yourself. I miss everything about you and can't wait to give you a big hug and kiss." It ended with: "I love you with all my heart, your wife."

In the letter from February 2012, Patsy read, "I just wanted to send this note so you could read it to Grant." She followed that with a request for more photographs. In the portion to her imprisoned husband, Amanda wrote that she wanted to set up a time that they could meditate simultaneously. She advised him to "get a pair of ear plugs if it's too noisy." She wrapped up with a message of love.

"Please take good care of yourself and know that I love you and miss you."

Then, for the first time in the trial, defense attorney Johnny Gaskins did not conduct the cross-examination. Instead, his cocounsel, Rosemary Godwin, asked the questions. "When Amanda was writing to you and talking to you on the phone, she never talked to you about any difficulties she was having with Grant, did she?"

"No, ma'am."

"It was only after hearing that when Amanda testified in court about being fearful of Grant, and that, he, in fact, threatened her in a letter while she was in jail that it prompted you to contact the district attorney's office?"

"My husband called."

Godwin asked if she'd been aware before of any problems between her son and Amanda, and Patsy replied, "No, she always said that she loved him and to tell him she missed him. She always spoke well of Grant."

"And you love your son very much, I'm sure."

"I love my son and I love Amanda very much."

"And you have stood by Grant throughout these difficult times?"

"I send him pictures just like I do Amanda."

Godwin established that Patsy had not testified at her son's trial or even come to her son's trial, then she asked, "Would it be fair to say, Mrs. Hayes, that when Grant was a teenager and in his younger years, Grant exhibited behavior that caused you and his father to have some concerns about the stability of his emotions or mental state?"

"Grant was a sweet child," Patsy said. "He was very docile and he was charming."

"Do you recall a time in the home when there was an altercation between Grant and Grantina? And Grantina became so concerned that your husband took Grant and left for a little while so that everyone could calm down?"

"I think I do recall some of that."

"And when he was involved with his first wife, Emily Lubbers, they, I believe, lived in Greenville . . . And she was in school and also working while she was in school. Do you remember that?"

"Yes, I do remember her working and going to school some."

"And do you remember that at that time Grant was having difficulty finding work that suited him? . . . And were you aware, that at one time, he did seek psychiatric treatment for depression and mood swings?"

"He was—I don't—I don't know. I don't think I recall that because, like I say, I try to stay out of their affairs."

When neither side had any more questions, Patsy turned to the judge. "Can I say something before I leave?"

"I don't know because I don't know what you're going to say," Judge Stephens replied.

"I want to go back to that last question."

"No, no. I don't want you saying anything in front of the jury, okay?"

"Okay."

"If you need to tell somebody, you can tell them later."

With that, the parts of the trial remaining were closing arguments, jury instruction and deliberations. Now, however, it was late on a Friday afternoon. The judge excused the jurors for the weekend. When they returned on Monday, the fiery rhetoric would keep them on their toes.

CHAPTER FIFTY

AMANDA Hayes's lawyer Johnny Gaskins began his closing remarks on Monday, February 17, 2014, by discussing the presumption of innocence and reasonable doubt. He claimed that there was no proof that Amanda was complicit in the crime committed by the convicted Grant Hayes and that the only decision the jury had to make was whether or not Amanda was guilty of being an accessory after the fact.

"I told you that this was a case of a sociopath and his two victims," Gaskins continued. "Grant Hayes is a classic example of a sociopath. One the one hand, he is a talented musician; he's witty, charming, charismatic. But on the other hand, he's controlling, manipulative and domineering and, worst of all, he's dangerous. I'll talk more about Grant Hayes, but first I want to talk to you about his two victims.

"First, I want to talk to you about Laura. We know that Laura had become involved with Grant and had become enamored, involved in a romantic relationship with him and the two of them had two children: little Grant and Gentle. Laura had some problems early in her life that led her to believe that it was in the best interest of the boys that they stay with him during the week and they stay with her on the weekends. But her life improved; and it improved once she became separate and apart from Grant. She got a job working, very much involved with the church—things for Laura were looking very good." He said that was why she challenged the custody agreement that turned into a bitter fight between the two of them and in which Amanda was not involved.

Turning to his client, he said "Amanda was a woman who had spent her entire life looking out for and caring for other people," and listed how she'd "looked out for her mother when her mother was sick," how she'd cared for her paralyzed husband, Nicky Smith, until his death, how she looked after her daughter, Sha, and her family. "When she became involved with Grant, she was the person who looked after little Grant and Gentle [while] Grant was off traveling around the world, doing either—doing musical gigs or pretending to do musical gigs—we don't know which."

He turned to the testimony of Heidi Schumacher, who described Grant as the personification of evil. "She told you that Laura had told her that 'if anything ever happens to me—if it's thought that I had committed suicide or that

I had disappeared—go look for Grant because Grant is the one who did it.'"

Then the defense attorney revisited some of the remarks from Laura's parental history about Grant, and about the anonymous Crime Stoppers tip. He moved on to the video of Grant's calm demeanor in Wal-Mart shopping for the reciprocating saw just hours after Laura's death. Then Gaskins brought up the many places Grant had visited as a musician and leaped to an incredible conclusion: "How many women do you think simply disappeared in those cities where Grant Hayes was there either doing gigs or pretending to do gigs? Did his demeanor walking down the aisles remind you of a man who'd made this same shopping trip before? I suggest to you that he knew exactly what he wanted, and he knew exactly what he wanted because he'd done it before."

He talked about Grant and Amanda meeting in St. John as a predator/prey relationship. He said that when they met, "Amanda had $188,000 in an investment account. By the end of July 2011, Grant Hayes had gotten all of that money. He had sold all of her jewelry. They were being evicted from her apartment. Grant Hayes had taken her for everything that she was worth."

He went on to read some of the testimony from John Sargeant, Laura's custody attorney, that pointed to Laura's lack of animosity toward Amanda.

He went through the events of July 13, 2011, tossing in a few assumptions not previously mentioned in court, such as the groundless theory that Laura stopped at Crabtree Valley Mall before coming to the apartment that night.

Then he ran down the phone calls Grant made that evening after Laura's call and then segued into Amanda's version of events. During that portion, he insisted that Grant was using his answering service to cloak the identity of a person whom the defense alleged he communicated with that night and later met at the Black Flower. However, no evidence had been produced during the trial to confirm the existence of the alleged accomplice or to prove the defense team's shadowy theory.

The hall bathroom was the next focus of Gaskins's attention. He claimed that the lack of blood in the room and the absence of saw nicks on the floor proved that Laura was not killed or cut up there. "The point that I'm making is that Grant Hayes and Grant Hayes alone killed Laura. Amanda didn't help him. She's looking after two little boys and her baby. But when you track Grant and you recognize the pattern of his purchases, you can tell exactly what he's done and how he did it."

He spoke next of the large rug under the dining room table that went missing, the one Amanda said the boys had made too dirty to salvage. "I suggest to you that the way that Grant has gotten her body out of the bathroom . . . is by using the rug to go down the stairwell. . . . Right next to the apartment door . . . the stairs go down one level; they turn and go down another level, directly to the parking lot. Grant Hayes, either by himself or through the help of a friend, could have taken her body out of that apartment in probably less than sixty seconds by rolling her up in that rug."

Grant's habit of using credit cards for innocuous purchases like gas and using cash to pay for suspicious purchases like the reciprocating saw, Gaskins said, proved that the Apple power adapter cord purchase was made for nefarious reasons associated with the death of Laura Ackerson. "Here is what I suggest to you has happened: He's sent Amanda out—she's gone to the Chick-fil-A. By the time she gets back, Grant Hayes has strangled Laura with the Apple adapter cord and disposed of [the cord] someplace, probably Kinston, which is why they can't find it. . . . There is absolutely no evidence that Amanda participated in his strangulation of Laura—the evidence is to the contrary."

Gaskins reminded the jurors that the dirty shirts, dirty underwear and goggles found in the Dumpster trash had no blood on them, and through a convoluted stretch of logic, he claimed that somehow proved that Amanda was not involved in the dismemberment. He then talked about the injury toward the back of Laura's neck and described it in a way no forensic pathologist ever would: "The reason for the knife wound is that he has cut Laura's throat and drained the blood from her body" before the dismemberment.

He disparaged the state's case over the credibility of Patricia Barakat as a rebuttal witness and attacked the testimony of Patsy Hayes. He explained that the only reason Amanda sent love letters to Grant via Patsy Hayes was so that she could maintain a conduit for information about her daughter Lily. He then voiced the defense's paranoia about the motivations of Grant's mother. "She came here to deliver the message: 'Amanda, you're right—you will never see Lily again. I have Lily. You have badmouthed Grant. Don't think for a second that you or anyone in your family will ever see her again.'"

Gaskins wrapped up by saying, "The state has absolutely failed to prove to you . . . beyond reasonable doubt or any other doubt in the world that Amanda participated in killing Laura—that just didn't happen. . . . That isn't even on the table. The only issue for you is whether she participated willingly in the disposal of Laura's body. . . . The state is looking for a . . . compromise verdict. They know you're not going to find her guilty of first degree murder. They know that that was never on the table. But by charging her with the more serious offense, what they're hoping is that you will compromise and give them something.

"Ladies and gentlemen, don't fall for it. It's a trick. We're asking that you find her not guilty on both charges." As far as the charge of accessory after the murder, the defense contended that Amanda acted "under duress, coercion and the threats that Grant made to her while they were in Texas."

The issues that Gaskins suggested the jury focus on were whether Amanda was "in fear of her own safety and the safety of her children? . . . You have to decide: did she act under duress? If she did, then she's not guilty."

ADA Boz Zellinger stood to present that first half of the closing for the state. His first words were: "'Laura's dead. I did it.' Those are the words of Amanda Hayes. Those aren't the words of Amanda Hayes to a foe or to someone who had an agenda on her. Those were the words to her own sister."

Zellinger introduced what he called the three principles of the case: that Amanda Hayes and Grant Hayes did this together; that the murder was premeditated; and that Amanda's story fell apart when all the evidence was examined. "It's hard to focus on those elements, because the defendant's story is so ridiculous. It's hard to pay attention to what the state's argument is when the defendant is stretching every little thing past where the truth was.

"You just heard the defense say . . . that there is no evidence that Amanda participated in this murder. Yet you also heard from Karen Berry that Amanda said, 'Laura's dead. I did it.' That's a bell you can't unring."

Zellinger continued on, highlighting the witnesses and evidence presented by the state. First, he pointed the jury's attention to the number of coincidences they'd have to accept to believe Amanda's story: that the bleach stain was caused by the little boys immediately after Laura's death; the frenetic cleanup of the scene that required her to insist that Sha take little Grant and Gentle out of the home immediately; that the electrical tape (most likely used to tape up tarps and plastic in the bathroom) just happened to be purchased in the immediate aftermath of the crime for use with Amanda's artwork; that Amanda was always facing the wrong way when Grant did anything suspicious; that although she was the one who disposed of the acid, she had nothing to do with it.

Zellinger later mentioned yet another fortuitous coincidence. "In the bathroom where Laura was dismembered, they coincidentally clean that. Grant and Amanda Hayes say that it was Gentle's fault—that feces had gotten in there. . . . It's a comical assertion that Amanda didn't know what was going on in this apartment."

He disparaged the defense arguments and said, "What we didn't do is claim things that there was no basis for. You heard the defendant say, 'Yeah, her body was dismembered in Kinston.' There's zero evidence of that at all." He played the video of Amanda unloading the heavy boxes containing the acid bottles, mocking the defense contention that Amanda couldn't do any heavy lifting because she'd just had a C-section.

Regarding prior intent, he said, "One of the biggest keys to the premeditation is this note that's found in the apartment," going on to wonder, "What happened with this note? Was there some sort of duress that made Laura sign this? . . . Most importantly about this note, I'd ask you: Why do we find this note? Why is it still in that apartment? Everything else that has Laura's blood on it, like those gloves, is gone. They throw everything else out. Why do we find it there? And I offer to you: The reason we find this at that apartment is because it makes it look like Laura fled. It makes it look like Laura Ackerson got the twenty-five thousand dollars and she's gone—she took the money and she ran."

He then suggested to the jury that from the moment that the note was drafted, premeditation existed. "I want to focus on some of the assertions of the defense because they're so ridiculous and farcical. Just because a question was asked of a witness doesn't mean it's evidence in this case. You heard some of those questions: 'Oh, was it a wink and a nod—is that why this plea deal was done?' Or 'Did you find the chain saw in the house?' This is a reciprocal saw. The reason the chain saw is thrown out is to get in your mind that it was a loud noise."

He reminded the jury that Patsy Hayes had told them that the rental properties were all occupied at the time of Laura's death, and the remaining pieces of real estate were vacant lots. "The defense, after getting their idea that the dismemberment of the body was done in Kinston blown up, they say maybe it was done . . . outside on one of those vacant lots, which is ridiculous, because that saw does not have a battery in it, so you'd need a really big extension cord."

Zellinger then mocked the sympathy plays made by the defense when they talked about Amanda caring for Nicky and others, and the subliminal attempt to plant concern in the jury's mind over the possibility of Amanda spending her life in prison. He replayed the message from Grant to his mother that the defense alleged to say that only Grant, Amanda and Lily were moving to the Hayes home in Kinston. However, a careful ear can pick up the words "and the boys" immediately after their half sister's name.

The prosecutor reviewed the telephone records for Grant and Amanda's one functional phone that night—the one belonging to Amanda. He said that if someone used that phone to call a messaging service, wouldn't it make sense for the person to access Amanda's messages, not Grant's? Sarcastically, Zellinger added, "I guess that somehow that makes her a drug dealer."

Laura's cell phone, he contended, would have told who left that message and it would have had a recording of what actually happened it that apartment. However, he said, it is somewhere "that we will never find. Additionally, there's no phone call to Amanda's phone at the time Amanda alleged that Grant called her to tell her to pick up bleach at Target."

Moving back to the charges before the defendant, the state's attorney said, "First degree murder is on the table. Mr. Gaskins told you it wasn't on the table. The judge will tell you that first degree murder is on the table. . . . The biggest issue is this acting in concert. And you know this team of Amanda and Grant committed this murder." He read the relevant passage from the judge's instructions and added, "The state, in this case, relies on the legal theory which can infer that for a person to be guilty of a crime, it is *not* necessary that she, herself, personally, do all the acts necessary to constitute that crime. . . . This wasn't a situation where Laura was killed and the body was just thrown in a lake or something along those lines. There was a deliberate effort to cut off her arms, cut off her legs, cut her torso in half and then, finally, to cut her head off so they would fit in these coolers. The kind of depraved mind for Amanda and Grant to do that shows this murder wasn't just an accident. You don't cut somebody's body up and drive it halfway across the country if it was an accident."

Zellinger circled back around to that note. He contended that Laura could have signed the note and made a tape recording of what had transpired, then turned to them "and said, 'Ha. I gotcha.' And Grant and Amanda say,

'Now we need to kill her.'" That, he alleged, was sufficient proof of premeditation. "It just has to be a short moment for Grant or Amanda to say, 'We can't let her go out that door.' And maybe that's why she's killed by that front door. Why would Laura start this fight with Amanda when this custody dispute is finally going her way?"

The prosecutor then ran through some of the other contentions made by the defense. He asked the jurors to consider that if Grant had been in Kinston dismembering the body, why didn't he buy the duffel bags there? Then he moved to Gaskins's insistence that the saw would leave marks on the tile floor. "You don't know, with two people, if you would necessarily make indentations. . . . What you did hear was that Grant Hayes bought a huge plastic tarp and a whole bunch of plastic sheeting. You can construe that was put down in that apartment and that the electric tape was used to seal it off. There just wasn't bleach at the front door, there's bleach leaking out of the bath and that has not been explained, either. And the reason for this is that Grant and Amanda Hayes bought this bleach and they dumped that bleach all over that bathroom.

"Mr. Gaskins gets up here and tells you luminol would still react to body fluids that were in there after they had bleach poured on them . . ." but the experts say that "bleach would have destroyed the body fluids that were in there and the only thing you'd find evidence of is bleach, and that's what happened in this case."

He turned then to the defendant's testimony. "How many times did Amanda Hayes say from the witness stand 'honestly'? I can't remember. 'Honestly' this and 'honestly' that. Focus in on those things 'cause that's what your job is as a juror, to listen to the evidence and determine what is believable."

Bringing his portion of the state's arguments to a close, Zellinger said, "You've seen a deliberate, orchestrated effort to avoid justice in this case by Amanda Hayes. From those eleven days in July 2011 to the past four weeks of this trial, Amanda Hayes has tried to duck justice.

"She's tried to put you on the wrong path. She's tried to hide from justice. She's tried to deceive it. Justice screamed out when Laura was being dismembered and murdered in that apartment. You know it waited for days and days as Laura's body was decomposing in that Texas creek, and you know that it covered its mouth when Amanda Hayes took the witness stand and swore to [tell] you the truth and told you what she told you.

"Ladies and gentlemen, today justice arrives. It is before you today. And it demands, on the behalf of law, reason and in the inhumanity of what happened to Laura, that you find Amanda Hayes guilty of first degree murder."

CHAPTER FIFTY-ONE

BECKY Holt stood to deliver the prosecution's final argument. "Grant and Amanda Hayes acted together on July the thirteenth in 2011 because by July 2011, Grant *and* Amanda Hayes were desperate."

She went through the dire financial situation facing the couple and the final blow to their hopes found in the psychological evaluation. Amanda had called Dr. Calloway's recommended two-three-two split "'ridiculous.' And what did that mean? It meant, not only were they not going to be free of Laura, not only were they not going to get custody and be able to move away and pursue their dreams . . . they were going to be stuck in Kinston."

Holt scoffed at Amanda's attempts at trial to appear as the peacemaker, to distance herself from the custody battle. She reminded the jurors that Amanda got married for the custody battle, moved to North Carolina for it and spent tens of thousands of dollars on it. "What does your reason and common sense tell you about that?"

Holt reread a few previously shared passages from Laura's journal that outlined the contentious nature of Laura and Amanda's relationship, before moving to the events of July 13. She alleged that the last phone call answered on Laura's phone was from Amanda telling her to come to the apartment. "We know that because that's what she told Patricia Barakat."

Holt referred to Grant and Amanda's need to stretch time, because if Laura got there at five thirty, that's four hours before Amanda is seen outside that apartment and that span did not fit with Amanda saying that she didn't know what happened to Laura. She mocked the contention that Laura arrived much later because of the stop for food at Crabtree Valley Mall, telling the jurors that the defense only told them that so they wouldn't question why Amanda was there so long with a dead body while claiming ignorance of the fact. She added that what actually happened in that apartment on that night will remain unknown, "because Laura is not here to tell us; because Grant has been convicted of first degree murder; and, we submit, because Amanda has not been truthful telling you about those events.

"We know that what she did in that apartment before she was murdered was that she signed an agreement that she never, ever would have signed. . . . Laura Ackerson did not voluntarily sign that agreement or write that in there that said 'I can get to see my children whenever [their] father says.' You know that."

Holt also focused on the "stab wound to C4. Mr. Gaskins explains that to you by saying her neck must have been cut so the blood could have drained out. That's not what Dr. Ross said. She said there was a stab wound." Holt moved her arm through the air, pantomiming a knife thrusting into her own throat. "We know that Dr. Radisch testified that she witnessed injuries to the neck muscles and the crushing of the cartilage. We know that the damage to her head was like you would get from a concussion—it was not fatal. We know that she was either strangled or stabbed or some combination of those two. We know that she was murdered in that apartment."

Holt turned to Gaskins's outline of Grant going out to stores and she asked, "What does that mean? It means that Amanda and the boys are home in that apartment with Laura's body. And what would Amanda say? She would say, 'No, I didn't know Laura was dead. I didn't know she was in that bathroom.' She would have you believe that for four days that hall bath, the main bath, is out of use and shut off and that she didn't know that Laura's body was in there. What does your reason and common sense tell you about that?"

Holt ran through Amanda's actions over the time they were in Texas, from the disposal of the clothing they wore when Laura's body parts were dumped in the creek to Amanda's careful concealment of the boxes of acid behind some trees. "Where's the duress? There isn't any—because they're in it together, from the beginning."

Holding up a photograph taken at the motel near Kinston on their arrival back in North Carolina, Holt said,

"Mr. Gaskins argues that she's haggard, that she's not happy. I'll tell you what this is—this is a celebration. This family is going to be together and Laura has finally, in their view, been erased. They've taken her halfway across the country. They chopped her up. They poured acid on her. And they fed her to the alligators in the creek. [Amanda] thinks they're home free. This isn't the face of someone," she said pointing to Amanda in the photo, "who's frightened of this man," she said as she shifted her finger over to Grant.

She directed her attention to the fact that Grant and Amanda were in separate cars with police officers when they were taken downtown. "That's important because if things had happened the way she told you they happened, don't you know that she would have told the police officers? She said she was scared. She was afraid. How much safer does it get? He's in a police car. She's in a police car with officers. She doesn't say a word about that."

Holt defended the testimony of Patricia Barakat and the state decision to call her. She said that the woman was a valuable witness because Amanda told her that she and Grant "both hated Laura.

"You also know that a year after they were arrested, Amanda doesn't say, 'I was afraid of Grant.' No. Patricia Barakat said she loved him. When Amanda could not adequately explain why she didn't call 911 or why they had to cut up Laura's body to Patricia, that's when Amanda changed her story and testified that she didn't know Laura was dead until that Monday night in Texas."

Holt reminded the jury of Patricia Barakat's observations

about Amanda in the courtroom when she was pressed, "and suddenly that little innocent-sounding, singsong voice was gone: 'that's how it was when we talked.'" The prosecutor noted that Patricia said Amanda's "little singsong voice" only appeared when she was trying to manipulate others.

Just like Zellinger, Holt disparaged the defense's groundless contention that the dismemberment occurred in Kinston and said that it was only common sense that Amanda was involved.

"Grant Hayes is a horrible person who did a horrible thing but he didn't act alone. Amanda Hayes and Grant Hayes decided that they were going to kill her and erase her. That she was going to stop being the barrier and the anchor them here and kept them from going forward. It's selfish. It's horrible. . . . What you have experienced through this court and through Amanda Hayes is a fine acting job. Amanda Hayes has come before you and tried to sell you on a role. She's tried to play a role in which she didn't know what was going on, in which she was controlled and manipulated by another person. And your reason and common sense says that's not what the evidence shows.

"She was not afraid then of Grant Hayes. She was not afraid a year later of Grant Hayes. She has given the performance of her life. . . . She has come here and constructed something that she thinks answers all the questions. And she's come concerned about her wardrobe. She asked Patsy Hayes for a baby pink blouse. . . . She's used a voice trying to manipulate you which is not her regular voice but one she uses when she wants to get something. Don't fall for it.

"Tell her that there will be justice for Laura Ackerson today—that it's not going to stop with Grant Hayes being held responsible for his actions. Tell her that she is going to answer for her part in the murder of Laura Ackerson. Tell her like you told all of us in jury selection that the law applies to her just like it applies to Grant Hayes—that the fact that she's a woman, the part of us that doesn't want to believe anyone could do this, especially a woman, is not going to get her out of this—that you're going to hold her responsible for her actions—that you're not buying this act she put on. Tell Amanda Hayes by your verdict that she is guilty of first degree premeditated murder."

CHAPTER FIFTY-TWO

AFTER forty-nine witnesses over thirteen days, the three-man, nine-woman jury received the case that same day at four P.M. on February 17, 2014. They deliberated for seventy-five minutes before adjourning. They were behind closed doors for another six hours a day on Tuesday and Wednesday. They requested Laura's diary and notebooks and the letter in which she purportedly relinquished custody in exchange for twenty-five thousand dollars. They also asked for the reciprocating saw that law enforcement purchased for scientific analysis of the tool markings and for dramatic demonstration during trial. Judge Stephens allowed them to view it in the courtroom from the jury box but would not allow it to be turned on, since neither side had done so during the trial.

Late in the afternoon of Wednesday, July 19, the jury announced they had reached a decision. They filed back into the courtroom. Foreperson Timothy Mock handed over the documentation.

Judge Donald Stephens read the verdict: guilty of second degree murder.

Afterward, jurors said that, at one point, there were nine people in favor of first degree murder, two who wanted acquittal and one who was undecided. All of them agreed, though, that they didn't want a hung jury and worked out their compromise. They said they were all willing to do so because not a single one of them believed Amanda's story that she didn't know Laura was killed and cut up until after they arrived in Texas.

DEFENSE attorney Rosemary Godwin stood before the judge to plead for his leniency. "Except for her relationship with Mr. Hayes, it is extraordinarily unlikely that Mrs. Hayes would have found herself in a courtroom of any kind." She continued talking about duress and coercion, mental and emotional abuse, and Amanda's upright character. "If Mr. Hayes had met Mrs. Hayes first and Ms. Ackerson second, it could very well be that Mrs. Hayes would be the victim in this case."

The judge appeared offended by that final suggestion. "But that would require Ms. Ackerson to participate in the killing of Amanda Hayes. My problem here is that I personally believe, with regard to the evidence, it is quite possible or likely that Amanda Hayes could have saved the life of Laura Ackerson and she chose not to. She chose instead to participate in her killing. Advise your client of her right to speak."

Amanda had something to say and she delivered it in the tiniest, sweetest voice she could muster. "Your honor, I would just like to apologize with my whole heart, being, soul. First to Laura. I apologize to her, to her family, to her children; to my family, to Grant's family, to everyone who had to work this case, to everyone who had to sit through this trial, to everyone in the media who had to watch this and, in fact, have it touch their lives. I am so sorry that this touched my life in any shape, form or fashion or anyone I love or care about or anyone. And I am truly, truly sorry with every ounce of my soul." She nodded her head as her lower lip quivered and lowered herself back into her chair.

The judge asked her to stand up. "Having pled not guilty to this charge of murder in the first degree, the jury having heard the evidence and returned a unanimous verdict of murder in the second degree, the state having prayed judgment, the defendant having no prior record . . . therefore, for a Class B felony, at the top of the presumptive range, can be sentenced by the court to a minimum term of one hundred fifty-seven months in the North Carolina Department of Corrections and a maximum term of one hundred ninety-eight months. This is an active prison sentence, give her credit for time served in jail awaiting charges. She is in custody of the sheriff." She definitely fared far better than Grant, who would be behind bars for the rest of his natural life.

———————

THE next month, Patricia Barakat's tale of the preferential treatment Amanda had received came home to roost for the Wake County Detention Center. An internal investigation concluded that Lieutenant Linda Hicks violated the fraternization policy prohibiting guards from having any kind of relationship with inmates outside the performance of their assigned duties. According to WRAL, several of their sources alleged that there were telephone recordings of romantic and sexual conversations between Lieutenant Hicks and Amanda Hayes. Hicks resigned on March 3. Five additional officers were also fired on March 7 for similar behavior with other inmates.

In April 2014, Amanda Hayes learned her legal tribulations were not over. A grand jury in Texas indicted her on a second degree felony for tampering with physical evidence in the state. If convicted of the offense relating to the dumping of Laura's remains in the creek, the sentence could range from two to twenty years in Texas on top of the time she is now serving.

On August 21, 2014, Amanda filed for divorce from Grant. Her petition was finalized that October.

Grant Hayes's appeals attorney filed a brief requesting a new trial on August 29, 2014. It claimed prejudicial and unfair evidence, testimony and actions in the court. They cited, among other items, the admission of the lyrics to "Man Killer," Ginger Calloway's custody evaluation, the testimony of Pablo Trinidad, the reading of the defendant's e-mails during trial and the judge's ruling that exhibits had to be viewed by the jury in the courtroom.

The state responded with a denial of any abuse of discretion by the trial court and then argued the grounds for inclusion of all evidence the defense team regarded as prejudicial. They contended that some of the points raised regarded testimony and exhibits that had been presented to show motive and ill will toward the victim, not to prove the truth of the charges against him. The higher court rejected his arguments and refused to hear them in a second appeal. Grant Hayes remains behind bars without hope of release.

SHA Elmer continued to work on rebuilding her life in New Mexico, the state of her birth. Little Grant, Gentle and Lily were being raised by their grandparents Grant and Patsy Hayes. Sha and the Hayes family all have an agreement that if something would happen to prevent the grandparents from caring for the kids any longer, it would be ideal if they could still remain together. Sha planned to travel east every summer for the children's big combined birthday party— since the siblings were born in May, June and August—and is committed to, at minimum, ensuring that little Grant, Gentle and Lily are together every year for their annual birthday celebration.

According to Sha, "All the children are healthy and doing well." She talked to four-year-old Lily on the phone every week, and said she'd reached a place where she felt that "it's the best possible solution that all three kids are together with Patsy and Grant II. I wouldn't have it any other way."

Patsy and Grant Hayes face years of parenting with a formidable burden waiting in the future. They will, one day, have to be totally honest with little Grant, Gentle and Lily about the dark side of their childhood. But how will they possibly explain that one parent is dead and the other two are in prison for taking that young mother's life?

AFTERWORD

Attempting to discern the truth through contradictory versions of events given by two defendants is always a difficult task. In this case, the poor state of the victim's recovered body added to the complications presented to investigators.

To me, the document signed by Laura Ackerson accepting twenty-five thousand dollars in exchange for custody of her children and putting all control of visitation in Grant Hayes's hands was the one item that cast immediate doubt on both of their stories. I feel certain that Laura would never participate in the drafting of that agreement of her own free will. When I close my eyes, the murder scene becomes vivid. A review of all the evidence and the application of common sense moved me to a conclusion about the events that led to her death.

I can see her walking through the front door of Grant

and Amanda Hayes's apartment. Little Grant, Gentle and Lily were all on the bed in the back bedroom while the two boys watched the animated movie *Cars*. Amanda and Grant were at the table with Laura.

At that point, Laura was threatened with the possibility of physical harm to herself or to her children or both. The stab wound to her throat could have been a part of the persuasion and would account for the disposal of the rug beneath the dining room table. It also could have been a part of the latter events.

No matter how terrified Laura was at that moment, she knew, in the end, she clearly had the upper hand. Like always, her tape recorder would have been rolling—she was capturing Grant and Amanda's coercion in audio. It would be the card she could play before the judge that would guarantee that she got full custody. There was even the distinct possibility that both of them would face criminal prosecution, and if Grant got any visitation at all, it would be supervised.

I can see Laura on her way out of their home, fear and jubilation forming an uneasy cohabitation that banished logical thought. I can picture her standing on that piece of carpet where the large bleach stain was found, allowing years of anger, frustration and self-doubt to overwhelm her common sense.

I can hear her crowing over her victory as she informed them that it was all on tape. I can imagine her turning to Amanda and saying, because of that audio, "You took my children, now I'll take your daughter from you." I believe that section of discolored carpet is where Laura lost her life. Did Amanda or Grant lunge and stab her to prevent her escape? Did Grant's rage and simmering thoughts of homicide finally burst forth, causing him to wrap the computer cord around her throat and squeeze until she went limp, maintaining his grip for the four or five minutes it would take until her physical death was apparent from the reaction of her body?

On a personal level, the exact way Laura died and who delivered the final deadly insult is irrelevant. The tragic outcome remains the same—Laura lost her life long before she should have, and her little boys lost their mother.

In the name of justice, it is not really vital to know, either. The evidence makes it apparent that Grant and Amanda acted in concert to achieve the common purpose of "obliterating" Laura.

Still, we are left with a bevy of questions that don't have comprehensive answers. How can someone see murder as the best solution? How can a person value his or her own wants over another individual's life? And how can anyone even conceive of the idea of cutting apart a human body like a cow in a slaughterhouse? What kind of a person could do that to another?

Experts cite a lack of empathy, an inability to properly experience emotions, poor integration in society and family, occupational problems, drug abuse and mental disease. Between Grant and Amanda, all of those points appear to be covered to one extent or another.

The experts go on to divide individuals who kill and dismember their victims into five types: 1) Aggressive, where the act is a continuation of the violence and rage of the murder itself; 2) Offensive, where the sole object of the killing is to obtain a body to dismember (this category includes necromantic obsessions as well as callous curiosity); 3) Psychotic, wherein the break with reality is so extreme that the perpetrator is driven to carry the act out by a disordered thought process or voices ordering that it be done; 4) Communication, where the sole aim is to deliver a gruesome threat or warning to another individual or group of people; and 5) Defensive, the most common of all, where the motive is to complicate the identification of the victim, to get rid of evidence or to make it easier to hide or move a body.

The latter seems to apply well to the crime against Laura Ackerson, both from the evidence available and from the words of Grant and Amanda, either in the courtroom, in interview or to acquaintances. In light of the fact that both of them indicated a desire for alligators to consume the last of the evidence, it seems that their mutual desire to "obliterate" or "erase" Laura was gratified by her dismemberment and disposal.

Grant Hayes had long exhibited a narcissistic attitude that his desires were of more importance than those of anyone else. He often referred to himself as one of the "chosen." Additionally, he demonstrated the desire to control and manipulate others—and he certainly controlled Laura's life to the point of its termination. That he had not been able to completely make every shred of her disappear was not because he didn't try—we owe that failure to some measure of luck and the dogged pursuit of the investigators in the case.

As a stepmother, I can understand the almost biological yearning for the children of the man you love to belong exclusively to the two of you. I can understand the wish that the other woman would simply disappear. In that, Amanda was just like many of us—but to act on those primitive desires is another matter entirely. Amanda had to have a cold, compassionless heart in order to even contemplate sacrificing Laura's life on the altar of her personal desire, ignoring the best interests of the children and throwing away any moral compass or law-abiding instincts.

Amanda's daughter, Sha Elmer, struggles, too, trying to find a new place in the world as she accepts the reality of what her mother has done. As Sha said, "Don't be fooled. Amanda was a manipulator, too. Grant was not the only one. Amanda met her match in Grant."

We are left with the mournful disquiet of those who cared for Laura Ackerson, the guilt-tinged anger of many who wished they had done more. And most important of all, the empty hole in the hearts of little Grant and Gentle, whose memories of their mother will fade and only a void will remain—a cold space with no capacity for comfort.

Keep those two little boys, as well as Lily, in your thoughts. Not one of them has a mother or father in their daily lives. Send them wishes for a much brighter future than this legacy of violence portends and a life in which they find happiness, acceptance and healing despite the scar on their souls.